The
HIDDEN INNS
of
THE NORTH OF ENGLAND

Edited by
Peter Long

Published by:
Travel Publishing Ltd
7a Apollo House, Calleva Park
Aldermaston, Berks, RG7 8TN
ISBN 1-902-00764-6
© Travel Publishing Ltd

First Published: 2002

Regional Titles in the Hidden Inns Series:

Central & Southern Scotland	Heart of England
Lancashire & Cheshire	North of England
Southeast England	South of England
Wales	Welsh Borders
West Country	Yorkshire

Regional Titles in the Hidden Places Series:

Cambridgeshire & Lincolnshire	Chilterns
Cornwall	Derbyshire
Devon	Dorset, Hants & Isle of Wight
East Anglia	Gloucestershire & Wiltshire
Heart of England	Hereford, Worcs & Shropshire
Highlands & Islands	Kent
Lake District & Cumbria	Lancashire and Cheshire
Lincolnshire and Nottinghamshire	Northumberland & Durham
Somerset	Sussex
Thames Valley	Yorkshire

National Titles in the Hidden Places Series:

England	Ireland
Scotland	Wales

Printing by: Ashford Colour Press, Gosport
Maps by: © MAPS IN MINUTES ™ 2001 © Crown Copyright, Ordnance Survey 2001
Line Drawings: Sarah Bird
Editor: Peter Long
Cover Design: Lines & Words, Aldermaston
Cover Photographs: St Patrick's Well, Bampton, Cumbria; The Allenheads Inn,
    Allenheads, Northumberland; The Sun Inn, Crook, Cumbria

FOREWORD

The *Hidden Inns* series originates from the enthusiastic suggestions of readers of the popular *Hidden Places* guides. They want to be directed to traditional inns "off the beaten track" with atmosphere and character which are so much a part of our British heritage. But they also want information on the many places of interest and activities to be found in the vicinity of the inn.

The inns or pubs reviewed in the *Hidden Inns* may have been coaching inns but have invariably been a part of the history of the village or town in which they are located. All the inns included in this guide serve food and drink and many offer the visitor overnight accommodation. A full page is devoted to each inn which contains a line drawing of the inn, full name, address and telephone number, directions on how to get there, a full description of the inn and its facilities and a wide range of useful information such as opening hours, food served, accommodation provided, credit cards taken and details of entertainment. *Hidden Inns* guides however are not simply pub guides. They provide the reader with helpful information on the many places of interest to visit and activities to pursue in the area in which the inn is based. This ensures that your visit to the area will not only allow you to enjoy the atmosphere of the inn but also to take in the beautiful countryside which surrounds it.

The *Hidden Inns* guides have been expertly designed for ease of use. *The Hidden Inns of the North of England* is divided into 5 regionally based chapters, each of which is laid out in the same way. To identify your preferred geographical region refer to the contents page overleaf. To find a pub or inn simply use the index and locator map at the beginning of each chapter which refers you, via a page number reference, to a full page dedicated to the specific establishment. To find a place of interest again use the index and locator map found at the beginning of each chapter which will guide you to a descriptive summary of the area followed by details of each place of interest.

We do hope that you will get plenty of enjoyment from visiting the inns and places of interest contained in this guide. We are always interested in what our readers think of the inns or places covered (or not covered) in our guides so please do not hesitate to write to us using the form at the back of the book. This is a vital way of helping us ensure that we maintain a high standard of entry and that we are providing the right sort of information for our readers. Finally if you are planning to visit any other corner of the British Isles we would like to refer you to the list of Hidden Inns and Hidden Places guides to be found at the rear of the book.

Travel Publishing

LOCATOR MAP

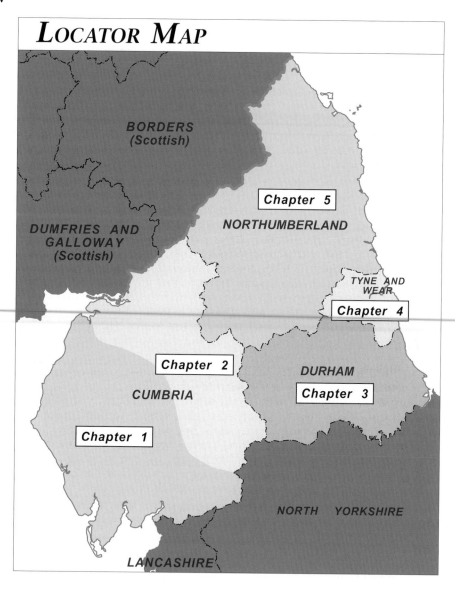

CONTENTS

1 The Lake District & Cumbrian Coast

PLACES OF INTEREST:

PUBS AND INNS:

The Hidden Inns of The North of England

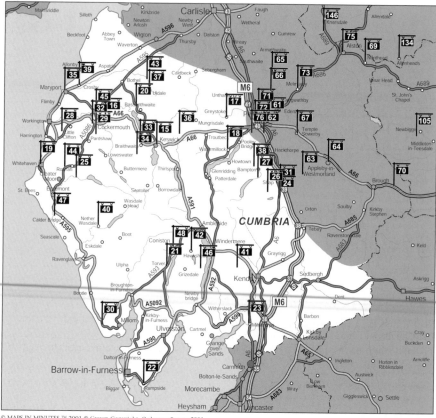

© MAPS IN MINUTES ™ 2001 © Crown Copyright, Ordnance Survey 2001

15 **Bank Tavern**, Keswick	**25** **The Fox and Hounds**, Ennerdale Bridge, Cleator
16 **The Black Bull**, Cockermouth	
17 **The Boot & Shoe**, Greystoke	**26** **The Greyhound Hotel**, Shap
18 **Brackenrigg Inn**, Watermillock, Ullswater, Nr Penrith	**27** **Haweswater Hotel**, Bampton
	28 **Hunday Manor Hotel**, Winscales, Nr Workington
19 **Cap'n Sennys**, Whitehaven	
20 **The Castle Inn**, Bassenthwaite	**29** **The Huntsman**, Cockermouth
21 **Church House Inn**, Torver, Coniston	**30** **King William IV**, Kirksanton, Nr Millom
22 **Clarke's Hotel & Brasserie**, Rampside Barrow-in-Furness	**31** **The Kings Arms**, Shap, Nr Penrith
23 **The Cross Keys Hotel**, Milnthorpe	**32** **The Manor House Hotel**, Cockermouth
24 **The Crown Inn**, Shap, Nr Penrith	**33** **Middle Ruddings Country Hotel**, Braithwaite, Nr Keswick

Please note all references refer to page numbers

3

The Lake District & Cumbrian Coast

Around 16 million visitors a year make their way to the Lake District, irresistibly drawn to its enchanting lakes, its picturesque villages and the most dramatic scenery in England. The highest mountain in the country, Scafell Pike (3,205ft), the largest and deepest lakes, Windermere and Wast Water respectively, are all found here, along with hundreds of other mountains, another 14 lakes, challenging crags and pastoral, wooded valleys.

Despite the huge influx of visitors, most do not venture far from the main tourist "honey-pots" so it's still easy to find the peaceful glades and windswept, isolated fells celebrated by the Lake Poets, Wordsworth, Coleridge and Southey. Between them, this lyrical trio transformed the pervading 18th century perception of the most northwesterly corner of England as an intimidating wilderness into an appreciation of its majestic scenery.

Almost exactly one third of Cumbria's 2,636 square miles lies within the boundaries of the Lake District National Park, created in 1951 to protect the area from "inappropriate development and to provide access to the land for public enjoyment". Not a single mile of motorway has penetrated its borders and only the very occasional stretch of dual-carriageway - barely a dozen miles in all.

But access to the area is very easy, with the M6 running right along its eastern edge. For many people travelling from the south into Cumbria, their first experience of the county is the area around Kendal and Kirkby Lonsdale. These ancient settlements both provide an excellent introduction to the history, people, and economy of Cumbria. Ideally placed for the Lake District National Park and the south Cumbrian coast, it is easy to forget that this area is also close to the northern Pennines and the Yorkshire Dales National Park. The North Cumbrian coast, from Workington to the Solway Firth, is one of the least known parts of this beautiful county but it certainly has a lot to offer. It is an area rich in heritage with a network of quiet country lanes, small villages, old ports, and seaside resorts.

PLACES OF INTEREST

ALLONBY

This traditional Solway village is backed by the Lake District fells and looks out across the Solway Firth to the Scottish hills. Popular with wind-surfers, the village has an attractive shingle and sand beach which received a Seaside Award in 1998. Allonby is well known for its

4

ponies which roam freely on the greens and if you fancy a foreshore ride there's a riding school located close to the beach. The **Allerdale Way** and the **Cumbrian Cycle Way** both pass close by, and the village is also on the Smuggler's Route trail. Smuggling seems to have been a profitable occupation around here - a Government enquiry into contraband trade reported in 1730 that "the Solway people were the first working-class folk to drink tea regularly in Britain".

In the early 1800s, Allonby was a popular sea-bathing resort and the former seawater baths, built in 1835 and now Grade II listed buildings, still stand in the old **Market Square**.

AMBLESIDE

Standing less than a mile from the head of Lake Windermere, Ambleside is one of the busiest of the Lakeland towns, a popular centre for walkers and tourers, with glorious walks and drives radiating from the town in all directions. Many of Ambleside's buildings are constructed in the distinctive grey green stone of the area which merges attractively with the green of the fields and fells all around. The centre of the town is now a conservation area and perhaps the most picturesque building here is **The Bridge House**, a tiny cottage perched on a packhorse bridge across Stock Ghyll. Today it's a National Trust shop and information centre, but during the 1850s it was the home of Mr and Mrs Rigg and their six children. The main room of this one-up, one-down residence measures just 13 feet by 6 feet. The popular panoramic view of Ambleside, looking north from the path up **Loughrigg Fell**, reveals the town cradled within the apron of the massive Fairfield Horseshoe which rises to nearly 3,000ft. Within the townscape itself, the most impressive feature is the rocket-like spire, 180ft high, of **St Mary's Church**. The church was completed in 1854 to a design by Sir George Gilbert Scott, the architect of London's St Pancras Station and the Albert Memorial. Inside the church is a chapel devoted to the memory of William Wordsworth and an interesting 1940s mural depicting the ancient ceremony of rush-bearing. The mural was painted by Gordon Ransome of the Royal College of Art during World War II when the college was evacuated to the town.

An experience not to be missed while staying at Ambleside is a boat cruise on Lake Windermere to Bowness. There are daily departures from the pier at Waterhead, about a mile south of the town. At Bowness, there are connections to other lakeland attractions and, during the summer months, evening wine cruises. Rowing boats and self drive motor boats can also be hired. Just to the west of the pier is Borrans Park, a pleasant lakeside park with plenty of picnic spots, and to the west of the park, the site of Galava Roman Fort. There is little to be seen of the fort but the setting is enchanting. Also well worth a visit is nearby **Stagshaw Garden** (NT), a spring woodland garden which contains a fine collection of shrubs, including some impressive rhododendrons, azaleas and camellias. Parking is very limited so it's best to park at Waterhead car park and walk.

Perhaps the most unusual visitor attraction in Ambleside is **The Homes of Football**, described by the *Sunday Times* as "a national treasure". It began as a travelling exhibition of football photographs and memorabilia but now has a permanent home in Lake Road. Photographer Stuart Clarke recorded games and grounds at every kind of venue from the Premier League down to amateur village teams. There are now 60,000 photographs on file and a massive selection on show, framed and for sale.

From Ambleside town centre, a steep road climbs sharply up to the dramatic **Kirkstone Pass** and over to Ullswater. The pass is so called because of the rock at the top which looks like a church steeple. Rising to some 1,489 feet above sea level, the road is the highest in the Lake District and, though today's vehicles make light work of the climb, for centuries the Pass presented a formidable obstacle. The severest incline, known as **The Struggle**, necessitated passengers to step out of their coach and to make their way on foot, leaving the horses to make the steep haul with just the carriage.

BASSENTHWAITE LAKE

Here's one for the Pub Quiz: Which is the only lake in the Lake District? Answer: Bassenthwaite, because all the others are either Waters or Meres. Only 70ft deep and with borders rich in vegetation, Bassenthwaite provides an ideal habitat for birds - more than 70 species have been recorded around the lake. Successful breeding is encouraged by the fact that no power boats are allowed on the lake and some areas are off limits to boats of any kind. Also, most of the shoreline is privately owned with public access restricted mostly to the eastern shore where the Allerdale Ramble follows the lakeside for a couple of miles or so.

Rising grandly above Bassenthwaite's eastern shore is **Skiddaw** which, ever since the Lake District was opened up to tourists by the arrival of the railway in the 19th century, has been one of the most popular peaks to climb. Although it rises to some 3,054ft, the climb is both safe and manageable, if a little unattractive lower down, and takes around two hours. From the summit, on a clear day, there are spectacular views to Scotland in the north, the Isle of Man in the west, to the east are the Pennines, and the greater part of the Lake District lies to the south.

COCKERMOUTH

No wonder Cockermouth is one of the 51 towns in Great Britain to be designated a "gem town" and recommended for preservation by the Department of the Environment. A market town since 1226, Cockermouth has been fortunate in keeping unspoilt its broad main street, lined with trees and handsome Georgian houses, and dominated by a statue to the Earl of Mayo. The Earl was Cockermouth's MP for ten years from 1858 before being appointed Viceroy of India. His brilliant career was brutally cut short when he was stabbed to death by a convict at a prison settlement he was inspecting on the Andaman Islands.

But Cockermouth boasts two far more famous sons. Did they ever meet, one wonders, those two young lads growing up in Cockermouth in the 1770s, both of them destined to become celebrated for very different reasons? The elder boy was Fletcher Christian who would later lead the mutiny on the *Bounty*; the younger lad was William Wordsworth, born here in 1770 at Lowther House on Main Street, an imposing Georgian house now maintained by the National Trust. Now known as **Wordsworth House**, it was built in 1745 for the Sheriff of Cumberland and then purchased by the Earl of Lowther who let it to his land agent, John Wordsworth, William's father. All five Wordsworth children were born here: William on 7th April 1770. Many of the building's original features survive, among them the staircase, fireplace, and fine plaster ceilings. A few of the poet's personal effects are still here and the delightful walled garden by the River Cocker has been returned to its Georgian splendour.

Wordsworth was only eight years old when his mother died and he was sent to school at Hawkshead, but later he fondly recalled walking at Cockermouth with his sister Dorothy, along the banks of the rivers Cocker and Derwent to the ruined castle on the hill. Built in 1134 by the Earl of Dunbar, **Cocker-mouth Castle** saw plenty of action against Scottish raiders (Robert the Bruce himself gave it a mauling in 1315), again during the Wars of the Roses and in the course of the Civil War it was occupied by both sides in turn. Mary, Queen of Scots, took refuge at the castle in 1568 after her defeat at the Battle of Langside. Her fortunes were so low that she was grateful for the gift of 16 ells (about 20 yards) of rich crimson velvet from a wealthy merchant. Part of the castle is still lived in by the Egremont family; the remainder is usually only open to the public during the Cockermouth Festival in August.

Opposite the Castle entrance, **Castlegate House** is a fine Georgian house, built in 1739, which hosts a changing programme of monthly exhibitions of the work of Northern and Scottish artists - paintings, sculptures, ceramics and glass. The works are for sale and interest free credit is usually available through the Northern Arts Purchase Plan. To the rear of the house is a charming walled garden which is open from time to time during the summer.

Just around the corner from Castlegate House is **The Toy & Model Museum** which exhibits mainly British toys from around 1900 to the present. There are many visitor operated displays including 0 and 00 gauge vintage tinplate trains, Scalextric cars, Lego models and even a helicopter to fly.

Almost next door, **Jennings Brewery** offers visitors a 90-minute tour which ends with the option of sampling some of their ales - Cumberland Ale, Cocker Hoop or the intriguingly named Sneck Lifter. The last independent brewing company in Cumbria, Jennings have been brewing traditional beers since the 1820s and today there are more than 100 Jennings' pubs across the north of England. In addition to the tours, Jennings has a shop selling gifts and leisure wear, the latter boldly emblazoned with the names of its various brews.

A short walk from the Brewery brings you to the **Kirkgate Centre** which is housed in a converted Victorian primary school. Run by

6

volunteers, the Centre offers a wide range of events and activities including live music, amateur and professional drama, films, dance, workshops, exhibitions of art and local history.

Two more visitor attractions stand either side of Wordsworth House in the Main Street. The **Printing House Museum** occupies a building dating back to the 16th century and has on display a wide range of historical presses and printing equipment, the earliest being a Cogger Press dated 1820. Visitors are offered the opportunity to gain hands-on experience by using some of the presses to produce cards or keepsakes.

On the other side is the **Mining Museum** which incorporates the Creighton Mineral Museum, based on the collection amassed by William Shaw. Mining for minerals in the area goes back to Roman times with Shap granite, garnet, andesite and the Cumberland Green Slate which is such a distinctive feature of many Lakeland houses. Also on display are miners' lamps, tools, vintage photographs and a dazzling display of fluorescent minerals in "Aladdin's Cave". The Museum shop stocks minerals and fossils for sale, as well as jewellery, original paintings, photographs and crafts.

Wordsworth House, Cockermouth

CONISTON

Beatrix Potter, John Ruskin, Arthur Ransome, Sir Donald Campbell - all of them have strong connections with Coniston Water, the third largest and one of the most beautiful of the central Cumbrian lakes. Beatrix Potter lived at Sawrey near Lake Windermere but she owned the vast Monk Coniston estate at the head of Coniston Water. On her death, she bequeathed it to the National Trust, a body she had helped establish and to which she devoted much of her time and fortune.

Ruskin came to Coniston in 1872, moving into a house he had never seen. **Brantwood**, on the eastern side of the lake, is open to the public and enjoys superb views across the water to the great crumpled hill of the **Old Man of Coniston**, 800 metres high. From its summit there are even more extensive vistas over Scotland, the Isle of Man, and on a clear day as far as Snowdonia.

Boats on **Coniston Water** are restricted to a 10 mph limit, which is an ideal speed if you're travelling in the wonderful old steamship, the *Gondola*. So called because of its high prow which enabled it to come in close to shore to pick up passengers, Gondola was built in 1859, abandoned in 1937 for many years and then restored by the National Trust in 1980. Up to 86 passengers can now travel in opulent comfort on its regular trips around the lake. Coniston Launch also offers lake cruises in its two timber launches, and at the boating centre craft of every kind are available to rent.

Just south of the village and beside the lake is Coniston Hall, the village's oldest building. Dating from the 16th century, it was the home of the Le Fleming family, the largest landowners in the area. Coniston's most famous inhabitant was, however, John Ruskin, the 19th century author, artist, critic, social commentator and one of the first conservationists. He lies buried in Coniston churchyard and the **Ruskin Museum** nearby contains many of his studies, pictures, letters, and photographs as well as his

Brantwood, Coniston

7

collection of geological specimens. You can also see a pair of his socks, his certificate of matriculation from Oxford, and his funeral pall made of Ruskin lace embroidered with wild flowers. The lace was so called because Ruskin had encouraged the revival of flax hand-spinning the area. Lace pieces made to his own designs and based on the sumptuous ruffs worn by sitters in portraits by Titian, Tintoretto and Veronese, were attached to plain linen to make decorative cushions, table covers and bedspreads - many of these are on display.

From the jetty at Coniston, a short ferry trip takes you to John Ruskin's home, **Brantwood**, which occupies a beautiful setting on the eastern shores of Coniston Water. It was his home from 1872 until his death in 1900. When he arrived for the first time he described the house, which he had bought for £1500 without ever seeing it, as "a mere shed". He spent the next 20 years extending the house, by adding another 12 rooms, and laying out the gardens. The view from the Turret Room he had built was, Ruskin declared, "the best in all England". Sadly, Ruskin's later years were blighted by mental illness, "He was" said a biographer "at times quite mad".

GRANGE-OVER-SANDS

Grange, as it's known locally, is an attractive little town set in a natural sun-trap on the north shore of Morecambe Bay. Much of its Victorian charm can be credited to the Furness Railway Company which developed the town after building the Lancaster to Whitehaven line in 1857. At that time, the whole of the Cartmel and Bowness Peninsulas were part of Lancashire, a detached area whose main link with the rest of the county was the dubious route across Morecambe Sands. The railway provided a safe

Promenade, Grange-over-Sands

alternative to this hazardous journey. At Grange the company built an elegant mile-long promenade (now traffic free) and set out the colourful ornamental gardens. Prosperous merchants built grand country homes here and it wasn't long before local residents began referring to their town as the "Torquay of the North".

Though Grange doesn't have a beach to rival that of its brash neighbour across Morecambe Bay, it does enjoy an exceptionally mild climate, the mildest in the northwest, thanks to the Gulf Stream. It is still a popular place particularly with people who are looking for a pleasant and quiet place to retire. It was a favourite with Beatrix Potter who recorded that on one visit to the town she met a "friendly porker" which inspired *The Tale of Pigling Bland*. There's no connection of course but today the town does boast a butcher's shop, Higginsons, which was recently voted the Best Butcher's Shop in England.

GRASMERE

In 1769 Thomas Gray described Grasmere as "*a little unsuspected paradise*". Thirty years later, Wordsworth himself called it "the loveliest spot that man hath ever found". Certainly, Grasmere enjoys one of the finest settings in all Lakeland, its small lake nestling in a natural scenic amphitheatre beside the compact, rough-stone village.

For lovers of Wordsworth's poetry, Grasmere is the pre-eminent place of pilgrimage. They come to squeeze through tiny **Dove Cottage** where Wordsworth lived in dire poverty from 1799 to 1808, obliged to line the walls with newspaper for warmth. The great poet shared this very basic accommodation with his wife Mary, his sister Dorothy, his sister-in-law Alice and, as almost permanent guests, Coleridge and De Quincey. (Sir Walter Scott also stayed, although he often sneaked off to the Swan Hotel for a dram since the Wordsworths were virtually teetotallers). Located on the outskirts of the village, Dove Cottage has been preserved intact: next door is an award-winning museum dedicated to Wordsworth's life and works. Dove Cottage, Rydal Mount, another of the poet's homes near Grasmere, and his birthplace, Wordsworth House at Cockermouth, are all owned by the Wordsworth Trust which offers a discount ticket covering entrance to all three properties.

8

Like Ambleside, Grasmere is famous for its **Sports**, first recorded in 1852, which still take place in late August. The most celebrated event in the Lake District, they attract some 10,000 visitors and feature many pursuits unique to Cumbria such as Cumberland and Westmorland wrestling as well as the more understandable, though arduous, fell running.

Dove Cottage, Grasmere

Collectors of curiosities who happen to be travelling north on the A591 from Grasmere should look out for the vintage black and yellow AA telephone box on the right hand side of the road. Still functioning, **Box 487** was recently accorded Grade II listed building status by the Department of the Environment.

KENDAL

In 1997, a survey by Strathclyde University revealed that the highest quality of life of any town in England was to be found in Kendal, the "capital" of South Lakeland. That assessment came as no surprise to the residents of this lively, bustling town which was once one of the most important woollen textile centres of northern England. The Kendal woollen industry was founded in 1331 by John Kemp, a Flemish weaver, and it flourished and sustained the town for almost 600 years until the development of competition from the huge West Riding of Yorkshire mills during the Industrial Revolution of the 19th century. The town's motto "Wool is my Bread" reveals the extent to which the economy of Kendal depended on the wool from the flocks of

Herdwick sheep that roamed the surrounding fells. The fame of the cloth was so great that Shakespeare refers to archers clad in Kendal Green cloth in his play *Henry IV*.

These archers were the famous Kendal Bowmen whose lethal longbows were made from local yew trees culled from the nearby limestone crags. It was these men who clinched the English victories at Agincourt and Crécy and fought so decisively against the Scots at the Battle of Flodden Field in 1513.

Kendal has royal connections too. The Parr family lived at **Kendal Castle** until 1483 - their most famous descendant was Catherine Parr, the last of Henry VIII's six wives. Today, the castle's gaunt ruins stand high on a hill overlooking the town, with most of the castle wall and one of the towers still standing, and two underground vaults still complete. Castle Hill is a popular place for walking and picnicking and in summer the hillside is smothered with wild flowers. From the hilltop there are spectacular views and a panorama panel here assists in identifying the distant fells.

The largest settlement in the old county of Westmorland, Kendal has always been a bustling town, from the days when it was on the main route to Scotland. Nowadays the M6 and a by-pass divert much of the traffic away from the town centre, but its narrow main streets, Highgate, Stramongate, and Stricklandgate, are always busy during the season. The fine coaching inns of the 17th and 18th centuries, to which Prince Charles Edward is said to have retreated after his abortive 1745 rebellion, still line these streets.

Anyone wandering around the town cannot help but notice the numerous alleyways, locally known as yards, that are such a distinctive feature of Kendal. An integral part of the old town, they are a reminder that the people of Kendal used to live under a constant threat of raids by the Scots. The yards were a line of defence against these attacks, an area that could be secured by sealing the one small entrance, with the families and livestock safe inside.

Shoppers are spoilt for choice in Kendal. In addition to all the familiar High Street names, the **Westmorland Shopping Centre**, **Blackhall Yard** and **Elephant Yard**, all in the heart of the town, and the **K Village Factory Shopping** complex on the outskirts, make it easy to shop until you drop. One local product well worth sampling is **Kendal Mint**, a tasty chocolate-coated confection which is cherished by climbers and walkers for its instant infusion of energy. Another once-popular local medication, Kendal Black Drop, is sadly no longer available. "A more than commonly strong mixture of opium and alcohol", Kendal Black Drop was a favourite tipple of the poets Samuel Taylor Coleridge and Thomas de Quincey.

Kendal's excellent sporting facilities include the **Kendal Leisure Centre**, which offers a one-week "tourist pass", **Kendal Wall**, which is one of the highest indoor climbing facilities in the country, an artificial ski slope, 3 local golf courses and a driving range. Drama, music and the visual arts are presented in a regularly changing programme of exhibitions, live music, theatre productions and craft workshops at the **Brewery Arts Centre**. The Centre also houses Kendal's cinema which presents a mixture of mainstream, classic and art house films.

A number of interesting museums and galleries are also located in Kendal: the **Museum of Lakeland Life and Industry** which is themed around traditional rural trades of the region, **Abbot Hall Art Gallery** forming part of a complex within Abbot Hall park and **The Museum of Natural History and Archaeology**, founded in 1796 and one of the oldest museums in the country.

Adjacent to the elegant Georgian Abbot Hall is the 13th century **Parish Church of Kendal**, one of the widest in England, with five aisles and a peel of 10 bells. The church also contains a sword thought to have belonged to Robert Philipson, a Cavalier during the Civil War. Whilst away fighting in Carlisle, Cromwell's supporters laid siege to Philipson's house at Windermere. On his return, the Cavalier attacked the Kendal church when he thought the Roundheads would be at prayer. Riding his horse right into the church, he found it empty save for one innocent man whom he ran through with this very sword.

Perhaps the most unusual attraction in Kendal is the **Quaker Tapestry Exhibition** at the Friends Meeting House in the centre of the town. This unique exhibition of 77 panels of community embroidery explores Quaker history from the 17th century to the present day. These colourful, beautifully crafted tapestries are the work of some 4000 people, aged between 4 and 90, from 15 countries. A Quaker Costume Display, embroidery demonstrations, workshops and courses, and a large screen colour video combine to provide a fascinating insight into the Quaker movement and its development.

KESWICK

For generations, visitors to Keswick have been impressed by the town's stunningly beautiful setting, surrounded by the great fells of Saddleback, Helvellyn and Grisedale Pike. Tourism, now the town's major industry, actually began in the mid-1700s and was given a huge boost by the Lakeland Poets in the early 1800s. The arrival of the railway in 1865 firmly established Keswick as the undisputed "capital" of the Lake District with most of the area's notable attractions within easy reach.

The grandeur of the lakeland scenery is of course the greatest draw but, among the man-made features, one not to be missed is the well-preserved **Castlerigg Stone Circle**. About a mile to the east of the town, the 38 standing stones, some of them 8ft high, form a circle 100ft in diameter. They are believed to have been put in place some 4,000 years ago and occupy a hauntingly beautiful position. In the riverside Fitz Park is the town's **Museum & Art Gallery** which is well worth a visit not just to see original

Friar's Crag, Keswick

10

manuscripts by Wordsworth and other lakeland poets but also for the astonishing "Rock, Bell and Steel Band" created by Joseph Richardson of Skiddaw in the 19th century. It's a kind of xylophone made of sixty stones - some a yard long -, sixty steel bars and forty bells. Four "musicians" are required to play this extraordinary instrument.

Surrounded by a loop of the River Greta to the northwest of the town is the surprisingly fascinating **Cumberland Pencil Museum** which, incidentally, boasts the six feet long "Largest Pencil in the World". The "lead" used in pencils (not lead at all but actually an *"allotrope of carbon")* was accidentally discovered by a Borrowdale shepherd in the 16th century and Keswick eventually became the world centre for the manufacture of lead pencils. The pencil mill here, established in 1832, is still operating here although the "wadd", or lead, is now imported.

Other attractions in the town centre include the Cars of the Stars Museum, ideal for movie buffs since it contains such gems as Laurel and Hardy's Model T Ford, James Bond's Aston Martin, Batman's Batmobile and Mr Bean's Mini; and **The Teapottery** which makes and sells a bizarre range of practical teapots in the shape of anything from an upright piano to an Aga stove.

KIRKBY LONSDALE

One fine day in 1875 John Ruskin came to Kirkby Lonsdale and stood on the stone terrace overlooking the valley of the river Lune. It was, he declared, "one of the loveliest scenes in England, therefore in the world". *He was equally enthusiastic about the busy little market town - "I do not know in all my country", he continued,* "a place more naturally divine than Kirkby Lonsdale".

Ruskin's View, Kirkby Lonsdale

Devil's Bridge, Kirkby Lonsdale

Ruskin had been inspired to visit the town after seeing JMW Turner's painting of that view, and Turner himself had come in 1816 on the recommendation of William Wordsworth. All three of them made a point of going to see the **Devil's Bridge** over the Lune, a handsome, lofty structure of three fluted arches reputedly built by Satan himself in three days. According to legend an old woman, unable to cross the deep river with her cattle, had asked the Devil to build her a bridge. He agreed but demanded in return the soul of the first creature to cross but his evil plan was thwarted by Cumbrian cunning. The old woman threw a bun across the bridge which was retrieved by her dog and thus she cheated the Devil of a human soul.

The bridge is at least 700 years old and although its exact age is a mystery we do know that some repairs were carried out in 1275, making it certainly the oldest surviving bridge in Westmorland. By the 1920s, this narrow bridge originally designed for pack-horses was quite inadequate for the growth in motor traffic. A new bridge was built and this, together with one of the country's first by-pass roads, has saved the lovely old town from further destructive road-widening schemes.

Kirkby's Main Street is a picturesque jumble of houses spanning several centuries, with intriguing passages and ginnels skittering off in all directions, all of them worth exploring. It's still a pleasure to stroll along the narrow cobbled streets bearing names such as Jingling Lane, past the 16th century weavers' cottages in Fairbank, across the Market Square with its 600-year-old cross where traders have displayed their wares every Thursday for more than 700 years, past ancient hostelries to the even more venerable **St Mary's Church** with its noble Norman doorway and massive pillars. In the churchyard, a Victorian gazebo looks across to the enchanting view of the Lune Valley painted by JMW Turner.

The town has 3 times been national winner of the "Britain in Bloom" competition and also attracts thousands of visitors for its **Victorian Fair**, held on the first full weekend in September, and again in December for the Yuletide procession through streets ablaze with coloured lights and decorated Christmas trees.

POOLEY BRIDGE

In Wordsworth's opinion Ullswater provides *"the happiest combination of beauty and grandeur, which any of the Lakes affords"*, an opinion with which most visitors concur. The poet also noted the curious fact that the lake creates a sextuple echo, a natural phenomenon that the Duke of Portland exploited in the mid-1700s by keeping a boat on the lake equipped *"with brass guns, for the purpose of exciting echoes"*.

The charming village of Pooley Bridge stands at the northern tip of **Ullswater**, and there are regular cruise departures from here during the season, stopping at Glenridding and Howton. Rowing and powered boats are available for hire and since Ullswater is in effect a public highway, you can also launch your own boat. Do make sure though that you observe the 10mph speed limit which applies over the whole of the 8-mile-long serpentine lake. Also, the greater part of the shoreline is privately owned and landing is not permitted. Licences are required for fishing: these can be obtained from the tourist offices at Pooley Bridge and Glenridding.

RAVENGLASS

The Romans built a naval base here around AD78 which served as a supply point for the military zone around Hadrian's Wall. They also constructed a fort, Glannaventra, on the cliffs above the town, which was home to around 1,000 soldiers. Little remains of Glannaventra except for the impressively preserved walls of the Bath House. Almost 12ft high, these walls are believed to be the highest Roman remains in the country.

In the 18th century Ravenglass was a base for smugglers bringing contraband in from coastal ships - tobacco and French brandy. Today, the estuary has silted up but there are still scores of small boats and the village is a

charming resort, full of atmosphere. The layout has changed little since the 16th century; the main street is paved with sea pebbles and leads up from a shingle beach. Once, iron-ore was brought to the estuary by narrow gauge railway from the mines near Boot, in Eskdale, about eight miles away.

11

One of the town's major attractions is the 15" narrow gauge **Ravenglass and Eskdale Railway** which runs for seven miles up the lovely Mite and Esk River valleys. Better known as "La'al Ratty", it was built in 1875 to transport ore and quarried stone from the Eskdale Valley and opened the following year for passenger traffic. Since then the railway has survived several threats of extinction. The most serious occurred at the end of the 1950s when the closure of the Eskdale granite quarries wiped out the railway's freight traffic at a stroke. However, at the auction for the railway in 1960 a band of enthusiasts outbid the scrap dealers and formed a company to keep the little railway running.

Today, the company operates 12 locomotives, both steam and diesel, and 300,000 people a year come from all over the world to ride on what has been described as "the most beautiful train journey in England". The La'al Ratty is still the best way to explore Miterdale and

Ravenglass & Eskdale Railway

12

Eskdale and enchants both young and old alike. There are several stops along the journey and at both termini there is a café and a souvenir shop. At Ravenglass station there is also the Railway Museum which brings to life the history of this remarkable line and the important part it has played in the life of Eskdale.

ULVERSTON

It was way back in 1280 that Edward I granted Ulverston its market charter: more than seven centuries later, colourful stalls still crowd the narrow streets and cobbled market square every Thursday. It's a picturesque scene but for an even more striking view of the town, follow the walk up nearby **Hoad Hill**. The great expanse of Morecambe Bay with a backdrop of the Pennines stretches to the south, the bulk of Ingleborough lies to the east, Coniston Old Man and the Langdale Pikes lie to the west and north. Crowning the hill is a 100ft-high **replica of the Eddystone lighthouse**, raised here in 1850 to commemorate one of Ulverston's most distinguished sons, Sir John Barrow. Explorer, diplomat and author, he served as a Lord of the Admiralty for more than forty years, his naval reforms contributing greatly to England's success in the Napoleonic Wars.

An even more famous son of Ulverston was Stanley Jefferson, born at number 3, Argyle Street on June 16th, 1890. Stanley, of course, is far better known to the world as Stan Laurel. His thirty-year career in more than one hundred comedy films with Oliver Hardy is celebrated in the town's **Laurel and Hardy Museum** in King Street.

Laurel and Hardy Museum

The oldest building in the town is the **Church of St Mary** which, in parts, dates from 1111. Though it was restored and rebuilt in the mid-19th century and the chancel was added in 1903, it has retained its splendid Norman door and some magnificent stained glass, including a window designed by the painter Sir Joshua Reynolds. The present tower dates from the reign of Elizabeth I as the original steeple was destroyed during a storm in 1540.

Ulverston also boasts England's shortest, widest and deepest **canal**. Visitors can follow the towpath walk alongside which runs dead straight for just over a mile to Morecambe Bay. Built by the famous engineer John Rennie and opened in 1796, the canal ushered in a half-century of great prosperity for Ulverston as an inland port. At its peak, some 600 large ships a year berthed here but those good times came to an abrupt end in 1856 with the arrival of the railway. The railway company's directors bought the canal and promptly closed it.

WHITEHAVEN

The first impression is of a handsome Georgian town but Whitehaven was already well established in the 12th century as a harbour for use by the monks of nearby St Bees Priory. This was a small-scale operation - most of the town was developed in the 17th century by the Lowther family to service their nearby mines. Whitehaven's growth in those years was astonishing by the standards of the time - it mushroomed from a hamlet of just 9 thatched cottages in 1633 to a sizeable, planned town with a population of more than 2000 by 1693. Its "gridiron" pattern of streets, unusual in Cumbria, will be familiar to American visitors and the town boasts some 250 listed buildings. By the mid-1700s, Whitehaven had become the third largest port in Britain, its trade based on coal and other cargo business, including importing tobacco from Virginia, exporting coal to Ireland, and transporting emigrants to the New World. When the large iron-steamships arrived however, the harbour's shallow draught halted expansion and the port declined in favour of Liverpool and Southampton. For that reason much of the attractive harbour area - now full of pleasure craft and fishing smacks - and older parts of the town remain largely unchanged.

The harbour and its environs have been declared a Conservation Area and it's here you'll

The Beacon, Whitehaven Harbour

Hood's Bay in North Yorkshire.

Long before the first lighthouse was built in 1822, there was a beacon on the headland to warn and guide passing ships away from the rocks. The present 99ft high lighthouse dates from 1866-7, built after an earlier one was destroyed by fire. St Bees Head is now an important Nature Reserve and the cliffs are crowded with guillemots, razorbills, kittiwakes, gulls, gannets, and skuas. Bird watchers are well-provided for with observation and information points all along the headland. There is a superb walk of about eight miles along the coastal footpath around the headland from St Bees to Whitehaven.

find **The Beacon** where, through a series of innovative displays, the history of the town and its harbour are brought to life. Visitors can also monitor, forecast and broadcast the weather in the Met. Office Weather Gallery, learn about the "American Connection" and John Paul Jones' attack on the town in 1772, or settle down in the cinema to watch vintage footage of Whitehaven in times past.

There's more history at **The Rum Story** which opened in early 2000 and tells the story of the town's connections with the Caribbean. The display is housed in Jefferson's, the oldest surviving UK family of rum traders.

Whitehaven's **Museum and Art Gallery** is particularly interesting. The museum deals with the history of the whole of Copeland (the district of Cumbria in which Whitehaven lies) with special emphasis on its mining and maritime past. The displays reflect the many aspects of this harbour borough with a collection that includes paintings, locally made pottery, ship models, navigational instruments, miners' lamps, and surveying equipment. The Beilby "Slavery" Goblet, part of the museum's collection, is one of the masterpieces of English glass-making and is probably the finest example of its kind in existence.

South of Whitehaven on the B5343, **St Bees Head**, a red sandstone bluff, forms one of the most dramatic natural features along the entire coast of northwest England. Some four miles long and 300ft high, these towering, precipitous cliffs are formed of St Bees sandstone, the red rock which is so characteristic of Cumbria. Far out to sea, on the horizon, can be seen the grey shadow of the Isle of Man and, on a clear day, the shimmering outline of the Irish coast. From here the 190-mile **Coast to Coast Walk** starts on its long journey across the Pennines to Robin

St Bees itself, a short walk from the headland, is a small village which lies huddled in a deep, slanting bowl in the cliffs, fringed by a shingle beach. The village is a delightful place to explore, with its main street winding up the hillside between old farms and cottages.

WINDERMERE

Birthwaite village no longer features on any map, thanks to the Kendal and Windermere Railway Company which built a branch line to it in 1847. With an eye on tourist traffic, and considering the name Birthwaite had little appeal, they named the station "Windermere" even though the lake is over a mile distant. In the early days carriages and, in later years, buses linked the station with the landing stages in the village of Bowness on the shores of the lake. As the village burgeoned into a prosperous Victorian resort, it became popularly, and then officially, known by the name of its station,

Steamer, Lake Windermere

14

while Windermere water was given the redundant prefix of Lake.

Windermere's railway is still operating, albeit now as a single track branch line. **The Lakes Line** is now the only surviving Railtrack line to run into the heart of the Lake District. Modern diesel railcars provide a busy shuttle service to and from the main line at Oxenholme. The route, through Kendal, Burneside and Staveley, is a delight and provides a very pleasant alternative to the often crowded A591.

It is from Bowness-on-Windermere, 2 miles south of Windermere, that most of the lake cruises operate. Lasting between 45 and 90 minutes, the cruises operate daily and provide connections to the **Lake District Visitor Centre** at Brockhole, the **Lakeside & Haverthwaite Steam Railway** and the **Fell Foot Country Park**. There are evening wine/champagne cruises during the summer months, and rowing boats and self drive motor boats are also available for hire all year round.

Not only is **Windermere** the largest lake in Cumbria but it is, at 11 miles long, the largest in England. Formed in the Ice Age by the action of moving glaciers, the lake is fed by the Rivers Brathay and Rothay, at the northern end, whilst the outlet is into the River Leven, at Newby Bridge. Windermere is actually a public highway or, more correctly, waterway and this stretch of water, with its thickly wooded banks and scattered islands, has been used since Roman times as a means of transport. Roman Legionnaires used it for carrying stone to their fort at Galava, near present day Ambleside, at the head of the lake. Later, the monks of Furness Abbey fished here for pike and char. The name Windermere, however, comes from Viking times and is derived from Vinand's Mere, Vinand being the name of a Nordic chief.

Across from Bowness, the lake is almost divided in two by **Belle Island** which is believed to have been inhabited by the Romans. During the Civil War, it was owned by Colonel Philipson (the Royalist supporter who disgraced himself by riding into Kendal Parish Church) and his family had to withstand an 80 day siege, successfully, whilst the colonel was away on another campaign. In 1774, the island was bought by a Mr English who constructed the round house which, at the time, caused such consternation that he sold the property and the island to Isabella Curwen, who planted the surrounding trees.

Fishermen, too, find great enjoyment practising their skills on this well-stocked lake. Once considered a great delicacy in the 17th and 18th centuries, the char, a deep-water trout, is still found here though catching it is a special art.

Away from the marinas and car parks is the old village where **St Martin's Church** is of particular interest. It has a magnificent east window filled with 14th and 15th century glass, and an unusual 300-year-old carved wooden figure of St Martin depicted sharing his cloak with a beggar.

On the lake shore just to the north of the village is the **Windermere Steamboat Museum**. The Museum grounds also includes a model boat pond, shop, tea room, picnic area, a self-catering flat for 2 persons, and free parking.

Just down the road from the Steamboat Museum is the Old Laundry Visitor Centre, the home of **The World of Beatrix Potter**, one of the top ten most popular visitor attractions in the country. Here visitors can enjoy fascinating recreations of the Lakeland author's books, complete with the sounds, sights and even smells of the countryside. Open all year, the complex also includes the Tailor of Gloucester Tea Room and the Beatrix Potter shop.

Bank Tavern | 15

47 Main Street,
Keswick, Cumbria
CA12 5DS
Tel: 017687 72663
Fax: 017687 75168

Directions:

Keswick stands on the A66/A59 at the northern end of Derwent Water. Bank Tavern is in the main street.

The father-and-son team of Ian and Stephen Dixon own and run **Bank Tavern**, which is one of the oldest established hostelries in Keswick. In the main street of this popular tourist centre, the tavern dates back to the early years of the 18th century, and behind the smart black-and-white exterior there's an abundance of old-world charm and atmosphere, with floors of wood or slate, well-upholstered seating and excellent lighting. The bar menu, which is available lunchtime and evening seven days a week, provides plenty of variety, and the dishes are all freshly prepared; fresh fish and local beef are among the highlights, and other choices include flavour-packed home-made pies, vegetarian options and a children's menu.

The town-centre location is convenient for both business and tourist visitors, and the tavern is open all day, every day. Keswick is certainly a place that deserves more than a passing visit, and under the eaves of Bank Tavern are five guest bedrooms, all very cosy and comfortable and full of character; they share two bathrooms. Keswick has two fascinating museums, one devoted to Pencils (the town was once the world centre for the manufacture of lead pencils), the other to the Cars of the Stars, and there are many other places of interest. The town is surrounded by glorious countryside and above it rises the majestic Skiddaw, one of the most popular peaks in the Lake District. A man-made feature not to be missed is the Castlerigg Stone Circle, believed to have been put in place 4,000 years ago.

Opening Hours: 11-11 (Sun 12-10.30).

Food: Bar meals lunchtime and evening..

Credit Cards: Mastercard, Visa.

Accommodation: 5 rooms, 2 bathrooms..

Facilities: Garden.

Entertainment: None

Local Places of Interest/Activities: Keswick Museums, Castlerigg Stone Circle 1 mile, Threlkeld (mountain walks, quarry & mining museum) 3 miles, golf, canoeing and many other outdoor activities nearby.

Internet/website:

e-mail:
stephendixon@banktavern.freeserve.co.uk

16 The Black Bull

Main Street,
Cockermouth,
Cumbria CA13 9LE
Tel: 01900 824071

Directions:
Cockermouth is close
to the A66 Penrith
road 6 miles east of
Workington and 30
miles west of Penrith.

The Black Bull is an 18th century inn on the main street of the superb little town of Cockermouth. The striking black-and-white frontage positively invites visitors inside, and what greets them will not disappoint. Stone and slate floors, beamed ceilings, and furniture in oak or pine all please the eye, and the setting is enhanced by judiciously placed concealed lighting. The Black Bull is owned and run by Beverley and Billy Kivell, and while Billy attends to dispensing drinks at the bar (including two cask ales and always something on promotion), Beverley is doing sterling work in the kitchen. She is half-Italian, and there are some Italian influences in the unpretentious, highly enjoyable dishes she produces every day of the week except Monday. Special theme nights are held every month, but any day is special at this most delightful, family-friendly pub, whose other assets include a beer garden and masses of parking space.

Cockermouth has two very famous sons, born a few years apart, in Fletcher Christian of *Bounty* fame and the poet William Wordsworth. The latter's house, with a walled garden by the River Cocker, is a much visited attraction in the care of the National Trust, and other places on the tourist trail include the Toy & Model Museum, Castlegate House, which has regular exhibitions of work by Northern and Scottish artists, and Jennings Brewery, home of the last independent brewing company in Cumbria.

Opening Hours: 11.30-11 (Sun 12-10.30).

Food: bar meals (not Monday).

Credit Cards: Amex, Mastercard, Visa.

Accommodation: None.

Facilities: Car park, beer garden.

Entertainment: Monthly theme nights.

Local Places of Interest/Activities:
Maryport 5 miles, Bassenthwaite 5 miles, Workington 6 miles.

The Boot & Shoe
17

Greystoke,
Cumbria
CA11 0TP
Tel: 017684 83343

Directions:
Greystoke is 5
miles west of
Penrith on the
B5288.

Occupying a substantial site in the centre of the village, the **Boot & Shoe** started life as a coaching inn almost 400 years ago. Externally, little has changed down the centuries, and even the old stables are still standing, now used as store rooms. The look also remains traditional behind the heavy outer door, and owner Paul Cobbe, who had a spell as manager a few years ago, likes to keep things the way they were while bringing the standards of comfort and amenity into the 21st century. Locals, walkers, cyclists and tourists meet in the convivial surroundings of the public and lounge bars, where well-kept ales - Jennings among them - are just the thing for quenching a fresh-air thirst.

Outdoor appetites are satisfied by a good selection of home cooking featuring as much fresh locally sourced produce as possible. Food is served lunchtime and evening, and all day in the summer months, when food and drink can be enjoyed alfresco in the beer garden. Thursday is quiz night, and the inn also hosts occasional live music evenings.

Greystoke is a very pleasant base from which to visit the many places of interest in the area, and the Boot & Shoe has a four bedrooms for Bed & Breakfast accommodation, all with en suite facilities, tv and tea/coffee tray. Greystoke is a real gem, its attractive houses grouped round a trim village green. The name is famously associated with the legend of Tarzan, whose ancestral home was Greystoke Castle. A real life connection is with the late trainer of racehorses Gordon W Richards, whose stables housed two Grand National winners, Lucius and Hello Dandy.

Opening Hours: 12-3 & 5.30-11; all day in summer.

Food: Bar meals.

Credit Cards: Amex, Mastercard, Visa.

Accommodation: 4 en suite rooms.

Facilities: Car park, garden.

Entertainment: Quiz Thursday.

Local Places of Interest/Activities: Penrith 5 miles, Dalemain (country mansion and gardens) 5 miles, Dacre Castle 5 miles.

18 | Brackenrigg Inn

Watermillock,
Ullswater, Nr Penrith,
Cumbria CA11 0LP
Tel: 017684 86206
Fax: 017684 86945

Directions:
Leave the M6 at J40
and take the A66 then
A592 along the
northern shore of
Lake Ullswater.

Stunning views of Lake Ullswater and the fells beyond are just one of the rewards of a visit to **Brackenrigg Inn**, where a warm welcome awaits from owner Garry Smith, John Welch and their staff. The 18th coaching inn has a friendly, relaxed atmosphere that is evident the moment guests step inside the bar with its cheerful open fire. Four real ales are always on tap to slake open-air thirsts, along with an excellent selection of wines, many of them served by the glass. The inn offers a choice of accommodation, residential or self-catering. The 11 bedrooms in the main building are all en suite, with central heating, tv and tea/coffee trays, and all enjoy the fabulous views. In the stables that once served the inn three spacious self-catering cottages have been created, each furnished in practical, traditional style and sleeping up to five guests in two bedrooms.

The inn has a small function room which can accommodate up to 30. Discounts are negotiable for group bookings, and feature weekends and special seasonal rates are also offered for individual bookings. A traditional Cumbrian breakfast is served in the lakeview dining room, and an excellent resident chef and his team prepare bar snacks and lunch and dinner meals using local produce as much as possible. Brackenrigg is an ideal base for discovering the delights of Ullswater and the surrounding area, and few visitors would disagree with William Wordsworth's opinion that Ullswater provides 'the happiest combination of beauty and grandeur which any of the Lakes affords'.

Opening Hours: 12-11.

Food: Bar and restaurant menus.

Credit Cards: Mastercard, Visa.

Accommodation: 11 en suite rooms and 3 self-catering cottages.

Facilities: Car park, terrace, garden

Entertainment: None

Local Places of Interest/Activities: Lake Ullswater, Aira Force waterfalls 2 miles, Lakelaw Bird of Prey Centre 4 miles, Penrith 5 miles.

Internet/website:

e-mail: enquiries@brackenrigginn.co.uk
website: www.brackenrigginn.co.uk

Cap'n Sennys   19

2 Senhouse Street,
Whitehaven,
Cumbria
CA28 7ES
Tel: 01946 62222

Directions:
Whitehaven is
situated on the
A595 on the
Cumbrian coast.

Cap'n Sennys and the road in which it stands take their names from Captain Senhouse, who was associated with the development of Whitehaven and Maryport. Granted to the Captain by the Lowther estate, the building later became the first distillery in Whitehaven. Now it has been revamped and virtually rebuilt so that it now resembles a warehouse, and the spacious, lofty interior features the finest oak in its handsome beams. It's a family business, with Andrew Conoley in charge of administration and cooking and other members of the family working equally hard in the background. The food is served in no-nonsense, good value portions, and among many popular choices the home-made lasagne and chicken & mushroom pie are favourites with the regulars.

Cask ales and a good selection of wines can accompany the food or of course can be enjoyed on their own. Major football matches are shown on a large screen in the bar, and there's live music for entertainment on Friday and Saturday, when the inn has a late licence. Cap'n Sennys is closed on Monday. Most of the town of Whitehaven was developed in the 17th century by the aforementioned Lowther family, and there's plenty for the visitor to see (there are, for example, 250 listed buildings). The town's history is recorded in two museums that deal with the maritime heritage and another - the Rum Story - tells the story of the town's connection with the Caribbean.

Opening Hours: 12-3 & 7-11 (to 1am Fri & Sat); closed Mon.

Food: Bar meals.

Credit Cards: None.

Accommodation: None.

Facilities: Car park.

Entertainment: Live music Fri & Sat.

Local Places of Interest/Activities:
Whitehaven Museums, St Bees Head 3 miles, Ennerdale Water 7 miles.

20   The Castle Inn

Bassenthwaite,
Cumbria
CA12 4RG
Tel: 017687 76401
Fax: 017687 76604

Directions:

From Keswick take the A591 along the eastern shore of Bassenthwaite Lake for about 7 miles. The hotel is through Bassenthwaite village on the lefthand side of the T-junction.

Overlooking Bassenthwaite Lake and some of the highest fells in England, the **Castle Inn** is an ideal base for a family holiday and for lovers of nature and the great outdoors. Part of the Corus & Regal Hotels group, the Castle has 48 well-appointed bedrooms including four-poster and family rooms. Children under 16 sharing with two adults stay free, paying only for meals taken; under-6s even eat free! A new team of chefs have devised interesting new menus of freshly prepared dishes available lunchtime and evening in Lakers Bar and in the evening in Sonnets Restaurant.

Guests at the Castle have temporary membership of Plimsoll's Leisure Club, whose amenities include an indoor swimming pool, sauna, solarium, gym and tennis. Guest parking is free, and the hotel can arrange bike hire. Walking/rambling packages are popular options, and the Castle offers many other special and seasonal deals. At nearby Dodd Forest there are trails for walkers, cyclists and horse riders, and among the amazing variety of local attractions are Trotters & Friends Animal Farm, the Cars of the Stars Museum in Keswick and, in Cockermouth, Wordsworth's House and museums devoted to mining, printing and toys. For the really energetic the challenge of Skiddaw beckons. Although it rises to over 3,000 feet, the climb is not too difficult, and the reward for reaching the summit is spectacular views to Scotland in the north, the Isle of Man in the west, the Pennines to the east and the Lakes to the south.

Opening Hours: 10 - 2 and 6 - 10

Food: Bar meals and evening table d'hote.

Credit Cards: All the major cards.

Accommodation: 48 en suite rooms.

Facilities: Car park, gardens, leisure club

Entertainment: Occasional live music.

Local Places of Interest/Activities:
Bassenthwaite Lake, Skiddaw 4 miles, Keswick 7 miles, Cockermouth 5 miles.

Internet/website:
website: www.regalhotels.co.uk/castleinn

Church House Inn   21

Torver, Coniston, Cumbria
LA21 8AZ
Tel/Fax:
   015394 41282

Directions:

Torver lies on the west side of Coniston Water on the A593. Two miles from Coniston village.

Church House Inn is a long, low building which originally housed monks from Furness Abbey. Steeped in 600 years of history, it was once the court for the area, and it has two ghosts - a monk and a landlord who was clearly reluctant to leave. The same is true of many of today's visitors, charmed by the setting, the warm, genuine welcome and the great food served at Patrick Hirst's inn. Garlic and herb mushrooms or crunchy potato skins with a spicy salsa dip could start the meal, with a main course of grilled plaice, a steak or the famous Church House Cumberland sausage served with a tangy apple sauce. Also on the menu are salads, scrumptious desserts and children's meals.

The location is a perfect centre for walking, climbing or just relaxing and drinking in the glorious scenery, and the inn has six rooms (four of them en suite) for Bed & Breakfast accommodation. The nearby village of Coniston, at the top of Coniston Water, is dominated by the great crumpled hill of the Old Man of Coniston, 800 metres high and affording fantastic views from its summit. Coniston's most famous inhabitant was the 19th century artist and writer John Ruskin, and the Ruskin Museum contains a large collection of his studies, pictures, letters and personal possessions. Coniston Water will always be associated with Sir Donald Campbell, who died here in 1967 when attempting to break his own water speed record in Bluebird.

Opening Hours: 11-11 (Sun 12-10.30).

Food: Bar meals and à la carte.

Credit Cards: All the major cards.

Accommodation: 6 rooms, 4 en suite.

Facilities: Car park, garden.

Entertainment: Quiz Sunday, occasional folk music evenings.

Local Places of Interest/Activities:
Coniston 2 miles, Hawkshead 4 miles, Grizedale Forest 3 miles.

Internet/website:
website: www.churchhouseinntorver.co.uk

22 Clarke's Hotel & Brasserie

Rampside,
Barrow-in-Furness,
Cumbria
LA13 0PX
Tel: 01229 820303
Fax: 01229 430954

Directions:

Leave the M6 at J36 and follow signs to Barrow (A590) to Ulverston. Turn left after pedestrian lights (signposted A5087). Follow coastal route for 10 miles, turn left at roundabout (Rampside). Hotel is 400 yards on the left.

Situated on the shore of Morecambe Bay, **Clarke's Hotel & Brasserie** provides a warm welcome and a pleasant stopping place in an area which abounds in facilities for all ages and tastes. Thomas Twigge's hotel, smartly painted in black and white and recently given a top-to-toe facelift, enjoys an excellent location, and the bedrooms - singles, twins and king-size - all have en suite facilities and multi-channel tv. Various seasonal and weekend special offers are available, and a 10% discount is offered to readers of Hidden Inns. A full English breakfast makes a good start to the day, and in the brasserie a good and varied menu is served lunchtime and evening. The hotel is very well placed for business within the Lakes and Furness area.

There's private parking and a beer garden. Children are always welcome at Clarke's, and there's plenty to keep them and grown-ups occupied and amused in Barrow, from the impressive Dock Museum and the ruins of Furness Abbey to superbowl and banger racing. Beyond Rampside, a road lead to the little island of Roa, while on the other side of Barrow the A590 runs across a bridge from the docks to the Island of Walney. This 10-mile island is home to two important nature reserves, one with the largest nest of herring gulls and lesser black-backed gulls in Europe, the other with 130 species of birds either resident or passing through, several species of orchid, the natterjack toad and the Walney geranium, a plant which grows nowhere else in the world.

Opening Hours: All day every day

Food: Brasserie menu, traditional Sunday lunch.

Credit Cards: Amex, Mastercard, Visa.

Accommodation: AA 3 star rooms en suite.

Facilities: Car park, garden.

Entertainment: None

Local Places of Interest/Activities: Furness Abbey 3 miles, Barrow Dock Museum 2 miles, Walney Island 4 miles, Ulverston 5 miles. Lake Windermere 10 miles

Internet/website:

e-mail: clarkeshotel@lineone.net
website: www.clarkeshotel.co.uk

The Cross Keys Hotel   **23**

1 Park Road,
Milnthorpe, Cumbria
LA7 7AD
Tel: 015395 62115
Fax: 015395 62446

Directions:
Milnthorpe is on the A6 7 miles south of Kendal. Leave the M6 at J35 from the south, J36 from the north. The hotel stands at a crossroads in the middle of town.

Unwinding and relaxing come easily at the **Cross Keys**, a traditional coaching inn on the doorstep of the English Lakes, the Lune Valley and the Cartmel and Furness Peninsulas. Recently refurbished to the highest standards by owners Ian and Sandra Mills, it has eight superbly appointed bedrooms (ETC 4 Diamonds), all en suite and some with sitting areas. The public rooms are equally appealing, particularly the limed oak-panelled bar, where an excellent selection of ale is served. The Cross Keys is a Hartley's house with real ale such as Hartley's XB on draught, Hartley's XB Smooth and Robinson's Best Bitter. While Ian attends to the liquid side of the business, Sandra and the resident chef take care of the kitchen. The inn offers an interesting à la carte menu and a traditional bar menu with familiar favourites such as steak & kidney pie or roast gammon. Most of the meat on the menus comes from an excellent local butcher who is the only Accredited Rare Breeds Butcher in Cumbria. Vegetarians are not forgotten, and for smaller appetites there's a menu of starters, salads and light bites.

The inn is fast becoming known for its scrumptious puddings, with most diners quite unable to resist the likes of treacle sponge and custard, sticky toffee pudding or sago, semolina and rice puddings. Overnight guests can start the day with a full English or lighter Continental-style breakfast, and the Cross Keys is open for morning coffee and afternoon tea as well as lunch and dinner. Milnthorpe, whose Friday street market dates from 1334, became an important staging post in the early 19th century; the Cross Keys had stabling for 36 horses and numbered a Russian Tsar and an Austrian Queen among its notable guests. Today, the Cross Keys can still unlock the door to a relaxed, civilised break in the most agreeable surroundings.

Opening Hours: 10.30am-11pm.

Food: Restaurant and bar meals.

Credit Cards: All the major cards.

Accommodation: 8 en suite rooms.

Facilities: Car park, outside seating, function suite (100).

Entertainment: None

Local Places of Interest/Activities: Kendal 7 miles, Carnforth (Steam Railway Centre) 6 miles, Arnside (estuary resort) 3 miles.

Internet/website:
e-mail: infocrosskeys@aol.com
website: www.thecrosskeyshotel.co.uk

24   The Crown Inn

Shap, Nr Penrith,
Cumbria
CA10 3NL
Tel: 01931 716229

Directions:

Leave the M6 at
J39 and turn right
on to the A6 for
Shap (2 miles).

Built in 1707, the **Crown** is certainly very old, but it's a mere stripling, not even half-a-crown, in comparison with its immediate vicinity as it sits upon the site of a stone age settlement. On the main street of Shap, the inn is run by a charming couple, Pam and Brian Beardall, who spent many years in South Africa before taking over here in the mid-1990s. The welcome is warm, and the whole place is cosy and neat as a new pin. Classical music adds to the peaceful, civilised ambience in the bar and in the lounge that overlooks the garden. Good wholesome food is served at very kind prices lunchtime and evening in the non-smoking dining room. Pam does the cooking, and she and Brian are rightly proud of the reputation they have built up and the high level of repeat business. Fish and meat comes from the best local suppliers, and among the favourite dishes are prize-winning Cumberland sausages and succulent lamb chops.

Pam has another, less expected string to her bow: she makes wonderful bespoke dolls, which are displayed in the bar, each one unique, much admired and suitably expensive, as befits a girl in a million. Shap has a superb location for walkers and lovers of the great outdoors, and guests making the Crown their base have a choice of three bedrooms, one of them en suite. The inn has a beer garden at the back and a good-sized car park. Among the attractions close by are Shap Abbey, just inside the Lake District National Park, and Haweswater, where golden eagles nest.

Opening Hours: Mon-Thurs 7-11 (summer from 6), Fri 4-11, Sat 12-11, Sun 12-10.30. In addition it is open lunchtimes in Summer but times vary so phone to check.

Food: Bar meals.

Credit Cards: Mastercard & Visa planned.

Accommodation: 3 rooms, 1 en suite.

Facilities: Car park, garden.

Entertainment: Occasional quiz nights and music nights.

Local Places of Interest/Activities: Lake District National Park, Shap Abbey 2 miles, Haweswater 5 miles, Penrith 8 miles.

Internet/website:
website: www.shap-cumbria.com

The Fox and Hounds | 25

Ennerdale Bridge,
Cleator, Cumbria
CA23 3AR
Tel: 01946 861373

Directions:

Ennerdale Bridge is
10 miles south of
Cockermouth off
the A5086.

Experienced publicans John and Veronica Webb have breathed new life into the **Fox &**
Hounds, which enjoys a picture postcard setting by an old stone bridge surrounded by the
beautiful Ennerdale Hills. The inn dates from the late 17th century, and the promise of the
location is more than fulfilled within, where black beams, small oak tables and chairs and
log fires in winter, create an inviting, traditional feel in the cosy bar and restaurant.

John and Veronica are both accomplished cooks, and the reputation they have built up
brings visitors from all over the region to sample the fine food. Dishes are fresh, wholesome
and appetising, served in generous helpings and firmly in the classic British tradition; their
Cumberland sausage with giant Yorkshire pudding is one of the many mouthwatering
delights that make a journey to this remote spot so worthwhile. Food is served lunchtime
and evening every day in summer and from Wednesday to Sunday in winter. The excellent
home cooking is complemented by a choice of well-kept real ales, and in summer both can
be enjoyed in the lovely beer garden.

This northern edge of the Lake District really is a walker's paradise, and the Coast to
Coast Walk runs the whole length of Ennerdale on its 190-mile journey from the west coast
across the Pennines to Robin Hood's Bay in North Yorkshire. The bridge by the Fox & Hounds
crosses the little River Ehen, which, a couple of miles downstream, runs into Ennerdale
Water, one of the most secluded, tranquil and beautiful of all the Cumbrian lakes. The coast
at Whitehaven is a short drive away, and to the south is St Bees Head, a red sandstone bluff
that is one of the most dramatic natural features along the entire northwest coast.

Opening Hours: 11-11 (Sun 12-10.30).

Food: Bar meals.

Credit Cards: None.

Accommodation: None.

Facilities: Car park, beer garden.

Entertainment: Live music at the weekend.

Local Places of Interest/Activities: Fishing
and golf available nearby; Ennerdale Water 2
miles, Cockermouth 10 miles, Whitehaven 7
miles, St Bees 7 miles.

26   The Greyhound Hotel

Main Street,
Shap,
Cumbria
CA10 3PW
Tel: 01931 716474
Fax: 01931 716305

Directions:
Leave the M6 at J39
and turn right on
to the A6 for Shap
(2 miles).

When newlyweds Richard and Ann Whinfel built the Greyhound in 1684 as a coaching inn, they also established a farm opposite to supply fresh produce. They thus began a tradition of hospitality that is being carried on in fine style by owners Derrick Newsome and Keith Taylor, who both spent many years teaching Hospitality and Catering at colleges of further education and before that had worked in top-of-the-range eating establishments. This charming old hostelry is still a welcoming sight for traveller and tourists as the first inn after crossing the once notoriously difficult route from Kendal over Shap Fell, and its reputation for highly quality food and comfortable accommodation has spread far and wide.

Local produce is used as far as possible on the menu of freshly prepared, no-nonsense dishes, which can be enjoyed in the cosy bar with its open fireplace or in the 50-cover restaurant. A wide selection of real ales, lagers and wines can be enjoyed with a meal or on their own in the pleasant, cosy surroundings. Food is served lunchtime and evenings, and all day at peak times of the season. The hotel can cater for private parties and small functions in the restaurant, back bar or meeting room. The 11 attractively furnished and decorated en suite guest bedrooms have tv and hospitality trays, and for those looking for budget accommodation there are bunkhouse facilities for up to 10 people. Shap, an interesting spot to explore, stands midway on the Coast to Coast Walk from St Bees to Robin Hood's bay, and with the M6 nearby, access to the Dales and the Scottish Borders is easy.

Opening Hours: 12-2.30 & 6-9.

Food: Extensive à la carte menu.

Credit Cards: Mastercard, Visa.

Accommodation: 11 en suite rooms and bunk facilities.

Facilities: Car park.

Entertainment: None

Local Places of Interest/Activities: Walking, cycling, fishing; Shap Abbey 1 mile, Northumberland National Park 1 mile, Penrith 10 miles.

Internet/website:
e-mail: postmaster@greyhoundshap.demon.uk

Haweswater Hotel 27

Bampton, Cumbria
CA10 2RP
Tel: 01931 713235
Fax: 01931 713145

Directions:
From the M6 (J39)
take the A6 to Shap.
In Shap, turn left and
go via Bampton
Grange and Naddle
Gate to the hotel on
the eastern shore of
Haweswater.

Set on the eastern shore of the most easterly of the Lakes, **Haweswater Hotel** offers a magical combination of quiet seclusion, comfortable surroundings, fine food and glorious views. The hotel was built from local stone in 1937 and its public rooms have recently been modernised. Ken and Jane Weller offer 15 centrally heated guest bedrooms, some of them en suite and most with magnificent views of the Lake and the surrounding countryside. Three rooms have private balconies. Also available is a self-catering flat for 2. Breakfast, lunch, bar and à la carte menus are served in the Mardale Restaurant overlooking the Lake, and in the Mardale Bar tea, coffee, light lunches and afternoon tea can all be enjoyed.

The main evening menu of 3 or 5 courses shows the full range of the kitchen team's skills with such imaginative delights as mixed grilled peppers filled with a medley of Continental cheeses or smoked duck breast with a damson and brandy sauce sharing the list with classics like pepper steak or trout with almonds. Haweswater is actually a reservoir, created in the late 1930s to meet the growing needs of Manchester and now managed as a nature reserve. Walkers have a good chance of seeing woodpeckers, buzzards and falcons, and perhaps even a golden eagle or two. The restaurant and bar of the hotel take their name from the village of Mardale, drowned when the reservoir was created - the ruined Holy Trinity Church can still be seen. Birdwatching, fishing, orienteering, painting, photography and walking are among the special activity breaks which the hotel can arrange subject to demand, but the real speciality is 'inactivity breaks' - relaxing, enjoying the excellent hospitality and revelling in the glorious scenery.

Opening Hours: All day, every day.

Food: Bar lunches, evening restaurant menus.

Credit Cards: Mastercard, Visa.

Accommodation: 15 rooms, 7 en suite; 1 self-catering flat.

Facilities: Car park, garden.

Entertainment: None

Local Places of Interest/Activities: Full range of outdoor activities on and off the Lake, Bampton 3 miles, Shap 5 miles.

28 Hunday Manor Hotel

Winscales,
Nr Workington,
Cumbria
CA14 4JF
Tel: 01900 61798
Fax: 01900 601202

Directions:

Winscales is 2 miles inland from Workington on the A595 between Whitehaven and Cockermouth.

Joe Wilson, who has owned the Manor House Hotel in Cockermouth since the early 1990s, added another string to his bow when he bought **Hunday Manor Hotel**. Set in 4 acres of woodland and landscaped gardens, the house was built in classic style in the early part of the 19th century, and a section of its handsome sandstone facade has a healthy covering of creeper. The hotel is coming to the end of a major upgrading programme that has included the outside, the ground floor and the bedrooms. Day rooms include a cosy bar, a spacious lounge amply supplied with sofas and armchairs, and a beautiful restaurant with well-spaced tables, pristine table linen and sparkling glass.

In these civilised surroundings guests can enjoy fine dining - the best of English and Continental cuisine on table d'hote and wide-ranging à la carte menus. Lunch and dinner are served every day. The hotel also has a function suite which can cater for up to 200 for private parties and special occasions. The overnight accommodation comprises 24 well-appointed bedrooms, all with en suite facilities, multi-channel tv, tea/coffee tray and hairdryer. Hunday Manor is a hotel of wide appeal, with a growing local clientele as well as business and corporate customers and tourists. Workington Golf Course is only a mile away, and the town itself is an easy drive away. The Helena Thompson Museum recalls life in the town's Victorian heyday, while Whitehaven, an easy drive down the A595, is famous for its elaborate old mine workings. Cockermouth is five miles away, and beyond it the lure of the Lake District beckons.

Opening Hours: 11-11.

Food: A la carte and table d'hote menus.

Credit Cards: Amex, Mastercard, Visa.

Accommodation: 24 en suite rooms.

Facilities: Car park, garden.

Entertainment: None

Local Places of Interest/Activities:
Workington 2 miles, Cockermouth 5 miles.

The Huntsman   29

*43 Main Street,
Cockermouth,
Cumbria CA13 9JP
Tel: 01900 826560*

Directions:
Leave the M6 at J40
and follow the A66
into Cockermouth.
The Huntsman is on
the main street in the
centre of town.

Sitting proudly on the main
street of the fine old town of
Cockermouth,   **The
Huntsman** has stood the test
of time very well. It
continues to flourish under
new tenants Ian and Sandra
Moore, who brought with
them many years experience in the licensed trade (and a serious love of golf) when they
took over the reins in the autumn of 2001. The pub extends over three floors, and in summer
hanging baskets and window boxes create a wonderfully colourful picture. Inside, all is
spick and span, with excellent carpets and curtains and comfortable, well-upholstered seats.
In the entrance bar and elevated lounge visitors can relax over a glass of excellent real ale,
which they can be sure is in good condition - Jennings Brewery is just across the street.

The food they serve every lunchtime and evening is simple and satisfying, offering real
value for money and a good choice on well-balanced menus to tempt all tastes and appetites.
Cockermouth is a good starting point for touring the Lake District and is well worth an
extended visit in its own right. It grew up round a castle built in 1134 at the junction of the
Derwent and Cocker rivers and has been touched by history down the years. Fletcher
Christian was born in Cockermouth, and so was William Wordsworth, whose handsome
Georgian family home is open for visits in the summer and at certain other times. Also on
the visitor's agenda are several museums and Castlegate House, which has monthly
exhibitions of work by Northern and Scottish artists; and for anyone as keen on golf as The
Huntsman's owners, Cockermouth Golf Course is a 5-mile drive from the inn.

Opening Hours: 11-11 (Sun 12-10.30).

Food: Bar meals.

Credit Cards: Planned.

Accommodation: None.

Facilities: None.

Entertainment: None

Local Places of Interest/Activities: Brewery,
museums and other attractions in
Cockermouth, golf 5 miles, Bassenthwaite 10
miles.

30 | King William IV

Kirksanton,
Nr Millom,
Cumbria
Tel: 01229 772009
Fax: 01229 775793

Directions:
Kirksanton lies just off the A595 2 miles north of Millom and 10 miles south of Ravenglass.

The 18th century **King William IV** has long been a great favourite with the local community, and its popularity has increased still further under the ownership of Pete and Karen Rodger. The exterior has changed little down the years, and inside, the look is also traditional Cumbrian with sturdy walls, a slate floor, open fires and neat little tables and chairs. The cooking, too, is reassuringly traditional, and the inn's steak & ale pie, cooked to an old local recipe, is always among the favourites on the menu. To accompany the food or to enjoy on their own there's a cask ale and a full selection of draught beers and lagers. This is a very peaceful corner of the county, a place to relax and unwind, and the King William IV offers comfortable, characterful accommodation in 3 guest bedrooms with en suite facilities, tv and tea/coffee tray.

The sea is just moments away, and rising above the village to almost 2,000 feet is the imposing Black Combe fell. Millom, 2 miles east of the inn, is a pleasant little town with an interesting folk museum, and at Bootle, a short drive up the A595, lies the Swinside Stone Circle, comprising 51 stones, either upright or fallen, and one of the best of its kind in Cumbria. Further up the A595 is the estuary town of Ravenglass, where the attractions for visitors include the 15" gauge Ravenglass & Eskdale Railway.

Opening Hours: 12-3 & 6-11 (winter 7-11only).

Food: Bar meals.

Credit Cards: None.

Accommodation: 3 en suite rooms.

Facilities: Car park, garden.

Entertainment: None

Local Places of Interest/Activities: Ravenglass 10 miles, Millom 2 miles, Bootle 4 miles.

Internet/website:
website: www.millom.org/kingbilly.htm

The Kings Arms | 31

Shap,
Nr Penrith,
Cumbria
CA10 3NU
Tel: 01931 716277

Directions:

Leave the M6 at J39 and turn on to the A6 for Shap (2 miles).

Larger-than-life landlord Ken Hind has ambitious plans for the **Kings Arms**, an imposing sandstone building on the main street of Shap. The large dining area/lounge was the first to be refurbished, and attention now turns to the other parts of the capacious public area - the main bar and the games area, where pool and darts are played. Ken loves his locals and they love him, and he has an equally warm welcome for new faces, and everyone enjoys the inviting ambience, the well-kept ales and the no-frills, good-value cooking. The bar food, served from 12 to 2 and 6 to 8 every day, is just what is needed for the hungry walkers and cyclists who come here, and for guests staying overnight the pub has five bedrooms for Bed & Breakfast, sharing two bathrooms. Pool and darts are played in the bar, and there are occasional live music nights.

The Kings Arms has a good car park, a beer garden and a play area for children. Shap, a small village on the once congested A6, was an important staging post for horses before they set out on the daunting climb up Shap Fell to its summit 850 feet above sea level. Not to be missed on a visit here are the imposing remains of Shap Abbey, built from the local granite that can be seen in many well-known buildings, including the Albert Memorial and St Pancras Station. In the nearby village of Keld is a chapel built by the monks from Shap Abbey and now in the care of the National Trust. The Kings Arms, built in the 18th century and rebuilt in the 19th, has enormous potential, and Ken Hind is certainly the right man to bring it to fruition.

Opening Hours: 12-11.

Food: Bar meals.

Credit Cards: Amex, Mastercard, Visa.

Accommodation: 5 bedrooms sharing 2 bathrooms.

Facilities: Car park, beer garden.

Entertainment: Pool, darts, occasional live music.

Local Places of Interest/Activities: Walking, cycling, fishing; Shap Abbey 1 mile, Lake District National Park 1 mile, Penrith 10 miles

32 The Manor House Hotel

Crown Street,
Cockermouth,
Cumbria CA13 0EH
Tel: 01900 828663
Fax: 01900 828679

Directions:

Leave the M6 at J40
on to A66. Turn right
at Cockermouth
roundabout, follow
road to Main Street
and left into Crown
Street at T-junction.

The Manor House Hotel is situated at the western end of tree-lined Crown Street, enjoying at one and the same time a quiet position and easy access to Cockermouth's shops and places of interest. A handsome 19th century building in Georgian style, the hotel offers quiet, comfortable accommodation (AA 3 Star) in 13 well-furnished en suite rooms with direct-dial telephone, tv, tea/coffee making facilities and hairdryer. Some rooms also have a trouser press and ironing centre. There is ample private car parking space directly accessible from the street.

The owner of the hotel is Joe Wilson, a trained chef who has expanded his talents to looking after this and another hotel, Hunday Manor near Workington. The restaurant at the Manor House has covers for 100 diners, who have a choice of very extensive à la carte or four-course table d'hote menus of dishes featuring the best of local produce. For less formal eating, a wide variety of lunch and supper dishes is available in the bar and adjoining lounge. The food is complemented by a carefully chosen list of wines. Joe and his team are happy to cater for special occasions and small conferences, and throughout the year the hotel offers a series of special breaks and provides very competitive rates for business guests. Terms for all guests can be Bed & Breakfast or Dinner, Bed & Breakfast.

Cockermouth, which grew up at the point where the Rivers Cocker and Derwent meet, combines the appeal of an essentially rural community with historic interest and modern amenities. Known most famously as the birthplace of William Wordsworth (his house can be visited), it also has some interesting museums and galleries and is an ideal base for tourists, with the Lake District in one direction and the coast and Solway Firth in the other.

Opening Hours: 11-11.

Food: Restaurant and bar menus.

Credit Cards: Amex, Mastercard, Visa.

Accommodation: 13 en suite rooms.

Facilities: Car park.

Entertainment: None

Local Places of Interest/Activities:
Maryport (maritime museums) 6 miles,
Bassenthwaite 6 miles, Keswick 10 miles.

Middle Ruddings Country Hotel 33

Braithwaite,
Nr Keswick,
Cumbria
CA12 5RY
Tel: 017687 78436
Fax: 017687 78438

Directions:
Braithwaite is 3
miles west of
Keswick on the
B5292.

Young, old and anyone in between - all are welcome at **Middle Ruddings Country Hotel**, where the friendly staff provide genuine country hospitality in the most delightful of surroundings. Braithwaite is a pleasant little village at the foot of the dramatic Whinlatter Pass, and the elevated position of the hotel affords tremendous views against the backdrop of the mighty Grizedale Pike rising to 2,600 feet. A large country house has been extended to offer abundant space and comfort for both residents and non-residents. For guests staying overnight there are 11 letting bedrooms, all tastefully decorated and furnished, with en suite facilities, tv and tea/coffee-makers. Everywhere is spick and span, both in the bedrooms and in the day rooms, which include a quiet, civilised lounge and a beautiful conservatory restaurant.

Well-priced bar and restaurant menus cater for all tastes and appetites, and the food is served lunchtime and evening seven days a week. Lovers of fresh air and the great outdoors are in their element at Middle Ruddings, whether relaxing in the garden or enjoying an invigorating walk while taking in the scenic glories of one of the most beautiful parts of the whole country. Bassenthwaite Lake, with Skiddaw looming above, and Derwentwater are very close by, and Whinlatter Forest Park, one of the Forestry Commission's oldest woodland, has a Visitor Centre, trails and walks for all energy levels, an orienteering course and an adventure playground.

Opening Hours: 12-2.30 & 6-11.

Food: Bar and restaurant menus.

Credit Cards: Mastercard, Visa.

Accommodation: 11 en suite rooms.

Facilities: Car park, garden.

Entertainment: None

Local Places of Interest/Activities: Keswick 1 mile, Whinlatter Forest Park 2 miles, Bassenthwaite Lake 2 miles.

Internet/website:
e-mail: middleruddings@aol.com
website: www.middleruddings.com

34   The Royal Oak Hotel

Braithwaite, Keswick,
Cumbria
CA12 5SY
Tel/Fax:
01768 778533

Directions:

Leave the M6 at
Junction 40 (Penrith)
and follow the A66
passing Keswick and
Portinscale junctions.
Braithwaite village is
situated just off the
A66 about 1 mile
further west.

The Royal Oak Hotel is a traditional country inn at the heart of Braithwaite village, set in spectacular scenery and within walking distance of some of the highest fells in the area. The hotel, owned and run by Terry and Paula Franks, is an ideal base for anything from a walking weekend to a family holiday, with the fells and the Lakes nearby and Keswick only a couple of miles away. The overnight accommodation, all en suite, with tv and tea/coffee makers, includes single, twin, double and four-poster rooms, all of them well appointed and tastefully decorated. A splendid Cumberland breakfast is served in the restaurant, where the full evening menu offers something for everyone.

The Royal Oak prawn cocktail ('served with a difference') is a popular starter, while the main courses include steaks, scampi, giant Yorkshire pudding filled with beef and Guinness and local specialities such as Cumberland sausage with apple sauce or a hotpot with lamb, black pudding and vegetables cooked in Jennings bitter. Light snacks and a bar menu are also available, and the food goes down particularly well with a glass or two of Jennings cask ale.

The village of Braithwaite is well worth taking time to explore (www.gobraithwaite.co.uk).It lies at the foot of Whinlatter Pass, one of Cumbria's most dramatic routes, with spectacular views and a forest park offering a range of activities for the energetic.

Opening Hours: 11-11 every day.

Food: Full menu and snacks.

Credit Cards: All the major cards.

Accommodation: En suite B&B rooms including a four-poster room.

Facilities: Car park, beer garden.

Entertainment: Occasional quiz and live music nights.

Local Places of Interest/Activities: Keswick 2 miles, Whinlatter Forest Park 2 miles, Skiddaw 2 miles, Bassenthwaite Lake 1 mile.

Internet/website:
e-mail: tpfranks@hotmail.com
website: www.royaloak-braithwaite.co.uk

Sailors Return   35

17 King Street,
Maryport, Cumbria
CA15 6AJ
Tel: 01900 813124

Directions:
Maryport is on the
coast on the A596, 6
miles north of
Workington.

Sailors are not the only visitors
who return time after time to
Dave and Moree Weir's homely
old pub overlooking the
recently redeveloped dock area
of Maryport. **The Sailors
Return** dates from 1884 and
was built in the old style, big
and bold and made to last. The
high-ceilinged open-plan
public area is warm and
inviting, but the real stars of the
show are Dave and Moree and
their son, whose genuine
Northern hospitality is second to none. Value for money is outstanding among the
straightforward bar meals that are served from noon to 7 o'clock seven days a week.
Sandwiches are popular choices for quick snacks, while main dishes include roast beef and
turkey, curried chicken, cheese and broccoli bake, home-made steak pie and lasagne (meat
or vegetarian).

Maryport, dramatically located on the Solway Firth, has a strong maritime history that
dates back to the Romans, who built a clifftop fort, Alauna, that is now part of the Hadrian's
Wall World Heritage Site. After a period of decline the town is now enjoying a revival shown
in the handsome restored Georgian quayside buildings and the bustling marina. Two
museums trace the maritime connection, and in the Lake District Coast Aquarium visitors
are introduced to the profusion of marine life to be found in the Solway Firth. The Sailors
Return is handily placed for all these attractions and offers budget overnight accommodation
in two letting bedrooms.

Opening Hours: 11-11 (Sun 12-10.30)

Food: Bar meals.

Credit Cards: None.

Accommodation: 2 budget rooms.

Facilities: Wheelchair access

Entertainment: Planned.

Local Places of Interest/Activities: Roman
fort and museums in Maryport, Allonby 4
miles, Workington (Helena Thompson
Museum) 6 miles.

Internet/website:
e-mail: dave@stationst.freeserve.co.uk

36   The Salutation Inn

Threlkeld,
Nr Keswick,
Cumbria
CA12 4SQ
Tel/Fax:
017687 76914

Directions:
Threlkeld is situated
on the A66 3 miles
east of Keswick.

The Salutation Inn is a
fine old coaching inn on
the main street of the
picture-postcard village
of Threlkeld, easy to find
on the A66 east of
Keswick. Behind the
smart frontage, painted
cream with black details for doors and windows, ancient beams testify to the inn's great age,
and an open fire, horse brasses and items of local history add to the appeal. The inn has
built up a long-standing reputation for hospitality and the excellence of its food, and that
reputation is being enhanced still further by the current owners John and Margaret, who
loves the inn and the region and has a genuinely warm salutation for all his customers. Real
ales and ciders satisfy thirsts, and there's a good selection of wines to enjoy with the splendid,
unpretentious home cooking. Lunch is served from 12 to 2, dinner from 6 to 9 every day,
and one of the great favourites at any time is the super steak, mushroom and ale pie.

A conservatory extension has recently been completed, and John plans add 4 en suite
guest bedrooms in the main building to the three-bedroom cottage that currently
accommodates guests. The village of Threlkeld, with its narrow streets and little alleyways,
is a delightful place to stay and a good base for touring. Close to the village is the mighty
Blencatha, one of the most exciting of all the Lake District mountains, and another popular
spot is the Threlkeld Quarry & Mining Museum with its collection of mining artefacts and
a re-created mine to explore. A pleasant walk along a disused railway line leads from Threlkeld
to Keswick, a beautiful town full of historical and cultural interest.

Opening Hours: 12-11 (may be seasonal
variations).

Food: Bar meals.

Credit Cards: Mastercard, Visa.

Accommodation: Cottage & planned rooms.

Facilities: Car park, beer garden.

Entertainment: None

Local Places of Interest/Activities: At the
foot of Blencathra, Keswick 4 miles.

The Snooty Fox | 37

Uldale,
Cumbria
CA7 1HA
Tel: 016973 71479
Fax: 016973 71910

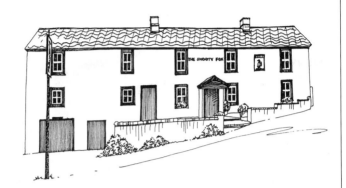

Directions:
From Keswick take
the A591 to
Bassenthwaite.
Uldale is reached by
a minor road that
leads north towards
the B5299.

To the northeast of Bassenthwaite Lake stretches the area known locally as the 'Land at back o' Skidda'. Well off the beaten tourist track, the region is both peaceful and picturesque, with fells and valleys and unspoilt villages. One such is Uldale, where the social hub is the **Snooty Fox** Country Inn. There are strong hunting traditions in this part of the county (John Peel married a girl from Uldale) and the name of the inn is taken up by images of the fox in the specially woven carpet. The inn, which dates from before 1700, is owned and run by Carol and Neil Tunstall, who offer their patrons an excellent choice of food served at lunchtime in the bar or non-smoking restaurant (don't miss the splendid Cumberland sausage!), three real ales (one brewed locally specially for the Snooty Fox) and comfortable accommodation in three en suite guest bedrooms with central heating, tv and tea-making kit.

The public bar has satellite tv and there are papers and magazines to read in the lounge; pool and darts are played in a separate games room. The bars and restaurant are accessible to wheelchair users. Packed lunches are available to make the most of the wonderful scenery and exhilarating air in this corner of the Lake District National Park. Bassenthwaite Lake, the mighty Skiddaw (3,054 feet) and the lovely town of Keswick are to the south, while to the north is the pretty village of Caldbeck. The Reivers Way and Coast to Coast (C2C) cycle route pass close to the Snooty Fox, which is open as both inn and hotel throughout the year.

Opening Hours: 12-2 & 6.30-11.

Food: Full menu available in all areas

Credit Cards: All the major cards.

Accommodation: 3 en suite rooms.

Facilities: Car park, beer garden.

Entertainment: Quiz Sunday.

Local Places of Interest/Activities:
Caldbeck 3 miles, Keswick 11 miles,
Bassenthwaite 5 miles.

Internet/website:
e-mail: snooty.fox@virgin.net

38 St Patrick's Well

Bampton,
Nr Penrith,
Cumbria
CA10 2RQ
Tel: 01931 713244

Directions:
Leave the M6 at J39
and take the A6 to
Shap. Turn left on
to a minor road
signposted Rosgil
and Bampton.

Peter and Cynthia Barry, here since the mid-1990s, make a splendid team at **St Patrick's Well**, where people meet from all over Cumbria to enjoy Cynthia's cooking. She sets great store by the quality of ingredients, seeking out the best local suppliers of meat and poultry for her excellent dishes. A good choice of wines is available to accompany the food, and the inn also keeps a good range of draught ales and lagers. In the roomy bar a treasured watercolour painting of the inn takes pride of place above the hearth, and on the beams and shelves is a collection of brasses, jugs and bottles.

The inn dates back to the early 18th century, and the long whitewashed frontage has original red sandstone steps leading up to the front door. Inside, all is equally delightful and shows the care and devotion bestowed on it by the owners. This is definitely a place to linger, to relax and unwind, and for guests staying overnight there are three letting bedrooms with tv, hospitality tray and hairdryer; two have en suite facilities, the other its own private bathroom adjacent. Both for food and the accommodation it is best to book ahead if possible.

There are plenty of good walks in this picturesque northern part of the Lake District National Park, and at nearby Haweswater, which looks like a lake but was actually created as a reservoir in the late 1930s, birdwatchers might spot woodpeckers and sparrowhawks, buzzards, peregrine falcons and even, if it's a lucky day, a golden eagle or two.

Opening Hours: Evenings only. Closed Monday.

Food: Bar meals.

Credit Cards: None.

Accommodation: 3 rooms, 2 en suite.

Facilities: Parking.

Entertainment: None

Local Places of Interest/Activities: Shap 3 miles, Haweswater 2 miles.

The Stag Inn

39

Crosby,
Nr Maryport,
Cumbria
CA15 6SH
Tel: 01900 812549

Directions:
Crosby is on the
A596 Carlisle road
about 3 miles out
of Maryport.

Hospitality is definitely the name of the game at the **Stag Inn**, a large and distinctive 100-year-old building off the A596 road out of Maryport. In the open-plan bar area, with thick-pile carpets, chunky tables and chairs and high-quality soft furnishings, regulars and visitors to the Cumbrian coast socialise and enjoy a glass of one of the regularly changing cask ales or something from the extensive choice of other draught beers and lagers. The Stag also has an excellent wine list to complement the good-value food served lunchtime and evening. There are separate bar and restaurant menus, both serving home-prepared classic pub fare in generous portions.

Darts, pool and dominoes are all played in the bar, and most days of the week bring entertainment of some kind - ladies darts on Monday, bingo on Tuesday, a quiz on Thursday, live music on Saturday. Not surprisingly, the Stag is a popular for parties and special occasions, and the function suite above the bar is in regular use. It's a quick and easy drive into Maryport, a charming Cumbrian coastal town where the Romans built a clifftop fort called Alauna. The Senhouse Roman Museum tells the story of life in those times, while two other museums are devoted to the port's maritime history. Windsurfers should head further up the coast to the popular resort village of Allonby.

Opening Hours: 11-11 (Sun 12-10.30).

Food: Bar and restaurant menus.

Credit Cards: Mastercard, Visa.

Accommodation: None.

Facilities: Car park, outside seating, function suite.

Entertainment: Something different most nights - see above.

Local Places of Interest/Activities:
Maryport 3 miles, Allonby 4 miles, Cockermouth 6 miles.

40   The Strands Hotel

Nether Wasdale,
Nr Gosforth,
Cumbria
CA20 1ET
Tel: 01946 726237

Directions:

Leave the A595 at
Gorforth and take
the minor road
through
Wellington to
Nether Wasdale.
The hotel is on the
righthand side in
the village.

1791 is the date inscribed above the entrance to the **Strands Hotel**, which is the largest and most conspicuous building in the tiny, picturesque village of Nether Wasdale. This is the first venture into the trade for Stuart and Laurie Sherry, who intend to retain as much of the inn's original character as possible. Thick walls divide the public area into a number of small rooms, each with tremendous charm, and in the restaurant good honest home-cooked food is served throughout opening times. Log fires keep the whole place warm and cosy, and in the summer the scene shifts to the lovely garden that surrounds the inn. Sellafield BNFL provides much of the business trade, while tourists, ramblers and cyclists also appreciate the hospitable atmosphere, the good food, the well-kept cask ales and the comfortable overnight accommodation.

There are eleven letting bedrooms, ten with en suite facilities and a single with adjacent bathroom. Walking and fishing are popular pastimes hereabouts for lovers of fresh air, there's golf a few miles away and it's only four miles to Scafell Pike, the highest peak in England at 3,205 feet. Wasdale is the wildest of the Lake District valleys but is nonetheless easily accessible by road. Nether Wasdale is at the southern end of Wast Water, which is just three miles long but is the deepest lake in England. At the northern end is Wasdale Head, whose village church is one of the smallest in the country.

Opening Hours: 6-11 on weekdays, 5-11 on Saturdays. Closed Sunday

Food: Home cooked

Credit Cards: Mastercard, Visa.

Accommodation: 10 en suite rooms, 1 with adjacent bathroom

Facilities: Car park, garden.

Entertainment: None

Local Places of Interest/Activities: Scafell Pike 4 miles. Walking, fishing, golf

The Sun Inn   **41**

Crook, Kendal,
Cumbria
LA8 8LH
Tel: 01539 821351

Directions:
The Sun Inn is
situated at Crook,
on the B5284
between Kendal
and Bowness-on-
Windermere.

In the early years of the 18th century the **Sun Inn** was a row of cottages, but when one of the cottagers started selling beer to travellers the stage was set for its future role. Today, in the ownership of Gill and Peter Sykes, the inn has two cosy rooms serving a wide range of traditional hand-drawn ales and home-cooked dishes. Mushrooms with a Dijon mustard sauce topped with croutons, and marinated anchovies with sliced tomatoes are typical tempting starters, while main courses on the bar menu could include almond-topped grilled salmon fillet, pepper steak, rack of lamb with minted gravy and chicken breast stuffed with cheese and wrapped in bacon with a Madeira sauce. Seafood and game make their appearances in season, and roast beef is a perennial favourite for Sunday lunch. The food is accompanied by an interesting choice of wines.

Children are welcome in the eating area (and they have their own menu), and the Sun has outside seating and a private car park. There are regular theme, food and quiz nights. The pub, a proper village local, enjoys a quiet setting away from the Lake District bustle, but all the attractions are nearby. Lake Windermere and the Grizedale Forest on its far shore are a short drive to the west, while in the other direction lies Kendal, whose attractions include the Museum of Lakeland Life and the ruins of a 12th century castle where Henry VIII's last wife Catherine Parr was born.

Opening Hours: 12-3 & 6-11.

Food: Bar and restaurant menus.

Credit Cards: Mastercard, Visa.

Accommodation: None.

Facilities: Car park, outside seating.

Entertainment: Monthly food and theme nights, occasional quiz nights.

Local Places of Interest/Activities: Golf, fishing; Kendal 4 miles, Bowness and Lake Windermere 4 miles.

42

The Sun Inn

Main Street,
Hawkshead,
Cumbria LA22 0NT
Tel: 015394 36236
Fax: 015394 36155

Directions:

Leave the M6 at J36
and take the A591 to
Ambleside then the
B5286 to Hawkshead.
The inn is in the
village centre.

Located in the centre of
the delightful village of
Hawkshead, the 17th
century **Sun Inn** has everything the visitor could want: the ambience is warm and welcoming,
the accommodation comfortable and characterful, the food excellent, the bar well stocked.
The inn has eight guest bedrooms, each individually furnished to make the best of the
traditional oak and Lakeland building features; all have private facilities, tv and tea/coffee-
makers. Six of the rooms are doubles/twins, one is a family room and one is a four-poster
room. Owners Tony and Doreen Pape also offer a superb range of cuisine, including local
specialities, and, as a free house, the inn keeps a good selection of local cask ales, lagers,
spirits and a wide choice of wines from around the world.

The Sun Inn is a popular base from which to tour the area, but the village itself has
much to interest the visitor. St Michael's Church is a grand 15th century building reflecting
the days when the village was a prosperous centre of the woollen trade; the Grammar School,
founded in 1585, numbers William Wordsworth among its star pupils and visitors can look
round the classrooms. In the same street as the Sun Inn is the Beatrix Potter Gallery with an
exhibition of her drawings and details of her life. Her home, Hill Top, is close by in Near
Sawrey. Hawkshead is situated at the head of Esthwaite Water and enjoys glorious views of
the 2,500 ft Old Man of Coniston. Grizedale Forest and Windermere are also close by, making
this a marvellous area for touring or walking holidays.

Opening Hours: 11-11 (Sun 12-10.30).

Food: Bar and restaurant menus.

Credit Cards: Mastercard, Visa.

Accommodation: 8 en suite rooms.

Facilities: Terrace.

Entertainment: None

Local Places of Interest/Activities: Fishing,
golf nearby, Near Sawrey (Beatrix Potter
home) 2 miles, Grizedale Forest 2 miles,
Windermere 2 miles.

Internet/website:

e-mail: thesuninn@hawkshead98.freeserve.co.uk
website: www.suninn.co.uk

The Sun Inn **43**

Ireby, Nr Wigton,
Cumbria CA7 1EA
Tel: 016973 71346

Directions:
From Cockermouth
take the A595 to just
after Bothel; turn
right on to minor
road signposted
Torpenhow and
Ireby. From the
north, take the A595
south to Mealsgate
then left on to the
B5299 and right on
to a minor road
signposted Ireby.

The Sun Inn lies in picturesque hunting country in a village above Bassenthwaite. It dates from 1594, and when the main Carlisle road ran through the village it was a popular coaching stop. The main road moved long ago, the village is quieter and The Sun is a delightful spot to seek out for a drink or a meal. It has been run for almost 25 years by a really charming couple Pam and Roland Medlicott, who are devoted to the inn and to this part of the county. The poet John Keats stayed here in 1818 on his walk north, and not a great deal has really changed since his visit. Behind the smart whitewashed frontage the scene is delightfully traditional, with a fire burning in the cast-iron grate, low beams hung with grass horns and ornaments, pictures and prints and plenty of comfortably upholstered chairs set at neat wooden tables.

Local farms produce all the meat and poultry to make the wholesome, tasty dishes that are served from 12 to 1.30 and from 6.30 to 9 each day. Two cask ales are on tap to enjoy with a chat or a game of darts or dominoes, or to take out into the beer garden. Minor roads lead from Ireby in all directions. To the south lie Bassenthwaite Lake and Trotters & Friends Animal Farm, home to many hundreds of animals and birds. Rising grandly above the Lake is Skiddaw, one of the Lake District's most popular peaks for climbers. The village next to Ireby is Uldale, from where Mary, the daughter of a local farmer, eloped to marry the renowned huntsman John Peel. This is the heart of John Peel country, and the man himself is buried in the churchyard at Caldbeck, a short drive along the B5299. In Ireby itself a horn, riding crop and stirrups belonging to John Peel are on display.

Opening Hours: 12-3 & 6.30-11.

Food: Bar meals.

Credit Cards: None.

Accommodation: None.

Facilities: Car park, beer garden.

Entertainment: None

Local Places of Interest/Activities: Uldale 1 mile, Bassenthwaite Lake 5 miles, Caldbeck 5 miles, Keswick 12 miles.

44   The Sun Inn

Spittal Square,
Lower Arlecdon,
Cumbria

Tel: 01946 862011

Directions:
Arlecdon is on the
A5086 Egremont-
Cockermouth road
4 miles north of
Egremont, 4 miles
east of
Whitehaven.

Lying just off the A5086 about a mile north of Frizington, the **Sun Inn** is a traditional country pub dating from the early part of the 19th century. Rural in every respect and totally without pretension, the inn is kept in apple pie order by the husband and wife team of Mike and Phyllis Deakin - he's a Cumbrian, she's from Antrim, and between them they provide an object lesson in just how a small country inn should be run. Two cask ales and a good selection of other draughts beers and ciders take care of fresh-air thirsts, and fresh fish and meat are to the fore in the straightforward home-cooked dishes that are served every session except Monday lunchtime, when the inn is closed.

The Sun is in an ideal location for ramblers and tourists and makes a good halfway house between Whitehaven and Cockermouth. Whitehaven, on the coast, is full of life and interest, while visitor attractions in the pretty town of Egremont, a short drive down the A5086, include the last deep working iron ore mine in Europe, and the annual Crab Fair, held on the third Saturday in September; celebrations at the fair include the parade of the apple cart, from which apples - originally crab apples - are thrown into the crowd, a greasy pole competition, wrestling and the world gurning championships. To the east of Arlecdon is the rather more tranquil and secluded Ennerdale Water on the most beautiful section of the Coast to Coast Walk.

Opening Hours: 12-2 (not Monday) & 6-11.

Food: Bar meals.

Credit Cards: None.

Accommodation: None.

Facilities: Car park, outside seats.

Entertainment: None

Local Places of Interest/Activities:
Whitehaven 5 miles, Egremont 4 miles,
Ennerdale Water 3 miles.

The Swan Inn

45

Kirkgate,
Cockermouth,
Cumbria
CA13 9PH
Tel/Fax:
01900 822425

Directions:

Leave the M6 at J40 and follow the A66 to Cockermouth town centre. Take Lorton/ Buttermere signs; turn right into Lorton Street then first left into Kirkgate.

Set among a warren of tiny streets in the old part of town, the **Swan Inn**, said to be the oldest in Cockermouth, is a traditional pub with quaint little cottages for neighbours. Inside, the scene is one of old-world charm, with thick walls, low, low ceilings, old oak beams, wooden or slate floors and an open fire by the bar, which is just about full when a dozen customers crowd in. Experienced publicans Glenn and Beryl Ireland, ably assisted by Jet the dog, have a warm welcome for all-comers, including children and dogs. Food is simple, quick and sustaining, with breakfast in a bun or egg and bacon butties among the favourites. This is a Jennings pub, one of more than 100 across the north of England, and the Jennings brews include Cumberland Ale, Cocker Hoop and Sneck Lifter.

The Jennings Brewery is actually in Cockermouth, and visitors can take a 90-minute conducted tour to see the beer being made, to do a spot of tasting and perhaps to buy a souvenir from the gift shop. Cockermouth's most famous son is William Wordsworth, whose imposing Georgian house is now in the care of the National Trust and is open to the public. Also not to be missed are the Toy & Model Museum, the Printing House Museum and the Mining Museum, and after taking in these and other attractions Glenn, Beryl and Jet are ready to take good care of you - but note that opening hours vary from day to day.

Opening Hours: Mon 6.30-11; Tue & Wed 12-3; Thur-Sat 11-11; Sun 12-4 & 7-10.30.

Food: Bar snacks.

Credit Cards: None.

Accommodation: None.

Facilities: None.

Entertainment: Occasional quiz nights.

Local Places of Interest/Activities: Jennings Brewery, Cockermouth museums, Bassenthwaite 10 miles.

46　The Tower Bank Arms

Near Sawrey,
Nr Hawkshead,
Cumbria
LA22 0LF
Tel/Fax:
　015394 36334

Directions:

Near Sawrey is
situated 2 miles
south of Hawskhead
on the B5285. From
Bowness, take the car
ferry across Lake
Windermere or head
for Newby Bridge
and drive up the
west shore of Lake
Windermere.

The Lakeland traveller will find no more hospitable a welcome than the one provided by Philip and Dorothy Broadley and their family at the 17th century **Tower Bank Arms**. Generations of children know it as the small country inn in Beatrix Potter's Tale of Jemima Puddleduck and a small country inn is what it remains today, carefully modernised to lose none of its period charm. Open throughout the year, the inn is ideally suited for walking, golf and sailing holidays, and it also has a fishing licence for two rods per day on some of the local tarns and lakes. There are three guest bedrooms, two with double beds and the other with twin beds. All three rooms have en suite facilities, tv and tea-making trays, and central heating keeps things cosy all year round.

　　Bar lunches are available every day and evening meals are served either in the bar or in the dining room. The inn is fully licensed and is renowned for its selection of beers including five real ales and a wide range from around the world, from an alcohol-free Erdinger Weiss to the super-strong Delirium Tremens from Belgium. Beatrix Potter lived for a time in the next-door Hill Top, which she bought with the proceeds from The Tale of Peter Rabbit. The house is much as it was on the day she died in 1943. Filled with Potter memorabilia and some of her original drawings, as well as her furniture and china, it is one of the most popular of all Lakeland attractions. Both Hill Top and Tower Bank Arms are owned by the National Trust.

Opening Hours: Summer: 11-3 & 5.30-11
(Sun 12-10.30); Winter 11-3 & 6-11 (Sun 12-3
& 6-10.30).

Food: Bar lunches, evening à la carte.

Credit Cards: All the major cards.

Accommodation: 3 en suite rooms.

Facilities: Car park, garden.

Entertainment: None

Local Places of Interest/Activities: Golf,
sailing, fishing; Hawkshead (B Potter Gallery)
2 miles, Lake Windermere 2 miles.

The White Mare

47

Beckermet,
Cumbria
CA21 2XS
Tel: 01946 841246
Fax: 01946 841100

Directions:

From Carlisle, take
the A595 past
Whitehaven and
Egremont until
picking up the
Beckermet sign.

Philip Ward is the friendly, energetic licensee at the **White Mare**, a small country pub and hotel set in the village of Beckermet. An ideal base for exploring the hidden places of the Westlakes and Lake District, it also attracts an appreciative local clientele. With its smart white-painted frontage and small-paned windows, the White Mare, which dates back to the early 1800s, is a place of considerable charm and character, and open fires in the main lounge make it a warm, inviting spot for a drink. On a lower level is a public bar with a pool table, while raised above the lounge is a delightful restaurant with a rich red carpet and oak furnishings. A dedicated team in the kitchen cater well for their customers, providing a good choice on bar and restaurant menus, including daily specials and a wide selection of vegetarian meals. Prices are very reasonable, and senior citizens get an extra special deal with a 2-course Sunday lunch for £6.

For overnight guests the White Mare has six double and two twin bedrooms, all with bath and shower en suite, tv and tea/coffee making facilities. Four of the rooms have convertible couches, making them particularly suitable for families, and all the rooms are non-smoking. The White Mare has an excellent car park and a beer garden. Local groups and singers perform in the restaurant once a month, and other social events include a quiz on Wednesdays and a knockout dominoes competition every Friday. The Lakes are within an easy drive, the sea even closer, and among the attractions in the vicinity are Egremont Castle, the Florence Mine Heritage Centre and the Sellafield Visitors Centre.

Opening Hours: Every lunchtime and evening.

Food: Bar and restaurant menus.

Credit Cards: All major credit cards

Accommodation: 8 en suite rooms.

Facilities: Car park, beer garden.

Entertainment: Quiz Wednesday, dominoes Friday, band and singers monthly.

Local Places of Interest/Activities:
Egremont 3 miles, Sellafield 2 miles.

Internet/website:
e-mail: phil@whitemare.co.uk
website: www.whitemare.co.uk

48   Yewdale Hotel

Yewdale Road,
Coniston, Cumbria
CA21 8DU
Tel: 015394 41280
Fax: 015394 41871

Directions:

From the M6 (J36) follow signs for Windermere (A591). After 4 miles turn left on to A590 signposted Ulverston. At Greenold turn right on to the A5092, then (2 miles) right on to the A5084 to Coniston.

The **Yewdale Hotel** is a small family-run concern situated in the centre of Coniston and therefore central for the scenic delights of the region. Built of local stone and slate in 1896, it was once part guest house and part bank. Owners Barbara and Ken Barrow and their son-in-law manager have invested time and care into improving the comfort and amenities while retaining much of its original charm including some fine oak woodwork (the hotel bar used to be the bank counter). Nine centrally heated bedrooms with en suite or adjacent bath/shower rooms, tv and tea-making facilities, provide comfortable, restful accommodation, and an excellent Cumbrian breakfast starts the day. In the 70-seat restaurant fresh seasonal produce features on a nicely varied menu that includes plenty of choice for vegetarians as well as children's dishes. A five-course dinner is served in the restaurant during the busy season, and at other times evening meals are taken in the lounge bar.

In high season the hotel is open daily for breakfast, morning coffee, snacks, lunches, afternoon tea and evening meals. Non-residents are welcome. All interests are catered for in the area, and the owners and staff are on hand to offer advice and information on how to enjoy them to the full. Fishing, boating, canoeing, walking and pony trekking are all available on or around Coniston Water, and those with energy to spare can tackle the climb up the 2,600' Old Man of Coniston. The Ruskin Museum in the village celebrates the life and work of the Victorian artist John Ruskin, and a short ferry trip across the Lake takes visitors to Brantwood, Ruskin's home for the last 28 years of his life.

Opening Hours: All day, every day.

Food: Bar and restaurant menus.

Credit Cards: Mastercard, Visa.

Accommodation: 7 rooms, 5 en suite.

Facilities: Car park.

Entertainment: None

Local Places of Interest/Activities: Many sporting/outdoor activities nearby, Windermere 5 miles.

Internet/website:

e-mail: yewdalehotel@virgin.net
website: www.yewdalehotel.com

2 North Cumbria and the Eden Valley

PLACES OF INTEREST:

PUBS AND INNS:

The Hidden Inns of The North of England

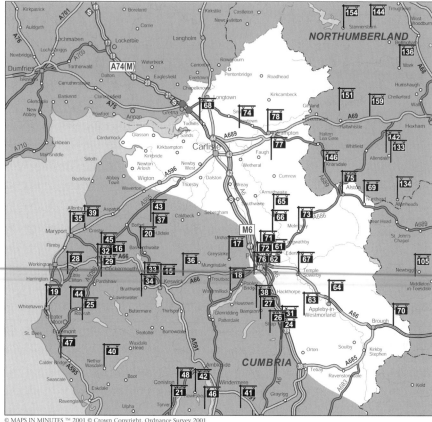

© MAPS IN MINUTES ™ 2001 © Crown Copyright, Ordnance Survey 2001

61 The Agricultural Hotel, Castlegate, Penrith

62 The Beehive Inn, Eamont Bridge, Penrith

63 The Butchers Arms, Crosby Ravensworth

64 The Crown & Cushion, Appleby-in-Westmorland

65 The Fetherston Arms, Kirkoswald

66 The Highland Drove Inn, Great Salkeld, Nr Penrith

67 The Kings Arms Hotel, Temple Sowerby, Nr Penrith

68 Metal Bridge Inn, Floristonrigg, Nr Carlisle

69 The Miners Arms, Nenthead, Alston

70 The Punch Bowl Inn, North Stainmore, Nr Kirkby Stephen

71 The Railway Inn, Low Row, Nr Brampton

72 The Royal, Wilson Row, Penrith

73 The Shepherds Inn, Melmerby, Nr Penrith

74 The Sportsman Inn, Laversdale, Nr Carlisle

75 The Turks Head, Alston

76 The Waverley Inn, Penrith

77 The Weary Sportsman, Castle Carrock, Nr Brampton

78 The White Lion Hotel, Brampton

Please note all references refer to page numbers

North Cumbria and the Eden Valley

This is the country of Hadrian's Wall, and not only are parts of the structure still visible but Birdoswald gives an excellent insight into Roman border life. The wall was built as a great military barrier across the narrowest part of Britain, from the mouth of the River Tyne, in the east, to Bowness-on-Solway, in the west. Guarded by forts at regular intervals, it was built between AD122-128 following a visit by the Emperor Hadrian who saw the then military infrastructure as insufficient to withstand the combined attacks of northern barbarians. Originally, much of the western side was built from turf, but by AD163 this had been replaced by stone. The wall was finally abandoned in the late 4th century. Carlisle is by far the largest and most important town in the region, while Penrith is the most historic of Lakeland towns and was almost certainly settled long before the Romans arrived. They quickly appreciated its strategic position on the main west coast artery linking England and Scotland and built a fort nearby although nothing visible remains today. Most of the town's oldest buildings have also disappeared, victims of the incessant Border conflicts. But Penrith today is a busy place, its location close to the M6 and within easy reach not only of the Lakes but also the Border Country and the Yorkshire Dales making it a hub of this north-western corner of England.

The Eden Valley is green and fertile - in every sense another Eden. But the valley was vulnerable to Scottish raids in medieval times and the number of pele towers and castles in the area are testament to a turbulent and often violent past. An attractive man-made feature of the valley is the collection of specially commissioned stone sculptures known as Eden Benchmarks dotted along its length. Each created by a different sculptor, they have been located beside public paths and, since they also function as seats, provide the perfect setting in which to enjoy the valley's unspoilt scenery.

PLACES OF INTEREST

ALSTON

For a few weeks in 1999 the small town of Alston, 1000ft up in the Pennines, became transformed into "Bruntmarsh", the fishing village in which the fictional Oliver Twist spent his early years. To recreate the squalid conditions of the poor in early 19th century England, production designers "dressed down" the town, so much so that anxious visitors noticing the soot-blackened buildings inquired whether there had been a major fire.

Alan Bleasdale's re-working of Charles Dickens' classic novel was for many the television highlight of 1999 and one of the mini-series' many strengths was the authenticity of the locations. Alston proved to be ideal since the town centre has changed little since the late 1700s when the story is set and there are many even older buildings. The town

Market Square, Alston

52

council has created an Oliver Twist's Alton Trail, with each of the 24 sites featured in the series marked by a picture of Mr Bumble.

The route includes some fascinating old buildings, a cobbled main street and, from the picturesque market cross, narrow lanes radiating out with courtyards enclosing old houses. Many of the older buildings still have the outside staircase leading to the first floor - a relic from the days when animals were kept below whilst the family's living accommodation was upstairs. This ancient part of Alston is known as The Butts, a title acquired by the need of the townspeople to be proficient in archery during the times of the border raids.

An unusual feature of Alston is the number of watermills in and around the town and the mill race was once the central artery of the old town. At High Mill, visitors can see the enormous **Smeaton water wheel** in action. The tall spire of St Augustine's Church is a well known local landmark and its churchyard contains a number of interesting epitaphs, as well as affording wonderful views of the South Tyne Valley.

Considering its small population, Alston supports an astonishing diversity of shops, pubs and craft centres.

Another popular attraction in Alston is the **South Tynedale Railway**. This narrow gauge (2ft) steam railway runs regular services during the summer months and at the northern terminus of the 3-mile long track travellers can join a stretch of the Pennine Way that runs alongside the River South Tyne. From Alston's restored Victorian station there's also a bus service ferrying passengers to the Settle and Carlisle railway.

Alston Moor, to the south of the town, was once the centre of an extremely important lead mining region, one of the richest in Britain. Lead and silver were probably mined on the moor by the Romans, but the industry reached its peak in the early 19th century when vast quantities of iron, silver, copper, and zinc were extracted by the London Lead Company. A Quaker company, it was a pioneer of industrial welfare and also built the model village of Nenthead to house the miners. Here, not only were the workers and their families provided with a home, but education was compulsory and there were some public baths.

APPLEBY-IN-WESTMORLAND

The old county town of Westmorland, Appleby is one of the most delightful small towns in England. It was originally built by the Norman, Ranulph de Meschines, who set it within a broad loop of the River Eden which protects it on three sides. The fourth side is guarded by Castle Hill. The town's uniquely attractive main street, Boroughgate, has been described as the finest in England. A broad, tree-lined avenue,

Appleby Horse Fair

it slopes down the hillside to the river, its sides lined with a pleasing variety of buildings, some dating back to the 17th century. At its foot stands the 16th century **Moot Hall** (still used for council meetings and also housing the Tourist Information Centre); at its head rises the great Norman Keep of **Appleby Castle** which is protected by one of the most impressive curtain walls in northern England. Attractions here include the dramatic view from the top of the 5-storey Keep; the stately Great Hall with its famous painting of Lady Anne Clifford and her family; and the attractive grounds which are home to a wide variety of animals and include a Rare Breeds Survival Centre.

BAMPTON

For several hundred years this small village was well-known for its Grammar School, two of whose pupils rose swiftly in the church hierarchy. One was Hugh Curwen who as a Protestant became Chaplain to Henry VIII, as a Catholic under Queen Mary was elevated to the Archbishopric of Dublin, and then prudently re-embraced Protestantism when Elizabeth succeeded to the throne. Another Bampton boy was less pliable. Edmund Gibson was baptised in the church here in 1669 and later became a

53

fiery Bishop of London who repeatedly denounced the degenerate morals of the age with little apparent effect.

A couple of miles south of Bampton, **Haweswater** is the most easterly of the lakes. It is actually a reservoir, created in the late 1930s to supply the growing needs of industrial Manchester. Beneath the water lies the village of Mardale and several dairy farms for which Haweswater Valley was once famous. By 1940, the lake had reached its present extent of 4 miles and Manchester Corporation set about planting its shores with conifers and today the area is managed as a nature reserve. Walkers have a good chance of seeing woodpeckers and sparrow hawks, buzzards and peregrine falcons, and with luck may even catch sight of golden eagles gliding on the thermals rising above Wallow Crag.

Above Haweswater runs the **High Street**, actually a Roman road, which is now one of the most popular fell walks in the Lake District. It overlooks the remote and lovely Blea Tarn and the lonely valley of Martindale, a cul-de-sac valley to the south of Ullswater, where England's last remaining herd of wild red deer can often be seen.

CARLISLE

According to a recent survey, if you are born in Carlisle you are more likely to stay here than the inhabitants of any other place in England. Its castle, cathedral, many other historic buildings, parks, thriving traditional market, shopping centres and leisure facilities all combine to endow Carlisle with the true feel of a major city. Carlisle is the largest settlement in Cumbria, (with a population of around 100,000), and is also its county town. The city stands at the junction of three rivers, the Eden, the Caldew and the Petteril, and was already fortified in Celtic times when it was named Caer Lue, "the hill fort". It became a major Roman centre: the military base for the Petriana regiment, Luguvallum, guarding the western end of Hadrian's Wall, and also an important civilian settlement with fountains, mosaics, statues and centrally-heated homes.

Today, the squat outline of **Carlisle Castle** (English Heritage), high on a hilltop overlooking the River Eden, dominates the skyline of this fascinating city. There has been a castle at Carlisle since 1092 when William Rufus first built a palisaded fort. The Norman Castle was originally built of wood but, during the Scottish occupation in the 12th century, King David I laid out a new castle with stone taken from Hadrian's Wall. The 12th century keep can still be seen enclosed by massive inner and outer walls. Entered through a great 14th century gatehouse, complete with portcullis, and with a maze of vaulted passages, chambers, staircases, towers, and dismal dungeons. Children, especially, enjoy the legendary "licking stones" from which parched prisoners tried to find enough moisture to stay alive. The castle is everything a real castle should be and is still the headquarters of the Kings Own Royal Order Regiment whose Regimental Museum is located within the castle walls.

During the Civil War, the castle was besieged for eight months by the Parliamentarians under General Leslie. When the Royalists finally capitulated, Leslie began repairing the castle and the city walls. The Puritans were no respecters of Britain's ecclesiastical heritage; stones from six of the eight bays of the cathedral were used for the repairs and the building of block-houses for the Puritan troops.

Partially for this reason, **Carlisle Cathedral** is now one of the smallest cathedrals in England but it has many interesting features, including an exquisite east window that is considered to be one of the finest in Europe. Below the beautifully painted wooden ceiling of the choir, with its gold star shimmering against deep blue, are the carved, canopied choir-stalls with their medieval misericords. These wonderful carved beasts and birds include two dragons joined by the ears, a fox killing a goose, pelicans feeding their young, and a mermaid with a looking glass.

Carlisle Cathedral

54

In the north transept is the superb 16th century Flemish Brougham Triptych which was originally in Cologne Cathedral. In the 19th century it was brought to Brougham Chapel near Penrith. The altar piece was later restored by the Victoria and Albert Museum in London and is now on permanent loan to Carlisle. It is a beautiful, intricate piece with delicately carved figures depicting scenes from the life of Christ.

It is hard to believe that it was here that Edward I solemnly used bell, book, and candle to excommunicate Robert the Bruce. It was here also that the church bells were rung to welcome Bonnie Prince Charlie in 1745. It is claimed that after the suppression of the Jacobite rebellion the bells were removed for their "treason" and only replaced in the 19th century.

Carlisle Cathedral is one of the few where visitors can enjoy refreshments actually within the precincts, in this case in the Prior's Kitchen Restaurant situated in the Fratry Undercroft. Seated beneath superb fan vaulting, customers have a good choice of home made soups, cakes and pastries, as well as morning coffee, lunches and afternoon teas.

Although an appointment is usually necessary, a visit to the nearby Prior Tower, if possible, is a must. On the first floor of this 15th century pele tower is a wonderful 45 panel ceiling incorporating the popinjay crest and arms of the Prior Senhouse. The 16th century Prior's gatehouse leads to a narrow lane called Paternoster which is named after the monks reciting their offices.

Like many great medieval cities, Carlisle was surrounded by walls. Guided walks and tours are available and the best view is to be found in a little street called West Walls at the bottom of Sally Port Steps, near the Tithe Barn. The walls date from around the 11th century and they remained virtually intact until the 1800s.

When the castle was under siege, the Sally Port allowed an individual to "sally forth". It was later used for access to the **Tithe Barn** to avoid paying city tolls. It is unusual to find a Tithe Barn within a city wall but this exception was probably made because of the Border raids. The barn dates from the 15th century and was used to collect and store taxes, or tithes, destined for the priory.

Close by is **St Cuthbert's Church**, the official city church of Carlisle and where the Lord Mayor's pew can be found. Although the present building dates from 1778, there has been a church on this site since the 7th century and the dedication is obvious since St Cuthbert was Bishop of Carlisle in AD680. It is a charming Georgian building with several interesting features including a moveable pulpit on rails.

The award winning **Tullie House Museum**, in the centre of the city close to the cathedral, is certainly another place not to be missed. Through skilful and interpretive techniques the fascinating, and often dark, history of the Debatable Lands, as this border region was called, is told. The museum's centrepiece is its story of the Border Reivers who occupied the lands from the 14th to the 17th century, with a law - or rather, a lack of it - unto themselves, being neither English or Scottish, unless it suited them to pledge, unscrupulously, allegiance to one or the other. These lawless, unruly people raged interfamily warfare with each other, decimating the lives of the local people and carrying out bloodthirsty raids. Their treacherous deeds have also added such words as "bereave" and "blackmail" to the English language.

The horrific stories of the Reivers have been passed down through the generations in the Border Ballads, and many of the Reivers family names are still known - the museum even offers a genealogy service, so that visitors find out if their ancestry goes back to these people. (Armstrongs, Bells, Charltons, Dacres and Elliots were just some of them). Perhaps the definitive Reiving story has been told in *The Steel Bonnets* by George MacDonald Fraser, author of the Flashman books. The city of Carlisle dates back far beyond those desperate days and Tullie House also has an extensive collection of Roman remains from both the city and the Cumbrian section of Hadrian's Wall.

A short walk from the Museum brings you to the **Linton Visitor Centre** (free) in Shaddongate which provides an insight into the city's industrial heritage. Standing next to a 280ft high chimney built in 1836 as part of what was once one of the largest cotton mills in Britain, the Centre has displays of hand weaving on original looms, informative displays and a selection of world famous fabrics and designer knitwear to buy.

The Old Town Hall, now an excellent Tourist Information Centre, dates from the 17th century and once housed the **Muckle Bell**, an alarm bell which, it was claimed, could be heard 11 miles away. The bell is now housed in the Tullie House Museum.

The **Guildhall Museum** (free) is housed in an unspoiled medieval building constructed by Richard of Redeness in 1407. Originally a town house, it provides an ideal setting for illustrating the history of both the Guilds and the City. Several rooms are devoted to creating the atmosphere of trade Guilds such as the shoemakers, the butchers, and the glovers. There is a splendid early 19th century banner of the Weavers Guild and an impressive collection of 17th and 18th century Guild silver. Displays also feature other items relating to the history of Carlisle and include a magnificent ironbound Muniment Chest dating from the 14th century. Conducted tours of this remarkable Guildhall are available.

Not far from the museum is the **Citadel** which is often mistaken for the castle. In fact, this intimidating fortress with its well-preserved circular tower was built in 1543 on the orders of Henry VIII to strengthen the city's defences. Much of it was demolished in the early 1800s to improve access to the city centre but what remains is mightily impressive.

Across the road from the Citadel is the railway station. The first railway to Carlisle opened in July 1836 and Citadel Station, which opened in 1850, was built to serve seven different railway companies whose coats of arms are still displayed on the façade. So elegant was its interior - and much of it remains - that Carlisle was known as the "top hat" station. Today it is still an important centre of communications; Intercity trains from Glasgow and London now link with lines to Dumfries, Tyneside, West Cumbria, and Yorkshire, and it is, of course, the northern terminus of the famous **Settle-Carlisle Railway** line.

One of the last great mainline railways to be built in Britain - it was completed in 1876 - the Settle to Carlisle line takes in some of the most dramatic scenery that the north of England has to offer. Scenic it may be but the terrain caused the Victorian engineers many problems and it is thanks to their ingenuity and skill that the line was ever finished. During the course of its 72 miles, the line crosses 20 viaducts and passes through 12 tunnels, each of which was constructed by an army of navvies who had little other than their strength and some dynamite to remove the rock.

Located on the north-western edge of the city, **Kingmoor Nature Reserve** occupies an area of moorland given to the city way back in 1352 by Edward III. Citizens enjoyed the right to graze sheep on the moors and to cut peat for fuel. Later, Carlisle's first racecourse was established here with annual Guild races being held up until 1850. Then in 1913, Kingmoor became one of the first bird sanctuaries in England and today provides a peaceful retreat away from the bustle of the city. A half-mile circular path wanders through the woodland with gentle gradients of 1 in 20 making it fully accessible to wheelchairs and pushchairs, and with seats every 100 yards or so providing plenty of resting places.

55

CROSBY-ON-EDEN

The tiny hamlet of High Crosby stands on the hillside overlooking the River Eden; the small village of Low Crosby sits beside the river, clustered around a Victorian sandstone church. Inside the church there's a modern square pulpit, intricately carved with pomegranates, wheat and vines. Apparently, it was carved from one half of a tree felled nearby; the other half was used to create a second pulpit which was installed in the newly-built Liverpool Cathedral.

A couple of miles east of Crosby, **The Solway Aviation Museum** is one of only a few museums located on a "live" airfield, in this case Carlisle Airport. Opened in 1997, the museum is home to several British jet aircraft of the 1950s and '60s, among them the mighty Vulcan. Other exhibits include a wartime air raid shelter where a video presentation explains the story behind the museum, displays of the Blue Streak rocket programme, testing for which took place only a few miles from here, and a very impressive engine room which houses one of Frank Whittle's first development jet engines.

GREYSTOKE

According to Edgar Rice Burroughs, Greystoke Castle (private) was the ancestral home of Tarzan, Lord of the Apes, a fiction which was perpetuated in the dismal 1984 film *Greystoke*, directed by Hugh Hudson. Tarzan's aristocratic credentials would have come as something of a surprise to the dignified Barons of Greystoke whose effigies are preserved in **St Andrew's Church**. As imposing and spacious as a cathedral, St Andrew's boasts a wonderful east window with much 13th century glass and, in the Lady Chapel, a figure of the Madonna and Child carved by a German prisoner-of-war.

About 100 yards from the church stands the **Plague Stone** where, during medieval times, coins were left in vinegar in exchange for food for the plague victims. An ancient **Sanctuary Stone**, now concealed behind a grille, marks the point beyond which fugitives could claim sanctuary.

Around the time of the American War of Independence, **Greystoke Castle** was bought by the 11th Duke of Norfolk, a staunch Whig who delighted in annoying his died-in-the-wool Tory neighbour, the Duke of Portland. Portland of course detested the American rebels so Norfolk built two curious castle/farmhouses close to Portland's estate, and named them Fort Putnam and Bunkers Hill after the two battles in which the British had been trounced. Norfolk displayed a similarly elegant disdain for one of his tenants, a religious bore who maintained that church buildings were an abomination. The Duke built a medieval-looking farmhouse for him and crowned it with a very ecclesiastical spire.

Greystoke village itself is a gem, its attractive houses grouped around a trimly-maintained village green. Nearby are the stables where Gordon Richards trained his two Grand National winners, *Lucius* and *Hello Dandy*.

KIRKBY STEPHEN

Surrounded by spectacular scenery, this old market town was established by the Vikings, who named it "Kirke and bye", meaning churchtown. Although essentially part of the Eden Valley, Kirkby Stephen has a strong Yorkshire Dales feel about it. Indeed, the **Church of St Stephen**, with its long, elegant nave, has been called the Cathedral of the Dales.

Dating from 1220 and with a 16th century tower, St Stephen's Church is one of the finest in the eastern fells, dominating the northern end of the town from its elevated position. Until the last century the Trupp Stone in the churchyard received money from local people every Easter Monday in payment of church tithes and, at eight o'clock, the curfew is still sounded by the Taggy Bell, once regarded by local children as a demon. Inside the church

are a number of pre-Conquest stones, some of which show Norse influence. The most remarkable is the 10th century **Loki Stone**, one of only two such carvings in Europe to have survived. Loki was a Norse God and presumably Viking settlers brought their belief in Loki to Kirkby Stephen. The carving of Loki shows a figure resembling the Devil with sheep's horns, whose legs and arms are bound by heavy irons, an image symbolising the overpowering of paganism by Christian beliefs. For many years the stone lay undiscovered, reused as a building stone. The church also boasts some interesting memorials, among them the Elizabethan tomb of Thomas, Lord Wharton and his two wives, and the earlier memorial to Sir Richard de Musgrave of Hartley Castle who died in the early 1400s. Sir Richard was the man reputed to have killed that last boar upon Wild Boar Fell, and the story was given credence when, some years ago, the tomb was opened to reveal the bones of a man and woman alongside two tusks from a boar.

Between the church and the market place stand the cloisters which served for a long time as a butter market. The market, still held every Monday, has existed since 1351 and has always been a commercial focus for the surrounding countryside. In the 18th century knitting - mostly of stockings - was the most important product of the town and a restored spinning gallery reflects the importance of the woollen industry.

There are many delightful walks from the town, to **Croglam Earthworks** for example, a prehistoric fort, or to nearby **Stenkrith Park** where the second of the Eden Benchmarks can be found. Created by Laura White in Ancaster limestone and titled *Passage*, the sculpture is deceptively simple, suggesting perhaps the course of a river bed. There are also some pleasant strolls along the riverside to a fine waterfall where the River Eden cascades into **Coop Karnel Hole**. Look out for the unusual shapes of the weathered limestone rock.

LITTLE SALKELD

A lane from the village leads to **Long Meg and her Daughters**, a most impressive prehistoric site and second only to Stonehenge in size. Local legend claims that Long Meg was a witch who, with her daughters, was turned to stone for profaning the Sabbath, as they danced wildly on the moor. The circle is supposedly endowed with magic so that it is impossible to count the same number of stones twice. Another superstition is that Long Meg will bleed if the stone is chipped or broken. The actual name, Long Meg, has been the subject of debate. It has been suggested that Meg may be a corruption of the word "magus" meaning a magician.

There are more than 60 stones in the Circle, (actually an oval), which is approximately 300ft across. The tallest, Long Meg, is a 15ft column of Penrith sandstone, the corners of which face the four points of the compass. Cup and ring symbols and spirals are carved on this stone which is over 3,500 years old. The circle is now known to belong to the Bronze Age but no one is certain of its purpose. It may have been used for rituals connected with the changing seasons since the midwinter sun sets in alignment with the centre of the circle and Long Meg herself.

In 1725 an attempt was made by Colonel Samuel Lacy of Salkeld Hall to use the stones for mileposts. However, as work began, a great storm blew up and the workmen fled in terror believing that the druids were angry at the desecration of their temple.

It was the same Colonel Lacy who gave his name to the **Lacy Caves**, a mile or so downstream from Little Salkeld. The Colonel had the five chambers carved out of the soft red sandstone, possibly as a copy of St Constantine's Caves further down the river at Wetheral. At that time it was fashionable to have romantic ruins and grottoes on large estates and Colonel Lacy is said to have employed a man to live in his caves acting the part of a hermit. Alternatively, the caves may have been intended to provide a wine store; Colonel Lacy used to entertain his guests here, and there were probably gardens around the caves. The rhododendrons and laburnums still flower every spring.

LONGTOWN

Situated on the north side of Hadrian's Wall, only a couple of miles from the Scottish border, this is the last town in England. Its position on the River Esk and so close to the border, has influenced its history from earliest times. The Romans occupied this land and they were followed by other conquerors. The legendary King Arthur attempted to organise the Northern Britons against the pagan hordes who tried to settle and control this territory. In 573AD the

mighty battle of Ardderyd was fought here and, according to legend, 80,000 men were slain.

57

Until 1750 Longtown was a small hamlet of mud dwellings. Dr Robert Graham, an 18th century clergyman, proposed the building of the Esk bridge which was completed in 1756, and it was this venture that led to Longtown's establishment as a bustling border town. These days it has some fine individual buildings and broad, tree-lined terraces of colour-washed houses.

On the outskirts of Longtown is **Arthuret Church**. The earliest records of the church date from 1150 and it was originally served by the monks of Jedburgh. But it is thought that the earliest church here may have been founded by St Kentigern in the 6th century and most recently, research has led people to believe that King Arthur was actually interred here after his last battle, Camboglanna, was fought a few miles east of Longtown at Gilsland. The present church, dedicated to St Michael and All Angels, was built in 1609, financed by a general collection throughout the realm which James I ordered after a report that the people of Arthuret Church were without faith or religion. The people that he referred to, of course, were the infamous Reivers, ungoverned by either English or Scottish laws.

LOW ROW

Within easy reach of the town is **Hadrian's Wall**, just 3 miles to the north. If you've ever

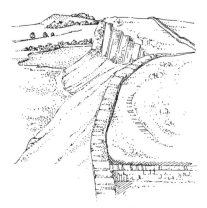

Hadrian's Wall

58

wondered where the Wall's missing masonry went to, look no further than the fabric of **Lanercost Priory**, just outside the town. An impressive red sandstone ruin set in secluded woodland, the priory was founded in 1166 by Robert de Vaux. In 1306, Edward I spent six months at the priory recuperating after his skirmishes with the Scots. Lanercost is well preserved and its scale is a reminder that it was a grand complex in its heyday. However, the priory suffered greatly in the border raids of the 13th and 14th centuries. One such raid is known to have been led by William Wallace, an early campaigner for Scottish independence from English rule. When the Priory was closed in 1536, the sandstone blocks were recycled once again for houses in the town. But much of the Priory's great north aisle remains intact, set in a romantic and hauntingly beautiful position in the valley of the River Irthing.

Also most impressive is **Naworth Castle**, built around 1335 in its present form by Lord Dacre as an important border stronghold. The castle passed through the female line to the Howard family after the last Lord Dacre was killed as a child, improbable as it might seem, by falling off his rocking horse. Now owned by the Howard family, Earls of Carlisle, the Castle is private but there are good views from the minor road off the A69 that passes in front of it - the scene is particularly attractive in spring when the lawns are ablaze with daffodils. Pre-booked parties are welcome all year round and the Castle has become a popular venue for weddings and corporate events.

The Castle's supreme glory is the Great Hall, hung with French tapestries and guarded by four unique heraldic beasts holding aloft their family pennants. The Long Gallery extends for 116ft and was used as a guardroom. It now houses an interesting collection of paintings, many brought together by the 9th Earl, George Howard. He entertained many pre-Raphaelite painters here, but the only surviving example of their work is Burne-Jones' *Battle of Flodden* - the rest were destroyed by a fire in 1844. In the courtyard there are some intriguing medieval latrines!

MELMERBY

Melmerby nestles at the foot of Hartside Pass, its spacious village green is dissected by three becks. Even today, every householder in Melmerby has grazing rights on the green. Horses are grazed more commonly now, but in the past it would have been more usual to see flocks of geese - indeed, there was once a cottage industry here making pillows and mattresses from goose feathers. Overlooking the 13-acre village green is **Melmerby Hall**, a defensive tower that was extended in the 17th and 18th centuries. The village church, with its tower, is a Victorian building, but the first known rector of the church came here in 1332.

A curious meteorological feature here is what are known as the Helm winds, localised gusts which sweep through the valley with the force of a gale whilst the surrounding countryside is perfectly calm.

From Melmerby the main road climbs out of the Eden Valley to the east and the landscape changes suddenly. The road passes **Fiend's Fell**, close to the highest point in the Pennine Chain, the summit of **Cross Fell**. Early Christians erected a cross on the highest point of the fell to protect travellers from the demons who haunted the moors. Today, a cairn marks the spot where the cross once stood.

PENRITH

In Saxon times Penrith was the capital of the Kingdom of Cumbria but after the Normans arrived the town seems to have been rather neglected - it was sacked several times by the Scots before **Penrith Castle** was finally built in the 1390s.

The much-maligned Richard, Duke of Gloucester (later Richard III) strengthened the castle's defences when he was Lord Warden of the Western Marches and responsible for keeping the peace along the border with Scotland. By the time of the Civil War, however, the castle was in a ruinous state. The Cromwellian General Lambert demolished much of what was left and the townspeople helped themselves to the fallen stones to build their own houses. Nevertheless, the ruins remain impressive, standing high above a steep-sided moat.

A short walk from the castle brings you to the centre of this lively town with its charming mixture of narrow streets and wide-open spaces, such as **Great Dockray** and **Sandgate**, into which cattle were herded during the raids. Later they became market places and a market is still held every Tuesday.

Penrith has a splendid Georgian church in a very attractive churchyard, surrounded by a number of interesting buildings. The oldest part of **St Andrew's Church** dates from Norman times but the most recent part, the nave, was rebuilt between 1719 and 1772, possibly to a design by Nicholas Hawksmoor. Of particular interest is the three-sided gallery and the two chandeliers which were a gift from the Duke of Portland in 1745 - a reward for the town's loyalty during the Jacobite Rising. A tablet on the wall records the deaths of 2,260 citizens of Penrith in the plague of 1597.

The church's most interesting feature however, is to be found in the churchyard, in the curious group of gravestones known as **Giant's Grave** - two ancient cross-shafts, each 11ft high, and four 10th century hogback tombstones which have arched tops and sharply sloping sides. They have clearly been deliberately arranged but their original purpose is no longer known. According to a local legend the stones mark the burial place of a 5th century King of Cumbria, Owen Caesarius. Also buried somewhere in the churchyard is Wordsworth's mother, but her grave is not marked. Overlooking the churchyard is a splendid Tudor house, bearing the date 1563, which is now a restaurant but was, at one time, Dame Birkett's School. The school's most illustrious pupils were William Wordsworth, his sister Dorothy, and his future wife, Mary Hutchinson. William is also commemorated by a plaque on the wall of the Robin Hood Inn stating that he was a guest here in 1794 and again in 1795.

Other notable buildings in the town include the **Town Hall** which is the result of a 1905 conversion of two former Adam-style houses, one of which was known as Wordsworth House as it was the home of the poet's cousin, Captain John Wordsworth.

The town is dominated by **Beacon Hill Pike**, which stands amidst wooded slopes high above Penrith. The tower was built in 1719 and marks the place where, since 1296, beacons were lit to warn the townsfolk of an impending attack. The beacon was last lit during the Napoleonic wars in 1804 and was seen by the author Sir Walter Scott who was visiting Cumberland at the time. Seeing it prompted Scott to hasten home to rejoin his local volunteer regiment. It is well worth the climb from Beacon's Edge, along the footpath to the summit, to enjoy a magnificent view of the Lakeland fells. It was, however, also on top of this hill, in 1767, that Thomas

Nicholson, a murderer, was hanged. The gibbet was left on the summit and so was Nicholson's ghost, seen in the form of a skeleton hanging from the noose.

About a mile southeast of the town, the substantial and imposing remains of **Brougham Castle** (English Heritage) stand on the foundations of a Roman fort. The castle was inherited in the 1640s by the redoubtable and immensely rich Lady Anne Clifford whose patrimony as Countess of Pembroke, Dorset and Montgomery, also included another half dozen northern castles. She spent a fortune restoring them all in medieval style and when told that Cromwell had threatened to destroy them replied *"As often as he destroys them I will rebuild them while he leaves me a shilling in my pocket"*. Brougham was her favourite castle and she died here in 1676 at the age of 86. From the castle there's a delightful riverside walk to Eamont Bridge and the circular Mayburgh Earthwork, which dates from prehistoric times. On the huge embankment, more than 100 yards across, stands a single, large stone about 10ft high. Close to the village, on the banks of the River Eamont, is Giant's Cave, the supposed lair of a man-eating giant called Isir. This local tale is linked with the legend of Tarquin, a giant knight who imprisoned 64 men in his cave and was eventually killed by Sir Lancelot. Some people also claim that Uther Pendragon, King Arthur's father, lived here and that he too ate human flesh. A nearby prehistoric earthwork has been known as King Arthur's Round Table for many centuries.

Penrith's latest and most spectacular visitor attraction, **Rheged Discovery Centre**, opened in Easter 2000 and dedicates itself to "a celebration of 2000 years of Cumbria's history, mystery and magic - as never seen before" .

3 miles southwest of Penrith off the A592, **Dalemain House** is one of the area's most popular attractions - an impressive house with a medieval and Tudor core fronted by an imposing Georgian façade. The house has been home to the same family since 1679 and over the years they have accumulated fine collections of china, furniture and family portraits. The grand drawing Rooms have fine oak panelling and 18th century Chinese wallpaper, and visitors also have access to the Nursery (furnished with toys from all ages) and Housekeeper's Room. The Norman pele tower houses the regimental collection of the

60

Westmorland and Cumberland Yeomanry, while the 16th century Great Barn contains an interesting assortment of agricultural bygones and a Fell Pony Museum. The extensive grounds include a medieval herb garden, a knot garden with a fine early Roman fountain, a deer park, and woodland and riverside walks.

SHAP

This small village on the once congested A6 enjoys some grand views of the hills. In coaching days Shap was an important staging post for the coaches before they tackled the daunting climb up **Shap Fell** to its summit some 850ft above sea level. Much earlier, in medieval times, the village was even more significant because of nearby **Shap Abbey**, constructed in the local Shap granite which has been used in many well-known buildings, St Pancras Station and the Albert Memorial in London among them.

The Abbey stands about a mile to the west of the village, just inside the National Park, and it's well worth seeking it out to see the imposing remains of the only abbey founded in Westmorland; the only one in the Lake District mountains; the last abbey to be consecrated in England (around 1199) and the last to be dissolved, in 1540. Henry VIII's Commissioners seem to have been especially thorough in their demolition of the Abbey and local builders continued the depredations. But the mighty west tower and some of the walls remain, and

they enjoy a lovely setting - secluded, tranquil and timeless.

From the Abbey there's a pleasant walk of well under a mile to Keld, a tiny village of just 17 houses. So quiet today, in medieval times Keld was a busy little place servicing the monks of Shap Abbey nearby. It was the monks of Shap Abbey who built the village's oldest building, the early-16th century **Keld Chapel** (NT). After the closure of the Abbey, the chapel fell on hard times and for two hundred years was used as a dwelling house. (That's when the incongruous chimney was added). In 1860 it was "serving as a cow-house" but was saved from this ignominious role in 1918 by the National Trust. A service is held in the chapel once a year in August; at other times, a notice on the chapel door tells you where you can obtain the key.

TALKIN

Talkin Tarn, now the focus of a 120-acre country park, has been a popular place for watersports for over 100 years. Glacial in origin, the Tarn was formed some 10,000 years ago and is continually replenished by underground streams. Modern day visitors can sail, windsurf, canoe or hire one of the original wooden rowing boats. Fishing licences are available, there's a Nature Trail and an orienteering course, a play area for children under 8, and guided walks are also available. The park is a peaceful place but, according to legend, beneath the surface of the lake there is a submerged village destroyed by a wrathful god, the ruins of which can still be seen below the water surface in a certain light.

The Agricultural Hotel 61

Castlegate,
Penrith,
Cumbria
CA11 7JE
Tel: 01768 862622
Fax: 01768 63985

Directions:
Penrith is very close
to J40 of the M6

Amanda Irving and her parents own and run the **Agricultural Hotel**, a large and handsome building close to the centre of the historic town of Penrith. A great favourite with local residents, business people and tourists, the hotel has a good-sized car park and a nice little beer garden. Inside, all is well laid-out and kept in excellent condition; the public bar has a little corner for pub games, and there's a roomy lounge and restaurant area. The food is very enjoyable - unpretentious, freshly prepared and well presented - and the home-made pies and hearty casseroles are high on the list in the popularity stakes. An upstairs function room is a pleasant venue for small parties and special occasions.

When entering Penrith from the M6, the Agricultural Hotel stands at the first roundabout, and with easy access to that motorway, this is a good base for both business and leisure visits. Overnight accommodation comprises four bedrooms that share a bathroom and separate WC. Penrith was the capital of the Kingdom of Cumbria in the 9th and 10th centuries, and reminders of its long history can be seen in the splendid Norman Church of St Andrew and the imposing ruins of its castle. In the spectacular Rheged Discovery Centre visitors can take a tour round 2,000 years of Cumbria's history, mystery and magic. A short drive out of town brings other attractions, including The National Trust's lovely gardens at Acorn Bank.

Opening Hours: 11-11.

Food: Bar meals.

Credit Cards: None

Accommodation: 4 bedrooms sharing facilities.

Facilities: Car park, outside seating.

Entertainment: None

Local Places of Interest/Activities: Rheged Discovery Centre 1 mile, Dalemain House 3 miles, Dacre Castle 4 miles, Lowther Country Park 4 miles.

62 The Beehive Inn

Eamont Bridge,
Penrith,
Cumbria
CA10 2BX
Tel: 01768 862081

Directions:
Eamont Bridge is
on the southern
edge of Penrith,
just off the A6, 1½
miles from J40 of
the M6.

Stephen Porter, at the helm since the early 1990s, creates a friendly, hospitable ambience at the **Beehive Inn**, which is at the heart of a small rural community just beyond the southern perimeter of Penrith. Close though it is the motorway and main road network, the Beehive is a pleasant haven of peace and tranquillity, little changed externally since its coaching inn origins of the 1760s. Inside, the bar space is divided between the public bar, lounge bar and dining area, and old beams and floorboards and open fires add to the homely, traditional feel that is generated and encouraged by Stephen and his always delightful staff.

Local residents, regulars attracted down from the town and the occasional tourist mingle to enjoy a chat, a glass or two of cask ale and perhaps something from the super value menus, which are available lunchtime and evening Monday to Saturday and all day on Sunday. Outdoor appetites are satisfied by generous portions of home-made pies or beef dishes served with plenty of vegetables; for smaller appetites or quicker bites, snackier items are also served. The Beehive has a good-sized car park and outside seating at the front; children are welcome and have a little area for playing and romping. Penrith has an abundance of places to see and things to do, and within an easy drive are Acorn Gardens, Lowther Country Park, Ullswater and Clifton Moor, site of one of the last battles fought on English soil.

Opening Hours: 11.30-3 & 6-11 (all day Sat & Sun).

Food: Bar meals.

Credit Cards: Planned.

Accommodation: None.

Facilities: Car park, outside seating.

Entertainment: None

Local Places of Interest/Activities: Rheged Discovery Centre 1 mile, Acorn Bank 5 miles, Clifton 3 miles, Ullswater 5 miles.

The Butchers Arms   63

Main Street,
Crosby Ravensworth,
Cumbria
CA10 3SP
Tel: 01931 715202

Directions:
Crosby Ravensworth
is situated 6 miles
north of Tebay off the
B6260; from J39 of
the M6 turn right on
to A6 to Shap then
right on to a minor
road back over the
M6 to Crosby
Ravensworth.

Truly a hidden gem, the **Butchers Arms** is the social hub of a tiny rural community east of Shap, just off the B6260 road that runs from Tebay to Appleby-in-Westmorland. But it's actually not at all difficult to find, and once found has for many become a regular rendezvous for enjoying the agreeable ambience, the good company and the good food and drink. The owners since 1997 are Melvyn and Judy Richardson, who know exactly what their customers want and who have worked hard to keep the place as they and their regulars want it. 1848 is the date above the front door of the inn, which has a sympathetic extension.

A wood-burning stove keeps winter at bay in the public bar, and across the hall is a lounge bar with massive feature stone walls and a collection of maps of the locality. Next to this is a 30-cover restaurant where good honest home cooking is the order of the day; Judy does the cooking with her sister. Crosby Ravensworth is the site of a prehistoric settlement of many ruined huts, one of which was 50 feet across. St Lawrence's Church, almost a cathedral in miniature, is another place not to be missed on a stroll around the village, and for motorists there are numerous nearby places of interest, including Appleby, Shap and Haweswater Reservoir. And for golfers, there's a course a few miles away.

Opening Hours: 12-3 and 7-11 every day

Food: Bar meals.

Credit Cards: None.

Accommodation: None.

Facilities: Off-street parking.

Entertainment: None

Local Places of Interest/Activities: Golf 7 miles, Shap 3 miles, Tebay 6 miles, Appleby 6 miles.

64 The Crown & Cushion

Boroughgate,
Appleby-in-Westmorland,
Cumbria CA16 6XA
Tel: 017683 51595

Directions:

Appleby-in-Westmorland lies on the B6542 (A66 bypasses town). From the south, leave the M6 at J38 and take the B6260 to Appleby. From the north leave the M6 at J40 and take the A66 and B6542 into town.

The Crown & Cushion stands next to the parish church in the delightful town of Appleby-in-Westmorland. Chris Wilson is the most charming, the most affable and the most professional of landlords, and his customer base covers a wide cross-section of the town and the surrounding district, as well as many of the thousands of tourists who visit the town each year. The Crown & Cushion, a listed building, occupies a prime site on the town's street, Boroughgate, one of the finest in England, which made many appearances in films and advertisements. Behind the typical Westmorland frontage the picture is one of slightly but delightfully cluttered country charm, with original wooden floor, brass rails at the bar, lots of oak, some pew-style seating and a display of local records - all just the way the regulars and Chris want to keep it. In this comfortable, convivial setting, real ales quench thirsts and good home cooking satisfies appetites. Fresh specials, steaks and pies are popular orders among a good choice of well-prepared, well-priced dishes.

Homely overnight accommodation comprises two guest bedrooms that share a bathroom. Appleby, formerly the capital of Westmorland, straddles the River Eden. At the foot of Boroughgate is the 16th century Moot Hall, while at its head rises the great Norman keep of Appleby Castle. Appleby is a station of the Settle-Carlisle railway, which takes in some of the most dramatic scenery that the north of England has to offer. At Long Marton, 3 miles north of Appleby, the line crosses a grand viaduct. A minor road leads north from Appleby through Brampton to Dufton, the nearest point on the Pennine Way.

Opening Hours: 12-3 & 6.30-11.

Food: Bar meals.

Credit Cards: Mastercard, Visa.

Accommodation: 2 rooms sharing a bathroom.

Facilities: Car park.

Entertainment: None

Local Places of Interest/Activities:
Brampton 2 miles, Brough 8 miles, Long Marton 3 miles.

The Fetherston Arms | 65

The Square,
Kirkoswald,
Cumbria
CA10 1DQ
Tel/Fax:
01768 898284

Directions:
Kirkoswald village
is on the B6413 8
miles north of
Penrith. From the
M6 J41 go to A6
roundabout, left to
Plumpton, right
on to B6413.

The social hub of a quiet village in the lovely Eden Valley, the **Fetherston Arms** is a charming little white sandstone inn dating from the early 19th century. The owners, Patricia and Peter Jackson, are attracting a growing band of local residents as well as tourists taking a break on their journey through this beautiful, tranquil part of the world. The public bar is small, cosy and convivial, a perfect spot for enjoying one of the real ales on tap. The stone-walled lounge, warmed by a log burning fire, has 50 covers where wholesome, tasty dishes are served at the weekend and during the week in summer, with a good selection of wines to accompany. The choice always includes daily specials, and children have a menu of their own. In the games room, winter nights often see darts and pool competitions, and other activities include monthly quiz nights and occasional live music at the weekend.

As well as being a very agreeable place for a drink and a meal, the Fetherston Arms is also a good spot to choose as a base for touring the delightful surrounding area. It has six letting bedrooms, three of them with en suite facilities, all with tv and tea/coffee makers. The locality is particularly rich in scenic and historic interest, with some fine old buildings and some evocative reminders of past local history. In Kirkoswald itself are a striking ruined 12th century castle and the Church of St Oswald, whose tower stands some 200 yards from the rest of the building. There is an open air swimming pool situated one mile away in the village of Lazonby.

Opening Hours: 12-3 & 7-11.

Food: Bar meals.

Credit Cards: Planned.

Accommodation: 6 rooms, 3 en suite.

Entertainment: Pool, darts, monthly quiz.

Local Places of Interest/Activities: Penrith 8 miles, Great and Little Salkeld 5 miles. Carlisle 16 miles, Alston 14 miles.

Internet/website:
e-mail: ppjackson@supernet.com

66 The Highland Drove Inn

Great Salkeld,
Nr Penrith,
Cumbria
CA11 9NA
Tel: 01768 898349
Fax: 01768 898708

Directions:

Great Salkeld is a small village on the A686 5 miles northeast of Penrith. The inn is secluded off the main street.

A Real Country Pub

In the heart of the picturesque Eden Valley, Great Salkeld stands on the old drovers' road from Scotland. The 14th century lookout tower in the village is a reminder that not all visitors from the north were welcome, but for the past 200 years the handsome **Highland Drove Inn** has been providing hearty hospitality to peaceful visitors from all directions. The inn has been run since 1998 by Donald Newton and his family, who have made the old place very smart and attractive while losing nothing of its traditional appeal.

In the bar or in the new 50-cover restaurant with a patio overlooking the garden an extensive selection of dishes is served lunchtime and evening; the main menu makes mouthwatering reading, and expectations are fulfilled in dishes such as Bantry Bay mussels with white wine, parsley and cream, Thai chicken or vegetable curry, steak & kidney pie with a double pastry crust and red wine gravy, or chargrilled tuna with crispy Parma ham, fried parsley, soft egg noodles and an anchovy cream sauce. There's always a choice of three real ales - Black Sheep, Theakston's and a guest - along with other draught beers, lagers and a selection of wines.

An ideal base for visiting the Lake District, the Northern Pennines and the Scottish Borders, the Highland Drove has five guest bedrooms, all en suite, with tv and tea/coffee-making facilities. The inn is closed Monday lunchtime.

Opening Hours: 12-2.30 & 6-11 (Sat 12-11, Sun 12-10.30). Closed Monday lunchtime.

Food: Bar meals.

Credit Cards: Mastercard, Visa.

Accommodation: 5 en suite rooms.

Facilities: Car park, garden.

Entertainment: None

Local Places of Interest/Activities: Little Salkeld (Long Meg and her Daughters prehistoric site) 1 mile, Penrith 5 miles.

Internet/website:

website: www.highland-drove.co.uk

The Kings Arms Hotel | 67

Temple Sowerby,
Nr Penrith,
Cumbria
CA10 1SB
Tel: 01768 361211

Directions:

Temple Sowerby is located on the A66 6 miles east of Penrith.

Owners Lee and Janice Ashworth ran a public house in Manchester for ten years, and their experience and natural hospitality are attracting a good trade, both local and passing, to the Kings Arms, which is easy to find on the A66 east of Penrith in the lovely Eden Valley. The exterior of their 300-year-old coaching inn is quite eyecatching and little changed down the years, and the Ashworths intend to keep the old-world look in the lounge and dining area. Log fires keep things cosy and comfortable, and there are lots of little alcoves for enjoying a quiet drink. But they also have plans, which include the possibility of adding a tea shop and Post Office in the adjoining premises. Black Sheep, Marstons Pedigree and regularly changing guest ales offer a good choice for those who know their beers, and there's also a well-chosen list of wines to accompany the excellent home cooked dishes prepared by the new chef.

This is definitely a place to relax and linger, and overnight accommodation is provided in seven comfortable bedrooms, all with en suite facilities, tv and tea/coffee tray. The inn has a beer garden and a car park with secure parking also for cycles and motorbikes. Walking, cycling are popular activities hereabouts, and fly fishing can be arranged on the nearby river.

One of the most popular attractions in the vicinity is the National Trust's Acorn Bank. This delightful garden has spectacular displays of shrubs, roses and herbaceous borders, sheltered orchards of traditional fruit trees and a herb garden with the largest collection of medicinal and culinary plants in the North. Also on site is a watermill. To the north is Cross Fell, the highest point in the Pennines.

Opening Hours: 12-3 & 6-11 (all day summer weekends).

Food: Bar meals.

Credit Cards: Mastercard, Visa.

Accommodation: 7 en suite rooms.

Facilities: Car park, garden.

Entertainment: None

Local Places of Interest/Activities: Golf 6 miles, Penrith 6 miles, Appleby 6 miles.

68 Metal Bridge Inn

Floristonrigg,
Nr Carlisle,
Cumbria
CA6 4HG
Tel: 01228 674044

Directions:

Floristonrigg is
situated on the A74
2 miles from J44 of
the M6. 2 miles
south of Gretna, 5
miles north of
Carlisle.

In acquiring the well-known **Metal Bridge Inn** local business is maintaining the inn's longstanding reputation for hospitality. Throughout its 220 years it has been a popular spot and an ideal place to break a journey to or from Scotland. The structure has changed little down the years and the interior is warm and welcoming, with plush carpets, comfortably upholstered seats and lots of cosy little alcoves. Food is an important part of the business, and customers have a choice of dining areas (150 covers in all) on several levels, some designated non-smoking. Some of the rooms overlook the River Esk. The menus provide plenty of variety, and for pushing the boat out the Metal Bridge Lamb Banquet - Highland lamb cooked with a special mixture of spices - is highly recommended. The Metal Bridge also offers a good choice for beer drinkers, with regularly changing guest beers from breweries both local and national.

The inn is an excellent venue for parties, meetings and special occasions, and for anyone wishing to tarry awhile there are five very well presented en suite bedrooms with tv, tea-makers, hairdryers and trouser presses - perfect for business or pleasure visits. The inn has a huge car park, and a bridle path running by the side of the building is a good spot for a stroll or walking the dog. The best known local attraction is Hadrian's Wall, built at the height of the Roman Empire and one of Rome's most northerly outposts, but there's plenty more for the visitor to see and do, including exploring the villages and the marshes of the estuary. Gretna Green, once a favourite spot for eloping couples to tie the knot, is close by, just over the border into Scotland, and Carlisle, a short drive south, is also well worth taking time to explore.

Opening Hours: 11.30-3 & 5.30-11.

Food: Bar and restaurant menus.

Credit Cards: Mastercard, Visa.

Accommodation: 5 en suite rooms.

Facilities: Car park.

Entertainment: Live music Saturday.

Local Places of Interest/Activities: Carlisle 5 miles, Gretna 2 miles, Burgh-by-Sands 8 miles.

The Miners Arms | 69

Nenthead,
Alston,
Cumbria
CA9 3PF
Tel: 01434 381427

Directions:
Nenthead is located
on the A689
Brampton-Durham
road between
Alston and
Killhope.

Standing at 1,500 feet above sea level in a designated Area of Outstanding Natural Beauty, the **Miners Arms** can probably lay claim to being the highest village pub in England. Owned and run by Alison Clark, it has a fast-growing and well-deserved reputation for genuine hospitality, homely accommodation, good real ales and excellent home cooking. Several of the dishes on the wide-ranging menu have won prizes, among them Alison's Alston pie, leek & stilton pots, mushroom & cheesebake and chocolate bread & butter pudding. Buttered trout and Cumberland sausage casserole are other favourites, and lovers of spicy food are in their element with chilli con carne and a variety of splendid curries (Curry Pub of the Year 1994). The full menu is on offer lunchtime and evening, and a snack menu wards off hunger pangs between 2 o'clock and 5.

Family, double, twin and single rooms are available for Bed & Breakfast at very reasonable rates, while truly low-price accommodation is provided in the Bunkhouse, which can sleep 12 in four three-tier bunks, with washing and changing facilities. The Miners Arms has a car park and beer garden, and there's a children's play area opposite. The pub is the official stamping post in Nenthead for the C2C (Coast to Coast) cycle route and the Alternative Pennine Way passes through the village. Many of the buildings in Nenthead date from around 1825, when the London Lead Company planned a 'model' village providing housing and amenities for its employees. The village's position on the main A689 puts the Lake District, North Pennines, Carlisle, Durham and Hadrian's Wall within easy reach, and there are several places of interest locally.

Opening Hours: All day May-Sept, lunch and evening Oct -Dec, evenings only Jan-Easter (but open all day at the weekend).

Food: Bar meals and snack menu.

Credit Cards: All the major cards.

Accommodation: B&B and budget Bunkhouse.

Facilities: Car park, beer garden.

Entertainment: None

Local Places of Interest/Activities: Killhope Mining Museum 2 miles, Alston 2 miles.

Internet/website:

website: www.theminersarms.org.uk

70   The Punch Bowl Inn

North Stainmore,
Brough,
Nr Kirkby
Stephen,
Cumbria
CA17 4DY
Tel/Fax:
01768341262

Directions:

North Stainmore is
situated just off the
A66 2 miles east of
Brough.

The local story is that the **Punch Bowl Inn** was one of the favourite hideouts of the notorious highwyman Dick Turpin, and there is said to be a 250-yard escape tunnel leading from the basement. Escape is far from the minds of today's visitors, as owners Andy and Julie Beagle are the friendliest of hosts, and the food and the real ales are guarantees of satisfaction. An accomplished cook, Julie offers an appetising menu of traditional pub fare, from sandwiches and light snacks to three-course meals; most of the dishes are available in smaller portions for children, and the food is served every day from noon to 11pm. To accompany the food is an excellent selection of draught keg ales, stouts, lagers, cider and a minimum of two real ales of which Black Sheep is always on tap.

The Punch Bowl was built in three different eras. The central part dates back to 1780, the wings were added exactly a century later and the modern bar a century after that. The inn offers all the traditional pub amusements - darts, pool, cards, dominoes - and overnight accommodation is available in three letting bedrooms. The Punch Bowl, with its location on the A66, is a good base for touring the Lake District, the Yorkshire Dales and the Scottish Borders. The village lies by Stainmore Pass and close to the summit are the remains of Maiden Castle, a Roman fort built to guard the pass; just over the border into County Durham is the stump of the ancient Rey Cross, which until 1092 marked the boundary between England and Scotland.

Opening Hours: 12-11 (Sun to 10.30).

Food: Bar menu and light snacks.

Credit Cards: None.

Accommodation: 3 rooms for B&B.

Facilities: Car park.

Entertainment: None

Local Places of Interest/Activities:
Stainmore Pass 1 mile, Brough Castle 2 miles, Kirkby Stephen 5 miles, Appleby 10 miles.

Internet/website:
e-mail: beagle@aol.com

The Railway Inn | 71

Low Row,
Brampton,
Cumbria
CA8 2LE
Tel: 016977 46222
Fax: 016977 46927

Directions:

Low Row is 3 miles
east of Brampton
off the A69.

Built as a byre and converted to an inn about 150 years ago, the **Railway Inn** is hidden away in its own grounds in the picturesque village of Low Row, a short drive east of Brampton and just off the A69. It's a great place to break a journey along that road and is well worth seeking out for the fine traditional ambience and for the banter of genial host Steve Doughty, who since taking over towards the end of 2000 has built up a loyal local trade. The inn, which takes its name from the main Carlisle-Newcastle line that runs nearby, serves a good variety of food lunchtime and evening, from quick snacks to excellent local beef; the traditional Sunday lunch always brings in the crowds, so booking is advisable.

In good weather a drink and a snack can be enjoyed at one of the picnic tables outside the inn. The delightful little market town of Brampton is close by, but even closer are two famous and intimately connected visitor attractions. Three miles to the north is an impressive stretch of Hadrian's Wall, while just under 3 miles from The Railway Inn is Lanercost Priory, founded in 1166 and built largely with stones cannibalised from the Wall. When the Priory was closed in 1536, some of the stones were recycled once again; but the great north aisle remains intact, in a beautiful setting in the Irthing Valley.

Opening Hours: 12-2.30 (Mon-Fri; Easter to October only); 6-11(Mon-Sat); 7-10.30 (Sun)

Food: Bar meals, Sunday lunches

Credit Cards: Mastercard, Visa, Switch, Solo

Accommodation: None.

Facilities: Car park, outside seating.

Local Places of Interest/Activities:
Brampton 3 miles, Hadrian's Wall 3 miles, Lanercost Priory 3 miles.

Internet/website:

e-mail: railwayinnlowrow@aol.com
website: www.therailwayinn.org.uk

72

The Royal

Wilson Row,
Penrith,
Cumbria
CA11 7PZ
Tel: 01768 862670
Fax: 01768 210813

Directions:
Penrith is 2 miles
from J40 of the M6.

The original **Royal** was a wooden structure dating from 1811, but the Royal of today is a spick-and-span, white-painted stone building opposite Penrith's magnificent Town Hall. The inn loses little in comparison with this noble edifice, and inside is an unqualified delight: old wood with classic tile flooring, brass window bars, ornate lamps, smartly refurbished oak table and chairs. Owners Wendy and Gary Sewell, who brought years of experience in the licensed trade when they came here in the summer of 2001, are devoted to the Royal and visitors can be assured of the warmest of welcomes in inviting, spotless surroundings. The couple are also interested in the history of the pub and the locality and are building up a collection of photographs and documents to be displayed in the bar.

Three real ales are always on tap, and a tempting menu of classic pub dishes - fresh, appetising and nothing too elaborate - is served lunchtime and evening Monday to Friday and all day at the weekend. Drinks and meals can be taken in the beer garden in the summer. Three en suite letting bedrooms with tv and tea-makers have widened the scope of this altogether super place, whose customer base is rightly broad and rightly growing. Guests who make it their base will find plenty to see and do in Penrith itself, while attractions out of town include the prehistoric site Long Meg and her Daughters at Little Salkeld, Lowther Country Park and the 7-mile long Ullswater.

Opening Hours: 11-11 (Sun 12-10.30).

Food: Bar meals.

Credit Cards: Mastercard, Visa.

Accommodation: 3 en suite rooms.

Facilities: Garden.

Entertainment: Occasional Irish evenings.

Local Places of Interest/Activities: Little Salkeld 6 miles, Ullswater 4 miles.

The Shepherds Inn 73

Melmerby,
Nr Penrith,
Cumbria
CA10 1HF
Tel: 01768 881217

Directions:

Melmerby is on the A686 Penrith-Alston road, 9 miles northeast of Penrith.

The Shepherds Inn is a classic village public house in a classic North Country village. Melmerby stands on the very edge of the Pennines, stretching out round a huge village green, and this fine old inn dating from the 17th century is a favourite place to find hospitality and refreshment of both local residents and the more than occasional tourist. Inside, the floor space is extensive and the look a combination of the traditional and the more modern, with stone floors and large, handsome pine tables and chairs. There's outside seating at the front and the inn has its own car park. Nick and Helen Baucutt have been here for 25 years - their youngest son is now in charge of the day-to-day running - so there's nothing they don't know about what their regulars expect.

Five real ales, including regularly changing guests, are always on tap, and in the elevated dining area, where some sections are designated non-smoking, fine home cooking features fish, poultry, meat and game from the best local suppliers. One of the favourite dishes is spicy chicken Leoni served with home-made pickles and chutneys. Melmerby stands on the A686, which leads northeastwards to Gilderdale Forest and Alston, said to be the highest market town in England; in the other direction lies the town of Penrith, whose attractions include a ruined castle and the spectacular Rheged Discovery Centre. Melmerby is in a part of the world full of possibilities for walkers and sightseers, and the more energetic could head for the 2,300ft Melmerby Fell. The most renowned establishment in the village is the wonderful Melmerby Bakery, but no visit here would be complete without a leisurely look-in at the Shepherds Rest.

Opening Hours: 10.30-3 & 6-11 (Sun 12-3 & 7-10.30).

Food: Bar meals.

Credit Cards: All the major cards.

Accommodation: None.

Facilities: Car park, outside seating.

Entertainment: Occasional theme nights.

Local Places of Interest/Activities: Village Bakery, Penrith 8 miles, Alston 3 miles, Ullswater 10 miles.

Internet/website:

website: www.shepherdsinn.net

74   The Sportsman Inn

Laversdale,
Nr Carlisle,
Cumbria
CA6 4PJ
Tel: 01228 573255

Directions:

Laversdale is five
miles northeast of
Carlisle on a minor
road between the
A689 and the
A6071.

Gordon and Christine Davidson are local farmers who bought the **Sportsman Inn** in 2001 and are gradually building up their customer base and increasing the amenities while retaining the period character and rural charm - and the friendly ghost. Built in 1828, the whitewashed inn occupies an elevated site in the tiny, picturesque village of Laversdale, located in lovely countryside yet less than a mile from Carlisle Airport and with good access to major roads. Thick stone walls and heavy oak beams create a splendid old-world atmosphere in the bar and lounge, and a wood-burning stove in a cobbled fireplace is an eyecatching feature. The 40-cover restaurant is a civilised setting for enjoying a very good leisurely meal with perhaps chicken with lemon and rosemary or a hearty steak and ale pie as the centrepiece. The delightful owners are still finalising their plans on the entertainment front, but quiz nights, live music and karaoke are all on the agenda. The inn has a pleasant garden and an excellent car park.

This is a great spot for lovers of the great outdoors; Hadrian's Wall is within walking distance and the scenic delights of the Lake District and the Pennines are an easy drive away. Three miles down the road is the little town of Brampton, where a market has been held ever since Henry III granted the town's charter in 1252, and where Bonnie Prince Charlie once had his headquarters. Carlisle, the largest town in Cumbria, is also well worth a visit for its castle, its cathedral and its museums.

Opening Hours: 6.45-11 (Sun 12-10.30); also open at lunchtime in summer.

Food: Restaurant meals.

Credit Cards: None.

Accommodation: Perhaps in future.

Facilities: Car park, beer garden

Entertainment: see above.

Local Places of Interest/Activities:
Brampton 3 miles, Carlisle 6 miles, Gretna 10 miles.

The Turks Head | 75

Market Place,
Alston,
Cumbria
CA9 3HS
Tel/Fax:
01434 381148

Directions:
From Penrith take the A69
then A686 to Alston. The
pub is in the centre of town
by the market cross.

The Turks Head was the first
pub in Alston and dates back
to 1679. Many original
features survive, which the
owners Colin and Sue
Wilson have been careful to
retain while adding modern
comfort such as central
heating (but log fires still
blaze a welcome in the
winter months). Whatever the season, the place has warm, inviting feel and visitors can
always look forward to a friendly greeting from the Wilsons, their staff and their springer
spaniel Ben. In the bar a regularly changing selection of real ales is on tap, and the menu
runs from sandwiches and light snacks to full meals and a traditional Sunday lunch. Classic
pub fare includes garlic mushrooms, jumbo haddock, home-made lasagne and chicken curry,
and for the really ravenous a full rack of ribs served in a BBQ sauce with onion rings, potato
wedges and salad.

For guests staying overnight the pub has two double rooms for Bed & Breakfast. The
pub sign illustrates the name: a Turks Head is a knot that was tied on to the edge of a ship's
wheel to mark the midships point. Its purpose was to act as a point of reference when
navigating in the dark. Alston is a good centre for shopping and a popular base for walkers
and lovers of the outdoor life. It was the setting for Alan Bleasdale's reworking of Charles
Dickens' Oliver Twist, and the town council has created an Oliver twist Trail, with each of
the 24 sites featured in the series marked by a picture of Mr Bumble.

Opening Hours: 11-4 & 7-11, Tue, Wed, Fri;
11-5 & 7-11 Thurs; All day Sat & Sun; 7-11
Mon

Food: Full menu and snacks.

Credit Cards: Mastercard, Visa

Accommodation: 2 B&B rooms; children
welcome, pets by arrangement.

Facilities: None.

Entertainment: Occasional quiz nights.

Local Places of Interest/Activities: Golf,
fishing, bird watching nearby, Killhope
Mining Museum 4 miles, South Tynedale
Railway in Alston, Alston Moor 1 mile.

76 The Waverley Inn

Crown Square,
Penrith,
Cumbria
CA11 7AB
Tel/Fax:
01768 891363

Directions:

Penrith is a short
drive from J40 of
the M6.

Rusty Lomas, young, enthusiastic and full of ideas, took over the **Waverley Inn** towards the end of 2001 with the intention of giving Penrith an entertainment pub. The Waverley, which was recently renovated, presents a solid, purposeful, up-to-date face next to a supermarket in what was the original town centre. It occupies a whole block, and the clean. no-nonsense appeal of the outside is echoed within, where the huge open space features bright carpets on slate floors, vibrant oil paintings and giant tv screens. In the dining area good-value, straightforward dishes are served, and a good selection of drinks is available at the bar.

Rusty, formerly a DJ, has themed the Waverley and its activities towards a younger clientele, with regular karaoke, disco and live music evenings, but its appeal spreads across the ages, and visitors to Penrith on business or on pleasure appreciate the chance to relax in completely informal surroundings and drink in the enjoyably 'different' atmosphere that prevails. The Waverley not only refreshes and entertains, but it also offers comfortable, practical Bed & Breakfast accommodation in eight letting bedrooms, four of them with en suite facilities; Rusty's plans include the installation of gym equipment for residents. Penrith has much to interest the visitor, including the splendid castle and the spectacular Rheged Discovery Centre, a celebration of 2,000 years of Cumbria's history. High above the town is Beacon Hill Pike, from whose summit there are magnificent views of the Lakeland fells.

Opening Hours: 11-11 (Thurs-Sat till midnight, Sun 12-10.30).

Food: Bar meals.

Credit Cards: None.

Accommodation: 8 rooms, 4 en suite.

Facilities: Car park.

Entertainment: Regular live music, disco and karaoke.

Local Places of Interest/Activities: Penrith Castle, Rheged DiscoveryCentre, Beacon Hill Pike, Ullswater 4 miles.

The Weary Sportsman | 77

Castle Carrock,
Nr Brampton,
Cumbria
CA8 9LU
Tel: 01228 670230
Fax: 01228 670089

Directions:
Leave the M6 at J43
and head east on
the A69. Turn right
on to the B6413 for
Castle Carrock,
which is 2½ miles
south of Brampton.

The Weary Sportsman, situated in the quiet village of Castle Carrock, has a history going back to the early coaching days of the 17th century, and its external appearance has changed little down the years. But inside, Ian and Gill Boyd have a surprise in store for visitors, as all is boldly, brightly contemporary in terms of decor, furnishings and fittings, a complete contrast to the whitewashed facade with its sign of an old-time angler, presumably weary after a long spell on the river with nothing to show for his patience. This weary sportsman would not need to move far from his sign to find everything needed to restore him: excellent food and drink and a comfortable bed for the night. In the very smart restaurant and conservatory (60 covers in all) the chef presents a menu that offers the best of cuisines from around the world, an adventurous menu that is quite in keeping with the distinctive, stylish surroundings.

The fine food is complemented by by an equally well-chosen selection of wines and ales, and when the sun shines visitors can take their drinks into the beer garden or the Japanese garden. Meals are served from 12 to 2.30 and from 6.30 to 9 every day. The Weary Sportsman is largely food-driven, but for the weary traveller the inn also offers three letting bedrooms for Bed & Breakfast accommodation. The go-ahead owners, who came in here in the autumn of 2001, have plans to bring more bedrooms on stream. The inn is a short drive from Brampton, in the heart of the lovely Irthring Valley, a little town closely connected with the exploits of Bonnie Prince Charlie. Even closer to the inn is Talkin Tarn, a country park with a nature trail, orienteering course, sailing, rowing, windsurfing and fishing......and at the end of the day lots of weary sportsmen.

Opening Hours: 12-3 & 6-11.

Food: Lunch and dinner menus.

Credit Cards: Mastercard, Visa.

Accommodation: 3 rooms.

Facilities: Car park, gardens.

Entertainment: None

Local Places of Interest/Activities: Talkin Tarn 1 mile, Brampton 2½ miles.

78 The White Lion Hotel

High Cross Street,
Brampton,
Cumbria CA8 1RP
Tel: 016977 2338
Fax: 016977 41618

Directions:

Brampton is about 8 miles east of Carlisle, just off the A69.

The people of Brampton, from youngsters to farmers, businessmen and retired folk, all give good support to the **White Lion Hotel,** which is also a perfect base for tourists. Louise and Paul Smith have invested a great deal of time and hard work in maintaining the highest standards at their mid-18th century coaching inn, which occupies a prime site in this fine little town in the heart of the lovely Irthing Valley. Behind the inviting exterior is a small hotel that offers a truly delightful ambience. There are two bars, with a choice of 150 malt whiskys, a good-sized lounge furnished with great style and taste, and a gem of a restaurant with pristine linen and sparkling glasses. A very dedicated and inventive chef does splendid work in the kitchen, producing an excellent variety of dishes on a well-balanced menu that really does offer something for everyone. Food is served every day from 12 to 2 and from 6 to 9.30.

For those with time to linger in this lovely part of the world the White Lion has ten well-appointed bedrooms, seven of them with en suite facilities, all with tv and tea/coffee trays. Whether it's for a quick drink, a meal or an overnight stay, a visit here will not disappoint: the owners are rightly proud of their staff and the service they offer, the staff are devoted to the owners and Brampton is devoted to them all. Brampton, where Bonnie Prince Charlie stayed during the siege of Carlisle, has plenty to interest the visitor, including the octagonal Moot Hall and the Church of St Martin, which has some superb Pre-Raphaelite stained glass.

Opening Hours: 10-11

Food: 12-2 & 6-9.30 (limited menu between 2 and 5)

Credit Cards: Most credit cards

Accommodation: 10 rooms, 7 en suite.

Facilities: Public car park, 2 sun bed rooms, restaurant, function room.

Entertainment: Occasional live music and theme evenings.

Local Places of Interest/Activities: Carlisle 8 miles, Hadrian's Wall 6 miles, Talkin Tarn country park 2 miles, Birdoswald Roman fort 7 miles.

Internet/website:

e-mail: wlionbrampton@aol.com
website: whitelionbrampton.com

3 County Durham

PLACES OF INTEREST:

PUBS AND INNS:

The Hidden Inns of The North of England

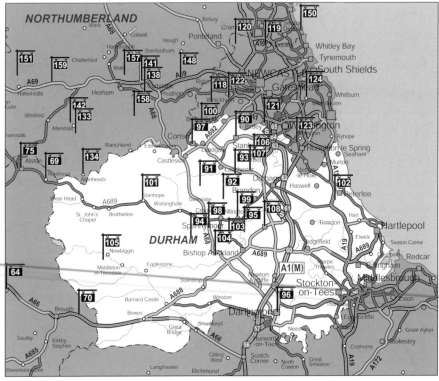

90 The Beamish Mary Inn, No Place, Stanley

91 The Black Horse, Old Cornsay

92 The Black Horse, Waterhouses

93 The Cross Keys, Esh Village

94 The Cross Keys, Hamsterly, Nr Bishop Auckland

95 The Fox & Hounds, Newfield, Bishop Auckland

96 The George, Darlington

97 The Grey Horse, Consett

98 Helme Park Hall Hotel, Nr Fir Tree, Bishop Auckland

99 The Lion & Unicorn, Willington

100 The Miners Arms, Medomsley

101 The Queens Head, Stanhope, Nr Bishop Auckland

102 The Royal George, Old Shotton, Nr Peterlee

103 The Saxon, Escomb, Nr Bishop Auckland

104 The Sportsmans Inn, Toft Hill, Bishop Auckland

105 The Strathmore Arms, Holwick, Middleton-in-Teesdale

106 The Village Inn, Sacriston

107 The White Tun, Witton Gilbert

108 The Winning Post, Spennymoor

Please note all references refer to page numbers

County Durham

County Durham's prosperity was founded on coalmining, and nowhere is this more apparent than in parts of Central and South Durham. Coal has been mined here for centuries, and no doubt the monks of Durham, Jarrow and all the other abbeys and priories in the area exploited the rich seams that underpin the landscape.

It wasn't until the 18th century, however, that the industry was established on a commercial basis. When the railways came along in the early 19th century, the industry prospered. It created great wealth for the land-owners, and sometimes great misery for the miners. Now that the industry has all but disappeared, the scars it created are being swept away. Spoil heaps have been cleared or grassed over, pit heads demolished and old industrial sites tidied up. The colliery villages, some with names that bring a smile to the face, such as Pity Me, Shiney Row, No Place, Bearpark, Sunniside, Quebec and Toronto, are still there however - tight-knit communities that retain an old-style sense of belonging and sharing. Coal may have been king, but County Durham's countryside has always supported an important farming industry, and Central and South Durham still retains a gentle landscape of fields, woodland, streams and narrow country lanes. It stretches from the coast in the east to the Pennines in the west, and from the old border with Yorkshire in the south to the edge of the Tyne and the Wear conurbations in the north. Within this area there are picturesque villages, cottages, grand houses, museums, snug pubs, old churches and castles aplenty.

Then there's the coastline. This too has been cleaned up, and now an 11-mile coastal footpath snakes through the district of Easington from Seaham Hall Beach in the north to Crimdon Park in the south. Most of it is along clifftops with spectacular views down onto the beaches. This coastal area has been designated as a National Nature Reserve, with some Sites of Special Scientific Interest along the way.

The railways were born in the county in 1825, with the opening of the famous Stockton and Darlington Railway. To the west, County Durham sweeps up to the Northern Pennines, a hauntingly beautiful area of moorland, high fells and deep, green dales. Part of the Pennine Way cuts through County Durham in the south, close to Barnard Castle and even closer to Middleton-in-Teesdale. It then follows Upper Teesdale west until it enters Cumbria. Further north, it enters Northum-berland to the west of Haltwhistle and then enters the Northumberland National Park.

Dominating the whole area is the city of Durham - surely one of Europe's finest small cities. And there are the towns of Darlington, Stockton-on-Tees, Hartlepool and Bishop Auckland to explore. All of these places were at one time within the borders of the county, but local government reorganisation placed two of them - Hartlepool and Stockton-on-Tees - in the upstart county of Cleveland. Now that Cleveland itself is no more, they, along with Darlington, are unitary authorities, and, strictly speaking, not part of County Durham at all, though old loyalties still exist.

PLACES OF INTEREST

BARNARD CASTLE

This old market town is a natural centre for exploring the central part of Teesdale. It is recognised as one of the 51 most important towns in Great Britain as far as history and architecture are concerned. It owes its existence to **Barnard Castle** itself, founded in the 12th century by Bernard, son of Guy de Baliol, one of the knights who fought alongside William I. This family's most famous - or infamous - son was King John Baliol, Edward I's puppet king of Scotland.

82

The ruins, with the massive, round keep overlooking the town's narrow, arched bridge of 1569 over the Tees, have a gaunt beauty. The castle has experienced its share of incidents,

Barnard Castle

perhaps most spectacularly during the ill-fated Catholic Rising of the North in 1569. At that time it was besieged by rebel forces for 11 days and, although it was finally forced to capitulate, this gave sufficient time for Queen Elizabeth's army, under the Earl of Sussex, to speed to York and force the rebels to flee. Many were executed and those leading families who had supported the plans to overthrow Elizabeth I lost their lands.

The town has an especially rich architectural heritage, with handsome houses, cottages, shops and inns dating from the 17th to the 19th centuries. There is an impressive **Market Cross** and an old town hall contained within an unusual octagonal structure, built in 1747. The

Barnard Castle Market Cross

area under the veranda has been variously used as a butter market, fire station or gaol, and the first floor as a courthouse. You can still see the bullet holes in the weather-vane, resulting from a wager by two local men in 1804, shooting from outside the Turk's Head, 100 yards away, to determine who was the best shot. The building was fully restored in 1999.

A walk along Newgate will bring the visitor to **Bowes Museum**, surely one of the most spectacular buildings in England. It looks like a French chateau, and is completely unexpected in a small English market town. It holds collections of paintings and objets d'art that are of international importance.

If visitors strike out along the A66 west of Barnard Castle, they'll eventually reach the small Cumbrian town of Brough. It was near this road that King Edmund erected the **Reys Cross** to mark the boundary between the kingdom of Northumbria and what was then the Scottish province of Cumbria.

BEAMISH

The award-winning **North of England Open Air Museum** is situated in 300 acres of landscaped parkland at Beamish, and here early life in County Durham has been vividly re-created. This is one of the county's major tourist attractions, with many features which were rescued from locations around County Durham - and even further afield - and re-erected on site.

Two miles to the NW is **Causey Arch**, claimed to be the world's first single-arch railway bridge. It was designed by Ralph Wood, a local stonemason, and carried the **Tanfield Railway** - opened in 1725 - between Sunniside and Causey. In those days the wagons were pulled by horses, though steam power eventually took over. Trains now run along three miles of line between Sunniside and East Tanfield. There is a car park and picnic area close by, and rights of way link them to Beamish.

BISHOP AUCKLAND

Bishop Auckland is an ancient town, standing on what was Dere Street, an old Roman road. Like many County Durham towns, it owed its later prosperity to coal mining. When the surrounding pits closed, the town went into decline, but it is now gradually rediscovering itself as new industries are established. As its name implies, up until the first part of the 19th century, this was part of the territory of the

Prince Bishops of Durham, who controlled what was then a scattering of small villages. Rapid expansion occurred during the 19th century and Bishop Auckland became an important market and administrative centre for the region. **Auckland Castle**, still the official palace of the Bishop of Durham, began as a small 12th century manor house. It was added to by successive bishops, and looking at it today, you would imagine it was largely 17th or 18th century. But the fabric is still basically medieval, though parts of it were destroyed during the Civil War, when it was the headquarters of Sir Arthur Hazlerigg, Governor of the North. Bishop Cosin set about making it wind and watertight after the Restoration, turning the Great Hall into a magnificent private chapel in 1665. Dedicated to St Peter, it is reputed to be the largest private chapel in Europe.

The palace grounds, within which is a deer house, are open all year round, though the palace itself is only open from May until September.

A market has been held in Bishop Auckland for centuries. Opposite the present market place is the imposing Franco-Flemish **Bishop Auckland Town Hall**, built in the early 1860s. Though the villages immediately surrounding Bishop Auckland are mainly industrial, there are still some attractions worth seeing. At South Church is the cathedralesque **St Andrew's Church**, 157 feet long and said to be the largest parish church in the county. And on display in a working men's club at West Auckland is an unusual trophy - the World Cup, no less.

In 1910 the village's football team headed off to Italy to represent England in the first ever "World Cup". It competed against teams from Germany, Italy and Switzerland, and surprisingly won the cup when it beat Juventus 2-0 in the final. The team returned the following year to defend their title, and again won the trophy, which they then retained for all time. But what you see is actually a replica, as the original was stolen.

BRANCEPETH

Brancepeth is a small estate village built by Matthew Russell in the early 19th century, with picturesque Georgian cottages and an 18th century rectory. To the south, in parkland, is the imposing **Brancepeth Castle**. Seen from a distance, it looks suitably medieval and grand,

but most of it dates from the same time as the building of the village. The original 13th century castle was owned by the Nevills, Earls of Westmorland.

83

Close to the castle is one of the saddest sights in County Durham - the remains of **St Brandon's Church**. In 1998 a fire destroyed everything but the four walls and tower of what was one of the county's most beautiful and historic buildings. The church's main glory, magnificent woodwork commissioned by its rector John Cosin in the early 17th century, was completely destroyed. Cosin went on to become Bishop of Durham, and restored many churches in the county.

CHESTER-LE-STREET

Chester-le-Street is a busy market town built around the confluence of Cong Burn and the River Wear. The street on which the town once stood was a Roman road, later replaced by the Great North Road. As the name suggests, there was a Roman fort here at one time.

The medieval **St Mary's and St Cuthbert's Church**, is built on the site of a cathedral established in AD883 by the monks of Lindisfarne carrying the body of St Cuthbert. His coffin rested here for 113 years until the monks took it to its final resting place at Durham. There are no less than 14 effigies (not all of them genuine) of members of the Lumley family within the church, though they don't mark the sites of their graves. Next to the church is the **Ankers House Museum**, situated in the medieval anchorite. Between 1383 and 1547, various anchorites, or Christian hermits, lived here at one time or another.

Lumley Castle, to the east across the River Wear, was built in 1389 by Sir Ralph Lumley, whose descendant, Sir Richard Lumley, became the 1st Earl of Scarborough in the 1690's. In the early 18th century it was refashioned by the architect Vanbrugh for the 2nd Earl, and turned into a magnificent stately home. But gradually the castle fell out of favour with the Lumley family, and they chose to stay in their estates in Yorkshire instead. For a while it was owned by Durham University until turned into the luxurious hotel it is today.

Waldridge Fell Country Park, two miles south-west of Chester-le-Street and close to Waldridge village, is County Durham's last surviving area of lowland heathland. A car park

84

and signed footpaths give access to over 300 acres of open countryside, rich in natural history.

COWSHILL

In a hollow between Cows-hill and Nenthead lies Killhope Mine. The Pennines have been worked for their mineral riches, particularly lead, since Roman times but until the 18th century the industry remained relatively primitive and small scale. The development of new techniques of mechanisation in the late 18th and early 19th century allowed the industry to grow until it was second only to coal as a major extractive industry in the region. Now the country's best-preserved lead-mining site, and designated an ancient monument, Killhope Mine is the focal point of what is now the remarkable **North of England Lead Mining Museum**, dominated by the massive 34-feet high water wheel. It used moorland streams, feeding a small reservoir, to provide power for the lead-ore crushing mills, where the lead-ore from the hillside mines was washed and crushed ready for smelting into pigs of lead.

Much of the machinery has been carefully restored by Durham County Council over recent years, together with part of the smelting mill, underground adits, workshops, a smithy, tools and miner's sleeping quarters.

Killhope Lead Mining Centre

DARLINGTON

Darlington, just off the A1(M). is an important regional centre serving the southern part of County Durham, Teesdale and much of North Yorkshire. It was founded in Saxon times, and has a bustling town centre with one of the largest market places in England. On its west side is the Old Town Hall and indoor market, with an imposing **Clock Tower**, designed by the famous Victorian Alfred Waterhouse in 1864, lording over it all, and on the south side is the Dolphin Leisure Centre, opened in 1983.

There are many fine buildings to be enjoyed in Darlington, perhaps most notably **St Cuthbert's Church** on the east side of the market place, with its tall spire. It is almost cathedral-like in its proportions, and was built by Bishop Pudsey between 1183 and 1230 as a collegiate church. Its slender lancet windows and steep roof enhance its beauty, which has earned it the name "The Lady of the North".

Perhaps Darlington's greatest claim to fame lies in the role it played with its neighbour Stockton in the creation of the world's first commercially successful public railway which opened in 1825. It was the Darlington Quaker and banker Edward Pease who became the main driving force behind the railway scheme to link the Durham coalfield with the port of Stockton.

The present Darlington Station at Bank Top came from a much later period in the railway age, as lines were being constructed to link England and Scotland. The original Darlington Station, built in 1842, was located at North Road Station. Today it is the **Darlington Railway Centre and Museum**, a museum of national importance which houses relics of the pioneering Stockton and Darlington Railway. This includes a replica of Stephenson's **Locomotion No 1**, a Stockton and Darlington first class coach carriage built in 1846, "Little Giant", (a 15 inch gauge miniature locomotive), a World War 11 newsstand, the **Derwent**, (the earliest surviving Darlington-built locomotive), a model of the Stockton to Darlington railway, and even Victorian urinals.

So much early railway history is to be seen in this part of County Durham that British Rail have named their local Bishop Auckland-Darlington-Middlesbrough line the **Heritage Line**.

To continue the railways theme, there's an unusual engine to be seen in Morton Park - it's

85

a full size model made of bricks, and was designed by sculptor David Mach. And above High Row at the foot of Post House Wynd, is a life-size floral replica of Locomotion No 1.

High Row, with its elevated street of shops makes an impressive sight, and forms part of a compact but characterful shopping centre. The tall buildings evolved because of the narrowness of the plots of land in medieval times. The façades are pierced by tunnels which at one time gave access to rear gardens. These have long since been built over as yards and lend their name to this part of town. The "yards" now contain shops and small businesses and are public rights of way between High Row and Skinnergate.

DURHAM CITY

Arriving in Durham by train, the visitor is presented with what must be one of the most breathtaking urban views in Europe. Towering over the tumbling roofs of the city is the magnificent bulk of **Durham Cathedral**, and, close by, the majestic **Durham Castle**.

No visit to the city is complete without time spent at the cathedral. It is third only to Canterbury and York in ecclesiastical significance, but excels them in architectural

splendour. Quite simply, it is the finest and grandest example of Norman architecture in Europe. This was the powerbase of the wealthy Prince Bishops of Durham who once exercised king-like powers in an area known the Palatinate of Durham. These powers were vested in them by William I, and they could administer civil and criminal law; they could issue pardons, hold their own parliament, mint their own money, create baronetcies, and give market charters. They could even raise their own army. Though these powers were never exercised in later years, they continued in theory right up until 1836, when the last of the Prince Bishops, Bishop William Van Mildert, died. The Palatinate Courts, however, were only abolished in 1971. It is little wonder that the County Council now proudly presents the county to visitors as "The Land of the Prince Bishops".

Even more significantly, in the cathedral are the tombs of two of the greatest figures of the early Christian church in England: the remarkable St Cuthbert (AD635-687), shepherd saint of Northumbria, and the Venerable Bede (AD673-735), saint, scholar and Britain's first and pre-eminent historian.

The cathedral owes its origin to the monks of Lindisfarne, who, in AD875, fled from Viking attacks, taking with them the coffin of St Cuthbert. In AD883 they settled at Chester-le-Street. However, further Viking raids in AD980 caused them to move once more, and they eventually arrived at a more easily defended site about ten miles to the south, where the River Wear makes a wide loop round a rocky outcrop. Here, in Durham, they built the "White Church", where St Cuthbert's remains were finally laid to rest.

The founder of the present cathedral, however, was a Norman, William de St Carileph, or Calais, Bishop of Durham from 1081 to 1096. He brought to the White Church not only holy relics but, in 1083, a group of monks and scholars from Monkwearmouth and Jarrow.

William fled to Normandy in 1088, having been accused of plotting against William Rufus, but returned in 1091 after a pardon, determined to replace the little church with a building of the scale and style of the splendid new churches he saw being built in France at that time. In August 1093 the foundation stones were laid, a witness being King Malcolm III of Scotland,

Durham Cathedral

86

famed as the soldier who slew Macbeth in battle.

The main part of the great building was erected in a mere 40 years, but over ensuing centuries each generation has added magnificent work or superb detail of its own, such as the 14th century Episcopal Throne, said to be the highest in Christendom, and the Neville Screen. Yet the impregnable fortress-like quality of the cathedral, with its famous carved columns, retains a visual splendour that makes it a very special place. Even so, nothing is more moving than the simple fragments of carved wood which survive from St Cuthbert's coffin, made for the saint's body in AD698 and carried around the North of England by his devoted followers before being laid to rest in the mighty cathedral. The fragments are now kept in the **Treasures of St Cuthbert Exhibition**, within the cathedral, with examples of the Prince Bishops' own silver coins.

Durham Castle, sharing the same rocky peninsula and standing close to the cathedral, was founded in 1072 and belonged to the Prince Bishops. Such was the impregnability of the site that Durham was one of the few towns in Northumbria that was never captured by the Scots using force. Among the castle's most impressive features are the Chapel, dating from 1080, and the Great Hall, which was built in the middle of the 13th century. Though the Keep was restored in Victorian times, it remains a remarkable building in its own right.

The importance of the whole area surrounding the cathedral and castle was recognised in 1987, when it was designated a UNESCO World Heritage Site.

The Castle is now used as a hall of residence for the students of Durham University and is only open to the public at limited times. But students and visitors should beware - the castle is reputedly haunted by no less than three ghosts. One is supposed to be of Jane, wife of Bishop Van Mildert, and takes the form of the top half of a woman in 19th-century dress. She glides along the Norman Gallery, leaving the scent of apple blossom in her wake. A second spirit is of university tutor Frederick Copeman, who, in 1880, threw himself off the tower of the cathedral. His ghost is said to haunt his former room off the Norman Gallery. A further apparition, which has been seen at various locations within the castle, is a cowled monk.

The university - the third to be established in England - was founded in 1832 by Bishop Van Mildert. In 1837 it moved into Durham Castle, though today its many buildings are scattered throughout the south of the city.

The rest of Durham reflects the long history of the castle and cathedral it served. There are winding streets, such as Saddler Street and Silver Street, whose names reveal their medieval origin, the ancient Market Place, elegant Georgian houses, particularly around South Bailey, and quiet courts and alleyways. There are also many churches, such as **St Nicholas's Church** in the Market Place, **St Margaret of Antioch Church** in Crossgate, **St Mary le Bow Church** in North Bailey (now **The Durham Heritage Centre and Museum**, which is well worth visiting), **St Giles Church** in Gilesgate, **St Oswald's Church** in Church Street and **St Mary the Less Church** in South Bailey, which shows that, in medieval times, this was a great place of pilgrimage.

In the western outskirts of the city, and straddling the A167, is the site of the **Battle of Neville's Cross**, fought in 1346 between Scotland and England. The Scottish army was heavily defeated, and the Scottish king, David 11, was taken prisoner. A leaflet has been produced which guides visitors round the site.

A favourite and famous walk past castle and cathedral follows the footpaths which run through the woodlands on each bank of the River Wear, around the great loop. You can begin either at Framwellgate Bridge or Elvet Bridge. The path along the inside of the loop goes past **The Old Fulling Mill**, sited below the cathedral, which now houses an archaeological museum containing material from excavations in and around the city. If walking isn't to your taste you can take a cruise along the river from Elvet Bridge.

The **DLI Museum and Durham Art Gallery** at Aykley Heads has been totally refurbished. It tells the story of the county's own regiment, the Durham Light Infantry, which was founded in 1758 and lasted right up until 1968. The horrors of First World War are shown, as is a reconstruction of a Durham street during the Second World War. Individual acts of bravery are also remembered, such as the story of Adam Wakenshaw, the youngest of a family of 13, who refused to leave his comrades after his arm was blown off. He died in action, and for this was awarded a Victoria Cross. The art gallery has a

Durham Light Infantry Museum and Art Gallery

riding and cycling (cycles can be hired). There is a visitor centre with displays on forestry, wildlife and timber usage, and large, grassy areas make splendid picnic spots. The forest is easily accessible from coach and car parks, and visitors are enthusiastically encouraged to enjoy the peace and quiet of this lovely place, which is now a Forest Nature Reserve.

87

changing exhibition of paintings and sculpture. A very different, but still outstanding, museum is the **Durham University Oriental Museum**, a collection of oriental art of international importance with material from Ancient Egypt, Tibet, India and China. The museum is located in parkland off Elvet Hill Road to the south of the city. The museum entrance is guarded by two stately Chinese lion-dogs.

The university also runs the 18-acre **Botanic Gardens**, on Hollingside Lane (off the A167) on the south side of the city. It is one of the newest in England, and has a large collection of North American trees, including junior-sized giant redwoods, a series of small "gardens-within-gardens" and walks through mature woodland. Two display greenhouses feature cacti and succulents and a tropical "jungle". The gardens are closed between Christmas and New Year.

Crook Hall and Gardens is on Frankland Lane, a ten minute walk north of the Millburngate Shopping Centre. Centred on a lovely 14th century medieval manor house, the gardens have such features as the Secret Garden, the Shakespeare Garden, the Cathedral Garden and the Silver and White Gardens. The hall itself, with its haunted Jacobean Room, is open to the public.

HAMSTERLEY FOREST

Hamsterley Forest is one of the Forestry Commission's most attractive Forest Parks. This huge area - over 5,500 acres - of mature woodland is managed for timber production, and has 1,100 acres available for recreation with a choice of rides and walks. Today it offers a wide range of activities for visitors, such as informal or guided walks, orienteering, horse-

Surprisingly enough, the Forest is largely artificial and relatively recent in origin. Much of it covers areas once worked by the lead-mining industry. It was planted some 40 to 50 years ago with European larch, pine and Norway spruce but, in the clearings, several self-sown species have become established - ash, birch and oak among them - adding variety and colour. This is a good area to discover a range of wild flowers and, in the damper places, fungi. There are still red squirrels as well as roe deer, badgers, adders and up to 40 species of birds including heron, woodcock, sparrow hawk, woodpeckers, fieldfare and goldfinch.

HARTLEPOOL

There are really two Hartlepools - the old town on the headland, and the newer part, which used to be called West Hartlepool. Up until 1968 they were separate boroughs, but they have now combined under the one name. This town, like Stockton-on-Tees and Darlington, is a unitary authority, though the border with County Durham is almost on its outskirts.

The old part of Hartlepool goes back centuries, and was at one time a walled town. Parts of these walls still exist on the shore line, and there is a particularly fine gatehouse, called the **Sandwellgate**, with solid turrets in either side. Go through the pointed archway, and you find yourself on the beach.

In the Middle Ages, Hartlepool was the only port within County Durham that was allowed to trade outside the Palatinate, which made it an important place. After the Norman Conquest, it was acquired by the Bruce family, whose most notable member was Robert the Bruce, King of Scotland. It received its charter about 1201 from King John, who ordered that the walls to be built to defend it against the marauding Scots.

The immense and ornate 13th century **St Hilda's Church** was built by the Bruces as a burial place, which may explain its size. Within

88 is the tomb of what is thought to be Robert Bruce, the church's founder. It sits behind the altar, and is made of Frosterley marble.

The church stands on the site of a monastery founded by St Aidan in AD647. Its most famous abbess was Hilda - hence the church's dedication - who subsequently went on to found the great monastery at Whitby, where the Synod of Whitby was held in AD664. Parts of its cemetery were excavated in the 19th century, and some of the finds are on show in Durham and Newcastle.

Hartlepool's harbour eventually went into decline, and by the early 18th century the place was no more than a fishing village. In 1835 work started on opening up the harbour once more, and rail links were established with the coalfields. But it had competition. In 1847 work started on the West Harbour and Coal Dock, and by 1860 it was thriving. Other docks were opened, and soon a new town grew up around them. So West Hartlepool was born. On December 16 1914 it was the first town in Britain to suffer from enemy action during the First World War when it was shelled from German warships lying off the coast.

Nowadays it is a thriving shopping centre, with some outstanding tourist attractions, including the **Hartlepool Historic Quay and Museum**. A small seaport has been constructed round one of the old docks, showing what life was like in the early part of the 19th century, when Britain was at war with France. Grouped round the small dock are various businesses and shops, such as a printer, gunsmith, naval tailor, swordsmith and instrument maker. Visitors can also go aboard **HMS Trincomalee**, Britain's oldest surviving warship (launched in 1817), and have coffee aboard the **PSS Wingfield Castle**, an old paddle steamer. The Trincomalee, strictly speaking, is a separate attraction, so there is an extra charge.

Attached is the Hartlepool Museum, with exhibits showing life in the town through the ages. It features "sea monsters", a medieval "round house", and interactive displays.

LANCHESTER

Lanchester owes its name to the Roman fort of Longovicium (The Long Fort), which stood on a hilltop half a mile to the south-west. The fort was built to guard Dere Street, the Roman road which linked York and the north. The scant remains sit on private land, however, and can't be visited. Stone from the fort was used in the mostly Norman **All Saints Church**, and Roman pillars can be seen supporting the north aisle. There is also a Roman altar in the south porch and some superb 12th century carvings over the vestry door in the chancel.

One place worth visiting near Lanchester is **Hall Hill Farm**, on the B6296 four miles south west of the village. It's a real working sheep farm which is open to the public all year round.

To the south of Lanchester is a typical County Durham mining area, with small colliery villages with names like **Quebec**, **Esh Winning**, **Tow Law** and **Cornsay Colliery**.

MIDDLETON-IN-TEESDALE

Middleton-in-Teesdale, the capital of Upper Teesdale, is a small, grey town in a dramatically beautiful setting with the Tees running below, while all around is a great backcloth of green hills. The town's links with the lead-mining industry are apparent in the Market Square, where there is a handsome cast-iron fountain which was purchased and placed there in 1877 by the employees of the Quaker-owned London Lead Mining Company. The expense was covered from subscriptions raised for the retirement of the company's local super-intendent, Robert Bainbridge. At the west end of Hude is **Middleton House**, the company's former headquarters.

Although the lead-mining industry disappeared long ago, Middleton still has the strong feeling of being a mining town, with company-built houses, shops, offices and sober chapels to keep the population suitably moral in outlook. The surrounding hills still bear the scars, with the remains of old workings, spoil-heaps and deep, and often dangerous, shafts. But the town's agricultural links remain strong, with streets still known as Market Place, Horsemarket and Seed Hill. Like Barnard Castle, it is increasing in popularity as a centre from which to explore both Teesdale and the entire North Pennines.

Middleton is also the centre for some magnificent walks in Upper Teesdale. The most famous of these is **The Pennine Way** on its 250-mile route from Derbyshire to Kirk Yetholm in Scotland. It passes through Middleton-in-Teesdale from the south, then turns west along Teesdale, passing flower-rich meadows which turn vivid gold, white and blue in late spring. It then goes past traditional, whitewashed farmsteads and spectacular, riverside scenery, including the thrilling waterfalls at **Low Force**, **High Force** and **Cauldron Snout**.

High Force is beautiful. While it isn't England's highest waterfall, it is its largest in terms of water flow, with the Tees dropping 68 feet over Great Whin Sill. When it's in spate, its rumble can be heard over a mile away. Low Force isn't so much a waterfall as a series of cascades, and is more beautiful, if less spectacular, than its neighbour. Cauldron Spout is a cascade that flows from Cow Green Reservoir, high in the hills, down into the Tees. As the road leaves the course of the River Tees and follows Harwood Beck before Cauldron Snout is reached. However, it can only be visited on foot.

STANHOPE

Stanhope, the capital of Upper Weardale, is a small town of great character and individuality, which still serves the surrounding villages as an important local centre for shops and supplies. It marks the boundary between the softer scenery of lower Weardale and the wilder scenery to the west. The stone cross in the Market Place is the only reminder of a weekly market held in the town by virtue of a 1421 charter. The market continued until Victorian times.

Stanhope enjoyed its greatest period of prosperity in the 18th and 19th centuries when the lead and iron-stone industries were at their height. The town's buildings and architecture reflect this. In an attractive rural setting in the centre of the dale, with a choice of local walks, Stanhope, in its quiet way, is becoming a small tourist centre with pleasant shops and cafés. The town itself is well worth exploring on foot and a useful 'walkabout' town trail is available locally or from information centres.

The most dominant building in the Market Square is **Stanhope Castle**, a rambling structure complete with mock-Gothic crenellated towers, galleries and battlements. The building is, in fact, an elaborate folly built by the MP for Gateshead, Cuthbert Rippon in 1798 on the site of a medieval manor house. In 1875 it was enlarged to contain a private collection of mineral displays and stuffed birds for the entertainment of Victorian grouse-shooting parties. In the gardens is the **Durham Dales Centre**.

Fossil Tree Stump, Stanhope

Stanhope Old Hall, above Stanhope Burn Bridge, is generally accepted to be one of the most impressive buildings in Weardale. This huge, fortified manor house was designed to repel Scottish raiders. The hall itself is part medieval, part Elizabethan and part Jacobean. The outbuildings included a cornmill, a brew house and cattle yards. It is now a hotel.

St Thomas's Church, by the Market Square, has a tower whose base is Norman, and some medieval glass in the west window. In the churchyard you'll find a remarkable fossil tree stump which was discovered in 1962 in a local quarry.

One of the most important Bronze Age archaeological finds ever made in Britain was at **Heathery Burn**, a side valley off Stanhope Burn, when, in 1850, quarrymen cut through the floor of a cave to find a huge hoard of bronze and gold ornaments, amber necklaces, pottery, spearheads, animal bones and parts of chariots. The treasures are now kept in the British Museum.

90 The Beamish Mary Inn

Front Street,
No Place,
Stanley,
Co Durham
DH9 0QH
Tel: 0191 370 0237
Fax: 0191 370 0091

Directions:

Stanley lies 5 miles
south of Newcastle at
the junction of the
A6076 and A693.

This sturdy stone inn on the main street was built in 1895 to serve what was then a close and mainly mining community, but **Beamish Mary**'s reputation has spread far outside the town. It has changed very little externally, and inside there's character in abundance, with exposed stone walls, original wooden floors, open fires and a massive clock rescued from the public baths at Stanley. The look may be late Victorian, but time certainly doesn't stand still here, and owner Graham Ford draws his clientele from near and far by offering the best in hospitality, entertainment, food and drink and accommodation. The selection of cask ales is among the very best in the region, with ten usually available, and there's also an impressive choice on the menus, which run from quick snacks and light bites to excellent seafood specials and juicy steaks.

The Beamish Mary is conveniently placed for both business and leisure visits to the area, and for guests staying overnight there are four letting bedrooms, three en suite, the other with adjacent bathroom, all with tv and tea/coffee facilities. Tuesday is quiz night at this most convivial of pubs, and there's live music on most of the other nights of the week: the jazz club meets on Sunday, the folk club on Wednesday, and blues and rock music is played on Thursday and Saturday. Newcastle, a thriving city with a long and interesting history, is a short drive north, but even closer are other attractions that recall the region's industrial heritage. Chief among these and less than a mile from the inn is the North of England Open Air Museum at Beamish, which illustrates life in the late 19th and early 20th centuries by means of streets and shops, trams, trains and a colliery village. For lovers of the great outdoors, the moors and fells of the Pennines are easily reached to the west.

Opening Hours: 12-11 (Sun 12-10.30).

Food: Bar meals.

Credit Cards: All major credit cards

Accommodation: 4 rooms, 3 en suite.

Facilities: Parking, beer garden.

Entertainment: Quiz Tuesday, music most evenings (see above).

Local Places of Interest/Activities: Beamish 1 mile, Newcastle 5 miles.

Internet/website:
e-mail: thebeamishmary@hotmail.com
website: beamishmary.co.uk

The Black Horse   91

Old Cornsay,
Co Durham
DH7 9EL
Tel: 0191 373 4211
Fax: 0191 373 3786

Directions:

Old Cornsay lies 3 miles south of the A691. Leave at Lanchester and take the B6301, Cornsay signposted after 2 miles, or the A68 to Tow Law and turn left just north of Tow Law.

The Black Horse is a rural 200-year-old coaching inn which has been lovingly restored and refurbished by owners Moira and Allen Cartmell, who took over the inn in May 1999. The Black Horse was built on a route that carried goods and mail from Weardale to the coast and thence overseas, and it is thought that two teams of black horses were at one time stabled here. Old sepia photographs from the early years of the 20th century are mounted on a wall in the lounge - a much more tangible link with the past than Mavis, the ghost who is said to haunt the cellars and the gents loo!

The owners have redesigned the quaint little bar area and the non-smoking restaurant, where the best of seasonal produce, much of it sourced locally, is used to create excellent dishes with both traditional influences. Booking is strongly recommended for a table on Saturday evening or Sunday lunchtime. The food, whose preparation is overseen by Moira, is an important part of the business, but the Black Horse also offers very comfortable overnight accommodation in three top-quality bedrooms, one with a four-poster bed, all with en suite facilities, tv and tea/coffee makers. Also available is a fully equipped self-contained, self-catering apartment which can sleep 4 guests. The pub has ample parking space and local brains are put to the test on quiz night, which takes place on the last Sunday of each month. The Black Horse is equally well placed for town and country, with Durham to the east and the fells and moors of the northeast Pennines to the west.

Opening Hours: 7-11 (Sun 12-3.00 & 7-10.30).

Food: A la carte menu and nightly specials.

Credit Cards: None.

Accommodation: 2 en suite rooms and self-catering apartment.

Facilities: Car park.

Entertainment: Quiz last Sunday of the month.

Local Places of Interest/Activities: Durham 10 miles, Hadrians Wall 15 miles, Beamish Open Air Museum(recently voted European Museum of the Year) 9 miles.

Internet/website:

e-mail: drcartmell@compuserve.com

92

The Black Horse

1 Hamilton Row,
Waterhouses,
Co Durham
DH7 7DA
Tel: 0191 373 4576
Fax: 0191 373 7124

Directions:
From Durham, take the B6302 to Esh Winning then the left fork to Waterhouses.

A short drive south from Esh Winning on the road to Crook, the **Black Horse** stands on a corner site in the tiny community of Hamilton Row, a 2001 County Durham Tidy Village winner. The pub itself is spick and span, its stone frontage whitewashed, with black details and black horses' heads above the ground-floor windows. Originally a mid-Victorian coaching inn (the stables are still there), the inn has been owned and run since 1994 by the affable, communicative husband-and-wife team of Barry and Pat Sims, who have an unfailingly friendly greeting for new faces as well as their regular patrons.

The old-world theme works well in the bar, whose walls are covered with pictures and prints of the area in bygone days. Real coal fires keep the whole place warm and cosy, and in the quaint little dining area traditional home-cooked dishes include the likes of gammon, pork chops and hearty, satisfying steak pies. To wash it all down there are two cask ales and a wide selection of draught and bottled beers. The Black Horse has a pool table, a beer garden and parking space across the road. The entertainment provided by the cheerful owners is supplemented on Friday by live music from a singer and a small band. The inn overlooks farmland and open fields, and the ancient Roman road now called Dere Street runs nearby. The moors and fells of the Pennines are a short drive to the west, while in the other direction lies Durham, a city full of historic interest for the visitor.

Opening Hours: 12-11 (Sun to 10.30).

Food: Bar meals.

Credit Cards: Mastercard, Visa.

Accommodation: 24 en suite rooms.

Facilities: Car park.

Entertainment: Live music Friday.

Local Places of Interest/Activities: Durham 5 miles.

The Cross Keys

93

Esh Village,
Co Durham
Tel: 0191 373 1279

Directions:
Esh village is located off the A691 or B6302 7 miles west of Durham.

Experienced proprietors Edwin and Davina Pickersgill know exactly what makes a good pub tick, and for 10 years they have been putting that knowledge to good use at the **Cross Keys**. In a former mining village west of Durham, their charming old coaching inn is a 'Pubs in Bloom' winner, and each spring Edwin spends a small fortune on plants and hanging baskets. The promise of the outside is more than fulfilled in the bar and lounge, where exposed stone walls, low oak-beamed ceilings and leather-backed alcove seating paint a picture of inviting old-world charm. The Cross Keys, a Vaux pub, serves two cask ales and a broad selection of other draught beers, and at lunchtime it does a roaring trade with its excellent home-made dishes typified by pasta bake and Durham lamb pie.

Booking is advisable to be sure of a table for Sunday lunch. The food is also available in the evening, from 7 o'clock to 9. Darts is the favourite pub game at the Cross Keys, which has ample parking space and some outside seating. Esh lies in what used to be a typical mining area, with other small colliery villages such as Quebec, Esh Winning, Tow Law and Cornsay. The main place of interest is Durham itself, with its superb Norman cathedral, majestic castle and numerous museums and galleries. A little way north of the pub is the village of Lanchester, where some of the houses and parts of the Norman church were built with stones from the nearby Roman fort of Longovicum.

Opening Hours: 12-3 & 7-11 (from 6.30 on Saturday).

Food: Bar meals.

Credit Cards: Mastercard, Visa.

Accommodation: None.

Facilities: Car park, beer garden.

Entertainment: None

Local Places of Interest/Activities: Durham 7 miles.

94   The Cross Keys

Hamsterly,
Nr Bishop Auckland,
Co Durham
DL13 3PX
Tel/Fax:
*   01388 488457*

Directions:

From Bishop
Auckland, B6282
then right on to the
A68 for 1 mile.
Hamsterly is
signposted off to the
left at Toft Hill.

Sitting opposite the vicarage in the picture postcard village of Hamsterly, the **Cross Keys** is a smart greystone building that started life in 1881 as two terraced houses. Food is a very important part of the business here, and the owners George and Hilary Hallimond, who previously ran a pub in Amble on the Northumberland coast, have the services of an excellent chef who has been here for 18 years. Fresh, wholesome cuisine is his trademark, and in the à la carte restaurant the menu offers something to please all tastes and satisfy all appetites. This fine food, which is served from 2 to 2 and from 6.30 to 9.30, is complemented by a well-chosen wine list, and ale connoisseurs can choose between a regular and a guest cask ale. The weekends, and in particular Sunday lunch, always bring in the crowds, so it's best to book to be sure of a table.

The closest major community to the inn is Bishop Auckland, where the castle is still the official palace of the Bishop of Durham. Hamsterly Forest, a short drive west of the village, is one of the Forestry Commission's most attractive forest parks, producing timber and providing an excellent range of activities for the visitor, including guided or informal walks, orienteering, horse-riding and cycling. The Forest is home to an abundance of animal, bird and plant life, and it has an interesting visitor centre with displays on various aspects of the forest. A day spent here in the fresh air is guaranteed to generate a thirst and an appetite which the owners and staff at the Cross Keys are ready and eager to satisfy. The inn has plenty of space for cars and a beer garden at the back.

Opening Hours: 12-3 & 6-11, all day in summer.

Food: Extensive menus.

Credit Cards: Mastercard, Visa.

Accommodation: Planned.

Facilities: Car park, beer garden.

Entertainment: None

Local Places of Interest/Activities:
Hamsterly Forest 2 miles, Bishop Auckland 5 miles.

Internet/website:
e-mail: hallimond@lineone.net

The Fox & Hounds 95

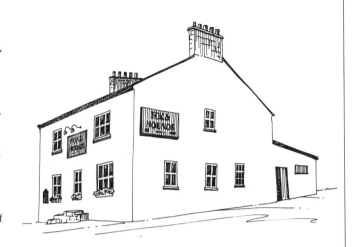

Stonebank Terrace,
Newfield,
Bishop Auckland,
Co Durham
DL14 8DF
Tel: 01388 662787

Directions:

Newfield is about 3 miles north of Bishop Auckland along the River Wear. Best reached by a minor road off the A689.

Outstanding food brings visitors from all over County Durham and North Yorkshire to the **Fox & Hounds**, which enjoys a secluded setting alongside the River Wear just north of Bishop Auckland. Dating from the early years of Queen Victoria's reign, the inn looks very smart in its coat of whitewash, and in spring and summer flower boxes and hanging baskets make a spectacular show of colour. Inside, an old Rayburn stove keeps things cosy in the bar, where customers can warm up before heading for the restaurant and the inn's great selling point - the food! The balanced menu provides a great choice of dishes prepared with care and flair by William Thompson, who runs the pub in partnership with Ray Henry.

The main blackboard menu is supplemented at lunchtime Tuesday to Friday by a splendid light lunch menu that runs from open baguettes sandwiches - grilled Brie with bacon and tossed salad - to scrambled egg with smoked salmon and spicy chorizo sausage, tuna and mushrooms with saffron risotto or sausages braised with borlotti beans and served with a mustard mash. Fine food deserves fine wine, and the Fox & Hounds has an excellent list. Walks along the banks of the River Wear are a pleasant way to build up an appetite, and after lunch or before supper there are plenty of places to see in the vicinity of the inn, among them the Roman fort at Binchester, the Saxon church at Escomb, Aukland Castle and Bishops Park, home of the Bishop of Durham.

Opening Hours: 12-3 & 7-11. Closed all day Monday

Food: A la carte and light lunch menus.

Credit Cards: Mastercard, Visa.

Accommodation: None.

Facilities: Car park.

Entertainment: None

Local Places of Interest/Activities: River Wear walks, Binchester 2 miles, Bishop Auckland 3 miles.

96

The George

Bondgate,
Darlington,
Co Durham
DL1 3HX
Tel: 01325 481686

Directions:

Close to the centre of
Darlington, just off the A1(M).
From the south J57 then A66;
from the north J59 and A167
or J58 and A68.

The George is a classic three-storey terraced building dating from Queen Victoria's coronation year, 1837. The prints and photographs on display in the bar show that it has changed little externally down the years, and the no-frills public area is roomy and comfortable, a proper non-nonsense ambience of which owner David Nicholls is justifiably proud. Draught cider and a huge selection of Northern-brewed ales are on tap to quench thirsts, and at lunchtime hefty portions of classic bar food are served. Evening meals are available to guests staying overnight in the well-priced accommodation, which comprises five rooms sharing facilities. The locals like a game of pool, and in the bar a jukebox provides a musical background and a television covers all the major sporting events.

Darlington, readily accessible from junctions 57, 58 or 59 of the A1(M), has a bustling town centre with one of the largest market places in England. It boasts a number of fine buildings, notably St Cuthbert's Church of almost cathedral-like proportions, but Darlington's greatest claim to fame is the role it played with its neighbour Stockton in the development of the world's first commercial passenger railway. It is that piece of history which brings railway enthusiasts and historians to the Darlington Railway Centre and Museum, housed in the original 1842 station and containing a replica of George Stephenson's Locomotion No.1, a carriage from 1846 and many other reminders of the earliest days of the railways.

Opening Hours: All day, every day.

Food: Bar meals.

Credit Cards: Mastercard, Visa.

Accommodation: 5 budget rooms.

Facilities: Car park.

Entertainment: None

Local Places of Interest/Activities: Railway Centre & Museum.

The Grey Horse

97

Sherburn Terrace,
Consett,
Co Durham
DH8 8NE
Tel: 01207 502585

Directions:
Consett is situated
on the A691 10
miles northwest of
Durham.

The Grey Horse is the oldest surviving pub in Consett, built in 1848 and originally called the Target Inn. Connoisseurs of fine ales know they've hit the target when they discover that the Grey Horse brews its own beer in the Derwentrose Brewery in an old stone building that was once a stable at the back of the pub. The pub has been owned and run since the late 1980s by Dubliner Paul Conroy and his wife Roseleen. They generate a cheerful, relaxed atmosphere in the public and lounge bars, which are a real delight, with beams, an open fire and a merry jumble of prints, pictures, jugs, beer bottles and general bric-a-brac. Simple snacks, headed by a great selection of sandwiches and toasties, provide the solid nourishment, but beer is the undisputed king here, and in 2000 the pub received the double accolade of Durham Camra Pub of the Year and the Evening Chronicle Best Beer Pub.

Among the dozen plus beers brewed on the premises are 3 Giants (3.2%), a dark mild first brewed the pub's 1999 Beer Festival; Red Dust (4.2%), tawny ruby-red coloured and named after the infamous red dust from the old Consett steel works; Angel Ale (5%), a golden premium bitter named in honour of the nearby Angel of the North; and the dark ruby Devil's Dip (a staggering 9%). There are plenty of opportunities nearby to work up a thirst in the open air: the C2C cycle route passes close by, as does Derwent Walk, which follows the valley along to a country park. To the west is Derwent Reservoir, where after a spell sailing the prospect of the fruits of the Derwentrose Brewery will be irresistible.

Opening Hours: 12-11 (Sun to 10.30).

Food: Bar snacks.

Credit Cards: None.

Accommodation: None.

Facilities: Car park, in-house brewery.

Entertainment: None

Local Places of Interest/Activities: Derwent Walk Country Park 4 miles, Derwent Reservoir 3 miles, Ebchester (Roman fort) 2 miles.

Internet/website:

e-mail: paul@thegreyhouse.co.uk
website: www.thegreyhorse.co.uk

98   Helme Park Hall Hotel

Nr Fir Tree,
Bishop Auckland,
Co Durham DL13 4NW
Tel: 01388 730970
Fax: 01388 731799

Directions:

From the A1(M) take the A689 from the south and the A690 from the north. The hotel is signposted just past Crook. From the A689 turn on to the A68 signposted Tow Law; the hotel is a few hundred yards on the left.

Helme Park Hotel is a country house hotel and restaurant set in the grandeur and beauty of rural County Durham between Teesdale and Weardale. Looking very smart after a top-to-toe refurbishment by owners Carolyn and John Wheeler, the hotel is a perfect venue for dining out, short breaks and functions of all kinds. Style and taste are evident throughout, from the foyer with its studded leather sofas to the beamed bar with open fires at each end and the elegant lounge with Regency-style fireplace, sumptuous carpets, Italian plasterwork and a bay window affording a superb view across the lawn to the wooded slopes of Weardale and the Pennines in the background. Informal meals are served in the bar and lounge, and in the restaurant the experienced head chef and his team have earned an excellent reputation for producing stylish, individual and tasty dishes reflecting the best of British and Continental cuisine. The finest and freshest ingredients, sourced locally as far as possible, are used on the à la carte and table d'hote menus, and an extensive, carefully chosen selection of wines from around the world perfectly complements the meal.

Accommodation at the Hall comprises 13 tastefully decorated and furnished bedrooms all with fully tiled bathrooms en suite, tv/radio, telephone, trouser press, hairdryer and hospitality tray. Top of the range is a wedding suite with a four-poster bed and double whirlpool bath. The picturesque setting, with its two acres of gardens and terrific views, makes the Hall a popular venue for functions and receptions, and a well-appointed conference facility can accommodate meetings of between 6 and 40 in various rooms and up to 150 theatre-style in the Stobart Suite. The hotel offers special breaks throughout the year, along with regular events such as dinner dances, cabaret suppers and murder mystery evenings.

Opening Hours: All day, every day.

Food: Bar and restaurant menus.

Credit Cards: Amex, Mastercard, Visa.

Accommodation: 13 en suite rooms.

Facilities: Car park, garden.

Entertainment: Dinner dances and regular special events.

Local Places of Interest/Activities:
Stanhope 8 miles, River Wear and Weardale Way 1 mile, Crook 2 miles, Bishop Auckland 8 miles.

Internet/website:

website: www.helmeparkhotel.co.uk

The Lion & Unicorn | 99

Commercial Street,
Willington, Co Durham
DL15 0AF
Tel: 01388 745512

Directions:
The inn is on the main street of Willington, 8 miles south of Durham on the A690.

Built in 1891 at a time when the town and its environs were centres of the coal-mining industry, the **Lion & Unicorn** continues to appeal to the local residents of Willington, which stands 8 miles south of the city of Durham. The tenants here are Mr & Mrs Hill, who since their arrival at the beginning of millennium year have been spending a great deal of time and effort in improving the decor and furnishings. Behind the terraced frontage on the main street of town, the bar is neat and compact, with new carpets, new tables and chairs and some handsome reclaimed oak flooring.

The kitchen has also been totally refitted and from late spring 2002 has been providing a range of straightforward dishes such as filled jacket potatoes, lasagne and meat pies. There's a full selection of draught and bottle beers, and always something on special promotion. It's an easy drive to the magnificent city of Durham, where the visitor will find a large number of churches, museums and galleries as well as the wonderful Cathedral (burial place of the Venerable Bede) and the majestic Castle. Halfway to Durham is the small estate village of Brancepeth, which also has a castle.

Opening Hours: 11-11 (Sun 12-10.30).

Food: Bar meals.

Credit Cards: None.

Accommodation: None.

Facilities: Parking at the rear.

Entertainment: Disco Friday & Sunday, live music Saturday, karaoke weekly.

Local Places of Interest/Activities: Durham 8 miles.

100 The Miners Arms

Manor Road,
Medomsley,
Co Durham
DH8 6QN
Tel: 01207 560428

Directions:

Medomsley is situated 2 miles north of Consett, where the B6278 meets the B6310.

Built in 1783 and considerably extended since, the **Miners Arms** is a recommended destination for anyone who appreciates good food and drink. Go-ahead young owner Phil Johnston has the services of an excellent chef who combines the traditional skills of his trade with a generous measure of flair and inventiveness. The pick of local produce is the basis of an exciting menu of dishes in the modern English style, which combines the best elements of British and European cuisines with influences from further afield. The wine list is every bit as interesting as the menu, with bottles from all over the world, and beer-lovers have a good choice of real ales and draught and bottle beers.

The public rooms of the Miners Arms are spacious and stylish, decorated and furnished to a very high standard that reflects great credit on owner Phil. There's a huge car park, a beer garden and a patio, and the inn is open for business all day, every day. It's a top spot not only for a local clientele but for a growing band of regulars drawn from outside the area. It's also a perfect place for tourists in an area that is rich in both scenic and historic interest. Nearby Shotley Bridge was where steel-making first started in this region and the legacy of the prosperous days can be seen in the many fine old houses in Consett. For lovers of the great outdoors, the Derwent Walk, open to walkers, cyclists and horse-riders, follows a disused railway line through woodland and along the Derwent Valley to a country park. Also close by is Derwent Reservoir, with sailing, fishing and bird-watching.

Opening Hours: All day, every day.

Food: Extensive à la carte menu.

Credit Cards: Mastercard, Visa.

Accommodation: None.

Facilities: Car park, beer garden.

Entertainment: Live music monthly.

Local Places of Interest/Activities: Consett 2 miles, Ebchester (Roman remains) 1 mile, Derwent Walk 1 mile.

Internet/website:
e-mail: michael@renshawmi.fsnet.com

The Queens Head 101

89 Front Street,
Stanhope,
Nr Bishop Auckland,
Co Durham
DL13 2LB
Tel/Fax:
01388 528160

Directions:
Stanhope is on the A689
Bishop Auckland-
Brampton road 2 miles
west of Bishop Auckland.

The Queen in question is a chess piece, which appears on the sign outside this classic mid-19th century building in a village-centre terrace. Inside, the decor is superb, with plush carpets and beamed ceilings contributing to the picture of comfortable, old-fashioned charm. Landlord Derek Storey has built up a loyal local clientele and he and his staff also have a warm welcome for the many walkers and tourists in this scenically attractive part of the world. Real ale enthusiasts will appreciate the excellent choice that is always on tap - two residents and three frequently changing guests - and the pub is also known for its fine home-cooked food, which is served every lunchtime and evening and typically includes lasagne, pies and other tasty dishes using the top-quality local beef and lamb.

The countryside hereabouts is very appealing, and lovers of the wide-open spaces will find the **Queens Head** a convenient and convivial base. It has four letting bedrooms, three of them en suite, the other with an adjacent private bathroom. The Weardale Way provides splendid walking and there are other footpaths along the rivers and into the open moorland. Stanhope itself, the capital of Upper Weardale, is a small town of considerable character and individuality, with many places of interest for the visitor. Notable among these are the Durham Dales Centre in the grounds of a mock-medieval castle, St Thomas' Church, where a famous fossil tree stump stands in the churchyard, and Heathery Burn, one of the most important Bronze Age sites in the whole country.

Opening Hours: 12-3 & 7-11 (seasonal variations).

Food: Bar meals.

Credit Cards: Mastercard, Visa.

Accommodation: 4 rooms, 3 en suite.

Facilities: None.

Entertainment: None

Local Places of Interest/Activities: Heathery Burn 2 miles, Turnstall Reservoir 6 miles.

Internet/website:
e-mail: derekstorey@supernet.com

102   The Royal George

Old Shotton,
Nr Peterlee,
Co Durham
SR8 1AT
Tel: 0191 587 0526

Directions:

Old Shotton is a
tiny hamlet just
outside Peterlee,
yards off the A19
and 10 miles north
of Middlesbrough.

Licensees Brian O'Connor and Christine Wanlevy and manager Ian Houghton make an excellent job of running the **Royal George**, a delightful inn dating from 1837, the year Victoria came to the throne. The outside is painted brilliant white, with arched windows and a pine main door, and within, the small bar and much larger lounge are decorated and furnished to a very high standard. A varied choice of draught beers and ciders takes care of thirsts, and there's an excellent selection of lunchtime and evening meals, with nothing frozen and everything prepared on the premises.

The evening menu combines classics such as garlic mushrooms, roast chicken, steaks, beef & ale pie and two sizes of mixed grill with some more esoteric delights like grilled tuna steak with a sherry and oregano sauce or aromatic roast duckling. Moussaka, lasagne and cannelloni come in vegetarian versions, and the dessert list includes gateaux, cheesecakes, ice creams and assorted steamed puddings. The weekend brings entertainment both musical and cerebral, with karaoke on Saturday and a quiz on Sunday. At other times the click of dominoes is often heard. The A19 offers ready access both north and south, but just a short walk from the pub is Castle Eden Dene Nature Reserve, one of the largest woodlands in the northeast that has not been much altered by man. It covers 500 acres in a steep-sided valley and is home to a wide variety of trees and shrubs, wild flowers and butterflies, including the very rare Castle Eden Argus.

Opening Hours: 11-11 (Sun 12-10.30).

Food: Bar meals, evening à la carte.

Credit Cards: None.

Accommodation: None.

Facilities: Car park.

Entertainment: Karaoke Saturday, quiz Sunday.

Local Places of Interest/Activities: Castle Eden 1 mile, Easington 2 miles.

The Saxon

Escomb,
Nr Bishop Auckland,
Co Durham
DL14 7SY
Tel: 01388 662256

Directions:

Escomb is located on the A689 3 miles northwest of Bishop Auckland. The inn is opposite the church.

Landlord Paul Hope, an experienced and accomplished chef, prides himself on the quality of the cooking at the **Saxon Inn**, which is set back from the main A689 road north of Bishop Auckland. Paul only took over the Saxon towards the end of 2001 but is already wooing the locals and the not-so-locals with a seasonally changing menu of wholesome dishes freshly prepared and attractively presented. All tastes are catered for, but the steak & ale pie has established itself as a firm favourite; the food can be enjoyed with a choice of real ales or something from a wine list that features some very good New World bottles.

The inn, which dates from 1671, looks very smart with its whitewashed facade and black window surrounds, and the decor inside is very much in keeping with its age and full of character. As well as satisfying the most discerning of diners, the Saxon is a very sociable place, with live music in the summer and quiz and bingo sessions on Sunday evenings. The inn takes its name from one of the true gems of County Durham right opposite. This is the Church of St John the Evangelist, one of only three complete Saxon churches in Britain, built using Roman stones from the old at nearby Binchester. Its treasures include a curious stone sundial next to the porch, topped with serpents and marked to show the times of the services. The fort itself, known to the Romans as Vinovia, has the best preserved Roman military bathhouse in Britain and is well worth a visit. There's good walking along the River Wear, and a short drive to the west is Hamsterly Forest, which offers a wide variety of outdoor activities and is home to an abundant wildlife and plantlife.

Opening Hours: 9-11 every day.

Food: Bar meals served from 12 noon to9pm

Credit Cards: None.

Accommodation: None.

Facilities: Car park, garden.

Entertainment: Quiz and bingo on Sunday, occasional live music in the summer.

Local Places of Interest/Activities: Saxon church opposite, Bishop Auckland 2 miles, Binchester Fort 2 miles.

104 The Sportsmans Inn

Toft Hill,
Bishop Auckland,
Co Durham
DL14 0JE
Tel: 01388 832938

Directions:

Toft Hill is on the A68 2 miles west of Bishop Auckland, 2 miles north of West Auckland.

An excellent site right on the A68 makes the **Sportsmans Inn** a very easy place to find on the route north from West Auckland. The inn has been here since the late 19th century, serving the needs of both the local community and those passing through, and the tradition of hospitality is being carried on by Isobel Brand and her partner John McMennum.. The Sportsman's bar is plain and unpretentious, with an open fire to warm the mixed clientele of country folk and those from the nearby towns who gather to swap news, put the world to rights and enjoy a glass of something from the good choice of real ales and draught beers and lagers that is always available.

The pub is open in the evenings only from Monday to Friday and lunchtime and evening Saturday and Sunday. Food is served Sunday lunchtime. The favoured games in the bar are darts and dominoes. Though the Sportsman is mainly a down-to-earth evening and weekend place for locals, its location means that it also caters for a thirsty passing trade. The ancient town of Bishop Auckland, where new industries have sprung up to replace coal mining, has some interesting buildings, including its castle, containing the largest private chapel in Europe, and the Franco-Flemish town hall. At West Auckland, just down the road from the Sportsman, is a replica of the first 'World Cup' which the village team won when representing England. They beat Juventus 2-0 and won again in the following year, thus retaining the trophy for all time.

Opening Hours: 7-11 (Sat 12-2 & 7-11, Sun 12-2.30 & 7-10.30).

Food: Sunday lunch.

Credit Cards: None.

Accommodation: None.

Facilities: Car park.

Entertainment: None

Local Places of Interest/Activities: West Auckland 2 miles, Bishop Auckland 3 miles, Hamsterly 3 miles.

The Strathmore Arms 105

*Holwick,
Middleton-in-
Teesdale,
Co Durham
DL12 0NJ
Tel: 01833 640362*

Directions:

Holwick is located off the B6277 4 miles west of Middleton-in-Teesdale.

Helen Osborne and Joe Cogdon offer traditional country hospitality at the **Strathmore Arms**, where visitors will also find satisfying home cooking, a good selection of cask and draught ales and a choice of overnight accommodation. The oldest part of the building dates back to the 1600s, and the pub took its present form two centuries later. Inside, it's everything a rural pub should be, with low beams, slate floors, an open fire and inviting couches. The food is served both sessions every day of the week during high season. The Strathmore offers home-cooked meals including hearty soups, sandwiches, steaks, boozy beef pies, fishcakes, a range of specials using Teesdale produce and an i nteresting selection of vegetarian options. The ales always include one guest and two permanent cask ales. For visitors using the Strathmore Arms for an overnight stop or a holiday base there are four well-appointed bedrooms, one with a four-poster, all with en suite facilities, tv and tea/coffee-makers. Alternatively, the inn has an adjacent campsite with toilet facilities, running water and space for up to 30 tents.

The area round Holwick is rich in Bronze Age and Roman remains and is a centre for some magnificent walks through glorious scenery. The most famous of the marked trails is the 250-mile Pennine Way, which runs from Derbyshire to Kirk Yetholm in Scotland; it runs along this part of the Tees, taking in spectacular riverside scenery that includes, very close to Holwick, the beautiful High Force waterfall, the largest in England in terms of water flow. Also close by are Bowless Visitor Centre near Newbiggin and the capital of the region, Middleton-in-Teesdale, a former mining town surrounded by hills that still contain remains of that once-thriving industry.

Opening Hours: 12-11 in high season. Times vary during low season

Food: Bar meals. Prior booking for groups required.

Credit Cards: None.

Accommodation: 4 en suite rooms + campsite.

Facilities: Car park.

Entertainment: Occasional folk music evenings.

Local Places of Interest/Activities: High Force 1 mile, Middleton-in-Teesdale 4 miles.

Internet/website:
e-mail: hojo@supanet.com

106   The Village Inn

Front Street,
Sacriston,
Co Durham
Tel: 0191 371 0477

Directions:

Sacriston is situated
3 miles north of
Durham. Take the
B6532 direct or turn
right off the A691 at
Witton Gilbert.

Owner and chef Michael Renshaw is passionate about the **Village Inn**, a mid-19th century hostelry in classic style located in the centre of Sacriston. Inside, the inn is roomy, bright and spotless, and the owner's warm welcome quickly makes visitors feel like old friends. The range of draught beers always includes at least one on promotion, and bar meals, which will be available all week during the summer, offer good honest flavours and excellent value for money. Michael works all hours at the Village Inn, for which he has some ambitious plans that will increase its scope and its customer base.

A new beer garden has recently been created, and Michael intends to make available six upstairs guest bedrooms for Bed & Breakfast accommodation. When these come on stream, the inn will be a good base both for tourists and for business people looking for somewhere with a bit of character. With its ready access the network of main roads, the inn is well situated for both town and country. The City of Durham, a place of great beauty and historical interest, is literally only minutes away to the north, and in the other direction lies the pleasant market town of Chester-le-Street. Even closer to Sacriston is Waldridge Country Park, the county's last surviving area of lowland heathland, with over 300 acres of open countryside and a wealth of wildlife.

Opening Hours: 11-11 Fri-Mon, 6-11 Tues-Thurs.

Food: Bar meals.

Credit Cards: None.

Accommodation: 6 rooms planned.

Facilities: Car park, beer garden.

Entertainment: Occasional disco.

Local Places of Interest/Activities: Durham 3 miles, Chester-le-Street 3 miles, Waldridge Country Park 2 miles.

The White Tun

Sacriston Lane,
Witton Gilbert,
Co Durham
DH7 6QU
Tel: 0191 371 0734

Directions:

Witton Gilbert is located 4 miles northwest of Durham off the A691.

The White Tun, a Vaux pub, is a large, low hostelry dating from the 1960s, with masses of space and a huge car park. Carol Turnbull and her husband arrived here as landlords at the beginning of 2002, full of fresh ideas to extend the scope of their pub. Behind the split-level facade - one storey in black and white, behind it a second floor with redbrick features - the look is big, bold and fresh, and the bar is a popular local meeting place where the regulars enjoy real ales and a wide variety of draught beers and lagers, perhaps over a game of pool or darts.

The bar food, served lunchtime and evening Monday to Saturday and lunchtime on Sunday, is appetising and full of good honest flavour, with mince and dumplings and braised steak among the most popular dishes. Parties are welcome, and the car park has more than enough room to accommodate all-comers. In the area around the White Tun there are many places of interest for visitors.

To the west is the town of Lanchester, where the church contains a good deal of Roman stonework, much of it taken from the Roman fort that once stood nearby. To the north is Chester-le-Street, and very quickly reached along the A691 is the city of Durham, whose Cathedral and Castle should be on the shortlist of any visitor to this part of the world.

Opening Hours: 11-11 (Sun 12-10.30).

Food: Bar meals.

Credit Cards: None.

Accommodation: None.

Facilities: Car park.

Entertainment: None

Local Places of Interest/Activities: Durham 5 miles, Lanchester 4 miles

108 The Winning Post

Merrington Lane,
Spennymoor,
Co Durham
DL16 1RY
Tel: 01388 811856

Directions:

The inn is situated
half a mile from
the centre of
Spennymoor, just
off the A688.
Durham is 5 miles
to the north,
Bishop Auckland 2
miles to the south.

South of the sprawling town of Spennymoor, just a furlong or two off the A688, the **Winning Post** is a super little inn built 150 years ago and now owned and run by golfing enthusiast Michael Hamilton and his wife. Behind the whitewashed frontage with tiny windows and doors, the bar is a real delight, with low ceilings, sturdy stone walls, smart carpets, an open fire and lots of little nooks. two cask ales are always on tap, along with a good selection of other beers and wines, and in the conservatory restaurant the resident chef satisfies the appetites of his regular customers and visitors with some really tasty, wholesome dishes.

Value for money is excellent, especially in the special deals for senior citizens and children and a 3-course Sunday lunch for £6.50. Food is served throughout opening hours. The Winning Post has a car park and a recently renovated beer garden. Friday night is quiz night. Spennymoor is within easy reach of both Bishop Auckland to the south and the city of Durham to the north; the River Wear is close by, with some very pleasant walks, and places of interest in the vicinity include Brancepeth Castle and Binchester Roman fort (Vinovia), whose remains include the best-preserved Roman military bathhouse in Britain.

Opening Hours: 11-11 (Sat 11-4 & 6-11, Sun 12-3 & 7-10.30).

Food: Bar meals.

Credit Cards: None.

Accommodation: None.

Facilities: Car park.

Entertainment: Quiz Friday.

Local Places of Interest/Activities: Bishop Auckland 2 miles, Durham 5 miles, Binchester Fort 3 miles, Brancepeth 4 miles.

4 Tyne and Wear

PLACES OF INTEREST:

PUBS AND INNS:

The Hidden Inns of The North of England

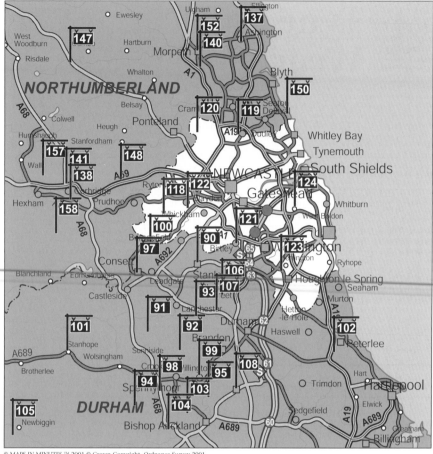

© MAPS IN MINUTES ™ 2001 © Crown Copyright, Ordnance Survey 2001

- 118 The Black Horse, Barlow
- 119 The Bridge, Annitsford, Cramlington
- 120 The Masons Arms, Dinnington
- 121 The Queens Head, Birtley
- 122 Run of the Mill & Chaplins Restaurant, Winlaton Mill, Blaydon-on-Tyne
- 123 The Stackyard, West Herrington, Houghton-le-Spring
- 124 The Wheatsheaf, West Boldon

Please note all references refer to page numbers

Tyne and Wear

The area south of the Tyne is largely industrial in character, encompassing large towns and cities in Tyne & Wear such as Gateshead, Sunderland and South Shields. But there is still plenty to see, as these places are re-discovering themselves and their heritage. And open space and countryside, especially to the south, are still there to be explored as well. The area inland from the north bank of the Tyne is mostly built up, though there are still areas of rural calm and beauty. Dominating it all is Newcastle-upon-Tyne, one of Britain's most important cities. It's built up area stretches out as far as the small towns of Tynemouth and Whitley Bay to the east, Longbenton to the north and Throckley to the west.

Industry made this area. It is real Geordie country, steeped in hard work and Newcastle Brown Ale. People found employment in coalmines, great engineering works and ship-yards, and didn't travel far to spend their leisure time or holidays. They headed for Whitley Bay or Tynemouth, eight miles east of Newcastle city centre on the North Sea coast, but a lifetime away from their harsh living and working conditions. Or they could head north into rural Northumberland, one of Britain's most beautiful and unspoilt counties.

PLACES OF INTEREST

GATESHEAD

Gateshead has perhaps suffered from its proximity to its big sister, Newcastle, for generations. Thanks to the **Metro Centre**, an impressive shopping and leisure complex, the borough is very much on the map as a place where Tynesiders and many other people go - not just to shop, but for entertainment in various forms.

The Metro Centre is really what Gateshead is most famous for. It is easy to fin-Borough of Gateshead and has achieved some notable successes in the Britain in Bloom competitions. The eight glasshouses, covering 3,034 square metres, have computer-controlled heating systems. Every year the nurseries host a major spring and summer flower show. An important part of the service offered is plant information for the general public. This is based in the showhouse which has pools, fish and ornamental planting. Visitors can enjoy the herb garden, rose garden, heather and conifer garden and tree and shrub nursery. There is also a picnic area.

But Gateshead is a town that is looking to the future, and there are some exciting new projects that should revitalise the area. Next to the A1 on Gateshead's southern approaches is one of North East England's most important modern icons - **The Angel of the North**. Commissioned by Gateshead Council and created by renowned sculptor Antony Gormley, this huge statue, made from 200 tonnes of steel, is 65 feet high and has a wingspan of 175 feet. It was erected in February 1998, and has attracted world-wide attention.

The **Gateshead Quay Visitor Centre** is housed in the former St Mary's parish church, where there is a display on Gateshead's history and future. It also incorporates a tourist information centre.

Due to open in 2003 is the **Gateshead Music Centre**, a £62 million project which will provide world-class facilities on a site overlooking the Tyne. There are plans for a 1650-seat auditorium, a 450-seat secondary hall and a school of music. It will cater for all tastes - jazz, classical, folk and rock. Close by will be the **Baltic Centre for Contemporary Arts**, based in an old grain warehouse on the banks of the Tyne. Linking the two will be a £30 million leisure complex with an 18 screen cinema, bowling alley, nightclubs, fitness suits and restaurants.

112

But perhaps the most spectacular new attraction in Gateshead is the £21 million **Gateshead Millennium Bridge** across the Tyne.

MARSDEN

The coast between South Shields and Roker is magnificent, with rocky cliffs projecting into the sea at Lizard Point and the impressive Marsden Bay. **Marsden Rock** was once a famous landmark - a rock formation shaped like an arc de triomphe which stood in the bay. In 1996, however, it finally succumbed to nature and collapsed, leaving two tall stumps. The smaller stump proved so unstable that in 1997 it was demolished.

Souter Lighthouse at Lizard Point was built in 1871, and was the first reliable electric lighthouse in the world. It's a perfect example of Victorian technology, and features an engine room, fog horns and lighthouse keeper's living quarters. It is open to the public, and owned by the National Trust.

NEWCASTLE-UPON-TYNE

Newcastle, the region's capital, is one of Britain's most exciting cities, and contains many magnificent public buildings and churches. Situated above the River Tyne, it is linked to its neighbour Gateshead by a series of road and rail bridges.

The most impressive is the **New Tyne Road Bridge**, commonly known as the "coat hanger bridge". This has become the icon by which Newcastle is internationally known, and was opened in 1928. It bears an uncanny resemblance to the Sydney Harbour Bridge, which isn't surprising - both were designed by the same firm of civil engineers.

Newcastle was, and is, many things - a Roman frontier station, a medieval fortress town with a "new" castle built in the 11th century, an ecclesiastical centre, a great port, a mining, engineering and shipbuilding centre and a focal point of the Industrial Revolution that changed the face of the world.

And, thanks to the **Metro Rapid Transport System**, the city and its surroundings are closely linked. It is the second largest underground rail network in Britain, though, like the London Underground, Britain's largest, most out of town

portions are above ground. The system takes in South Shields and Gateshead south of the city, and goes as far east as Tynemouth and Whitley Bay north of the Tyne. It even links up with Newcastle International Airport, and it takes a mere 20 minutes to go from the airport to the city centre - the shortest time of any city centre-airport link in Europe. **The Quayside** is the first view of Newcastle for visitors from the south, whether travelling by road or rail. This area is the symbolic and historic heart of this elegant city and boasts 17th-century merchants' houses mingling with Georgian and classical Victorian architecture. The area has been revitalised in recent years with some sensitive and imaginative restoration of the river front area. There are now a number of lively cafes and wine bars, with craft stalls and street entertainers as well. This is also the venue for a regular Sunday market.

The **Castle Keep** at Castle Garth was started by Henry II in the 12th century on the site of the 'new castle which gave the city its name, with King John completing the work. This earlier new castle was probably made of wood, and was built by Robert, eldest son of William 1, in 1080 on the site of a Roman fort called Pons Aelius. This is thought to have been the start of Hadrian's Wall before it was extended east. The wooden castle was built after uprisings against the new Norman overlords, and after the killing of Bishop Walcher in Gateshead at a meeting to discuss local grievances.

Newcastle's Quayside Market

Henry's massive new structure was built entirely of stone, and reached 100 feet in height. Although the battlements and turrets were added in the 19th century, most of it is Norman. The only other remaining castle building is **Black Gate**, dating from 1247 onwards. If at first glance the structure looks a little unusual, it is because of the house built on top of it in the 17th century. The castle was in use during the Civil War, when it was taken by the Scottish army after the Royalist defeat at the Battle of Newburn, five miles west of Newcastle, in 1640.

Many of the other medieval buildings were demolished in the mid 19th century to make way for the railway, and the Castle and Black Gate were almost demolished as well. Today the main Scotland rail line runs between the two, and the London branch passes to the west of the Castle Keep before crossing the river over the High Level Bridge.

Newcastle was at one time surrounded by stout walls that were in places 20 to 30 feet high and seven feet thick. Parts of these survive and include a number of small towers which were built at regular intervals. Begun in 1265, the walls were eventually completed in the mid-14th century. They were described as having a "strength and magnificence" which "far passeth all the walls of the cities of England and most of the cities of Europe". The best remaining section is the **West Walls** behind Stowell Street. Another good section is between Forth Street and Hanover Street, south of Central Station. This leads you to spectacular views of the River Tyne from the "Hanging Gardens of Hanover Street" perched on the cliff side.

One unusual feature of the walls was that they passed right through the grounds of the monastery of the Black Friars, or Dominicans, which caused the prior to protest loudly. To keep the peace, a door was cut through to allow the monks to reach their orchards and gardens, and the monastery was given a key to it.

Newcastle has two cathedrals - the Anglican **St Nicholas's Cathedral** on St Nicholas Street, and the Roman Catholic **St Mary's Cathedral** in Clayton West Street. St Nicholas, dating from the 14th and 15th centuries, was formerly the city's parish church, and it still has all the feel of an intimate parish church about it. St Mary's was designed by Pugin, and opened in 1842. The spire he designed was never built, the present one dating from 1872.

The city centre is compact, lying mostly within about a square mile, so it is easy to explore. For the most part the streets are wide and spacious and, like the later **Quayside** developments after the great fire of 1855, much of the architecture is in the Classical style. The focal point is Earl Grey's monument of 1838 which stands at the head of Grey Street about which John Betjeman wrote "not even Regent Street in London, can compare with that subtle descending curve."

During the 17th and early 18th centuries, Newcastle was a major coal port, with its core - still basically medieval in layout - near the riverside. But by the late 1700s the city began moving north, and in the early 1800s architects like William Newton, John Stokoe and John Dobson began designing some elegant Georgian buildings and spacious squares.

This is the core of modern day Newcastle, a city that is renowned for its shopping. In fact, **Eldon Square** is one of the largest city shopping centres in Europe, and contains department stores, restaurants, pubs and cafes, bus and Metro stations, and a sports and recreation centre. The adjoining Eldon Garden is smaller, with a number of specialist shops. A little further out is **Blackfriars**, a former Dominican monastery dating from 1239. It was earmarked for demolition in the 1960s, but was eventually saved. The church is long gone, but the rest has now been renovated and opened as a craft centre and restaurant grouped around a small square. It's another of the area's hidden places, and well worth a visit.

This is a metropolitan city of great vibrancy and activity, and there's plenty to do, with a rich variety of entertainment on offer. There is a choice of theatres, cinemas, concerts and opera. The nightlife has quite a reputation too - the pubs are so popular that queues form to get into them on a Saturday night. In fact, the city was voted by an American magazine as the eighth best place in the world to party. There are some fine restaurants too, with every type of cuisine on offer, and like many large cities there is a Chinatown.

The modern **Civic Centre** has won architectural awards, and there is a whole cluster of museums and art galleries, in fact, too many to describe them all in detail. There's the **Discovery Museum** (the North's largest

114

museum complex), **Laing Art Gallery** on New Bridge Street (with its **Proctor and Gamble Children's Gallery**), **The International Centre for Life** near Newcastle's main railway station, the **Hatton Gallery** at the Quadrangle, Newcastle University, the **Hancock Museum** at Barras Bridge, the **Museum of Antiquities** on King's Road, the **Trinity Maritime Centre** on Broad Chare, the **Military Museum** at Exhibition Park, and the **Newburn Hall Motor Museum** at Townfield Gardens in Newburn, on the western edge of the city, to name some of the best known.

And down near the quayside is a unique group of half-timbered houses known as **Bessie Surtees House**, owned by English Heritage. The rooms are richly decorated with elaborate plaster ceilings, and there is some beautiful 17th century wall panelling.

To the west, on the south bank of the Tyne, is **Blaydon**, famous for its races, which inspired one of Newcastle's anthems - "*The Blaydon Races*". But horse racing hasn't been held here since 1916, and the racecourse is no more. Gosforth, or more properly, High Gosforth, to the north of the city, is where horse racing now takes place. Near Blaydon is the **Path Head Water Mill**, a restored 18th century mill that can be visited.

Newcastle is more than just a regional centre. It's a northern capital - a proud city that doesn't look to the south (or to anywhere else, for that matter) for inspiration and guidance. It is one of the great cities of England, if not Europe, and such is its confidence that, with its neighbour Gateshead across the Tyne, it is bidding to become **European City of Culture** in the year 2008.

SOUTH SHIELDS

South Shields stretches out along the southern shore of the Tyne estuary. Though close to Newcastle and Gateshead, the North Sea coastline here is remarkably unspoiled, and can be walked along for many miles. No less a personage than King George V declared that the beach at South Shields was the finest he had seen. This is a stretch of fine firm sand behind which a small but pleasant resort thrives.

However, it is the older part of South Shields that has given the town a new claim to fame,

thanks to the work of one of the world's most popular novelists - Dame Catherine Cookson, who died in 1998. She was born Katie McMullen in 1906, in a house in Leam Lane amid poverty and squalor, the illegitimate child of a woman called Kate Fawcett. The house is gone now, but a plaque has been erected marking the spot.

Catherine Cookson wrote a series of popular novels - the world sales are in now in excess of 120 million - which captured the world of her own childhood, and that of her parents and grandparents, with vivid clarity. It was a world which was shaped in the 19th century around the narrow streets and coal-mines - a world of class warfare and conflict, passion and tragedy, violence and reconciliation.

A **Catherine Cookson Trail** has been now laid out in the town, showing places associated with her and her books, and a leaflet is available to guide you round. There is also a Catherine Cookson exhibition in the **South Shields Museum**. The mean streets she describes no longer exist. The old Town Hall is now part of a pedestrianised area, served by a station on the Tyneside Metro, and the town has a clean, modern image. In Baring Street you can see the extensive remains of the 2nd-century Roman fort, **Arbeia**. The West Gate has been faithfully reconstructed to match what experts believe to be its original appearance, with two three-storey towers, two gates and side walls. It is the biggest reconstruction of its kind in the country, and a truly magnificent achievement. It also incorporates the **Commander's Accommodation and Barracks**.

Much of the old harbour area at South Shields is now being restored, particularly around the **Mill Dam** area along the riverside, where fine Georgian buildings and warehouses survive. The river itself, like all great river estuaries, is a constant fascination as boats come around the breakwaters into the spectacular mouth of the Tyne heading for one of the docks, a reminder of the importance of the Tyneside ports.

SUNDERLAND

Sunderland is one of Britain's newer cities, and much of its history is told in an exhibition in the **Winter Gardens** and **Sunderland Museum and Art Gallery** in Burdon Road, where examples of works by Lowry and JW Carmichael, plus the maritime paintings of Sunderland-born Royal Academician and theatre-set designer Clarkson Stanfield are on display. The Winter Gardens is a green oasis in a glass rotunda, with exotic plants from all over the world. All are contained within **Mowbray Park**, which has been fully restored with themed walkways, poetry inscriptions, historical monuments, a lake and a bowling green. In the summer months, there is a full programme of entertainment. On Ryhope Road, south of the city centre, is the university-owned **Vardy Art Gallery**.

Three miles south of the city centre is the **Ryhope Engines Museum**, based on a pumping station which supplied the city and surrounding areas with water (see panel opposite).

On the north side of the Wear, in the suburb of Monkwearmouth, is **St Peter's Church**, one of the most important sites of early Christianity in the country. This tiny Saxon church was founded in AD674 by Benedict Biscop, a Northumbrian nobleman and thane of King Oswy, who had travelled to Rome and was inspired to found a monastery on his return. This was to become a great centre of culture and learning, rivalled only by Jarrow. The Venerable Bede, England's first great historian, lived and worked here for a time and described the monastery's foundation in his "Ecclesiastical History of England". The west tower and the wall of this most fascinating church have survived from Saxon times and the area around the church, where shipyards once stood, has been landscaped.

Close by, in Liberty Way, is the **National Glass Centre**. Glass was first made in Sunderland in the 7th century at St Peter's Church, so it's fitting that the centre was built here. Visitors can see how glass was made all those years ago, and watch modern glassblowing. There is a Glass Gallery, devoted to all forms of glass art, and in the Kaleidoscope Gallery there are plenty of interactive exhibits showing glass's many amazing properties. Walking on the roof is not for the faint hearted, as it's made of clear glass panels 30 feet above the riverside. However, some panels are opaque, so people with vertigo can still walk there and enjoy the view.

Monkwearmouth Station is one of the most handsome small railway stations in the British Isles. Built in imposing neo-classical style, it looks more like a temple or a town hall. Trains no longer call here, and it has been converted into a small museum of the Victorian railway age.

115

Roker is one of Sunderland's suburbs, located to the north of the great breakwaters that form the city's harbour. The northern breakwater, known as **Roker Pier**, is 825 metres long and was opened in 1903. Roker Park has been carefully restored to its former Victorian splendour, and from Roker and Seaburn through to Sunderland there is a six-mile-long seaside promenade.

It is worth making your way to Roker to visit **St Andrew's Church** in Talbot Road, described as "the Cathedral of the Arts and Crafts Movement". Built early this century, it is crammed with treasures by the leading craftsmen of the period - silver lectern, pulpit and altar furniture by Ernest Gimson, the font by Randall Wells, stained-glass in the east window by HA Payne, a painted chancel ceiling by Macdonald Gill, stone tablets engraved by Eric Gill, and Burne-Jones tapestry and carpets from the William Morris workshops.

Art of another kind is to be found in the **Sculpture Trail**. It was established in 1990, and has placed various works of outdoor sculpture along the banks of the Wear - mostly on the Monkwearmouth side. A leaflet has been produced that explains the exhibits as visitors go round.

By the beginning of 2002, Sunderland will be linked to the Tyneside Metro system, with stations at Sunderland Central, Monkwearmouth, the University, the Stadium of Light (Sunderland football ground) and Park Lane Transport Interchange.

TYNEMOUTH AND WHITLEY BAY

These two towns form a linked resort. Overlooking the river at Tynemouth is the notable **Collingwood Monument**, the grand statue of Admiral Lord Collingwood, Nelson's second in command at Trafalgar, who went on to win the battle after Nelson's death. The four guns below the statue are from his ship, the "Royal Sovereign". **Tynemouth Priory** was built over the remains of a 7th-century monastery which was the burial place of St Oswin, king of Deira (the portion of Northumbria south of the Tees), who was murdered in 651. The priory was as much a

116

fortress as a monastery, which explains the existence of the adjoining 13th century castle ruins.

The Long Sands lead on past Cullercoats, an old fishing village, to the seaside resort of Whitley Bay. On a small island, easily reached on foot at low tide, is **St Mary's Lighthouse**, now converted into a museum and run by North Tyneside Council. Visitors can climb the 137 steps to the top and get magnificent views of the Northumberland coast. The island is now a bird sanctuary. The town has some excellent, safe beaches.

towns are not especially interesting, two attractions make the place worth a visit. One is the **Stephenson Railway Museum** in Middle Engine Lane, and the other is a reconstruction of **Segedunum Roman Fort** on Buddle Street.

George Stephenson began his career as a humble engine-man at Willington Ballast Hill, before moving to Killingworth where he eventually became engine-wright. He was the engineer on the world's first passenger rail line - the Stockton to Darlington railway, opened in 1825. The museum remembers the man and his achievements, as well as explaining railway history in the area.

Segedunum (which means "strong fort") stood at the eastern end of the Hadrian's Wall. Originally the wall only went as far as Newcastle, but it was decided to extend it to deter sea attacks. There are only scant remains of the structure in the district nowadays.

Segedunum is a reconstruction of what the Roman fort would have looked like. Over 600 Roman soldiers would have been garrisoned here at any one time, and the area must have been a bustling place. Now visitors can explore the reconstructed fort, get a stunning view from a 114-feet viewing tower, and watch archaeologists uncovering yet more foundations of the original wall.

St Mary's Island

WALLSEND AND NORTH SHIELDS

This was where Hadrian's Wall ended, at a fort called Segedunum. The two communities of Wallsend and North Shields are wedged between Tynemouth and Whitley Bay to the East and Newcastle to the west, and though the

WASHINGTON

Present-day Washington is a new town with modern, self-sufficient districts scattered over a wide area surrounding the town centre. The town was built to attract industry into an area whose mining industry was in decline, and in this it has succeeded. The architecture is uninspiring, though within the old village of Washington to the east of the town centre there is one attraction well worth visiting - **Washington Old Hall**, ancestral home of the Washington family, ancestors of George

Washington, the first American president.

People tend to think that Sulgrave Manor in Northamptonshire was the Washingtons' ancestral home, but the family only lived there for about 100 years. Before that they had been in Lancashire and Westmorland, and before that they had lived at Washington Hall for 430 years. The Hall was originally a manor house built in the 12th century for the de Wessington family, whose descendants through a female line finally quit the house in 1613, when it was acquired by the Bishop of Durham. The present house, in local sandstone, was rebuilt on the medieval foundations in about 1623. In 1936 it was to be demolished, but a hastily formed preservation committee managed to save it, thanks to money from across the Atlantic. In 1955 it was officially reopened by the American Ambassador and two years later it was acquired by the National Trust. The interiors recreate a typical manor house of the 17th century, and there are some items on display which are connected to George Washington himself, though the man never visited or stayed there.

Washington is also the home to the **Washington Wildfowl and Wetlands Centre**, a conservation area and bird watchers' paradise covering some 100 acres of ponds, lakes and woodland sloping down to the River Wear. There are over 1,200 birds representing 105 different species, including mallard, widgeon, nene (the state bird of Hawaii), heron, Chilean flamingos, redshank and lapwing. There is also the **Glaxo Wellcome Wetland Discovery Centre**, with displays and exhibits, hides, a waterfowl nursery, an adventure play area and the Waterside Café.

118   The Black Horse

Barlow,
Tyne & Wear
NE21 6JH
Tel: 01207 542808

Directions:
Barlow lies off the A694 Newcastle-Consett road 6 miles south of Newcastle city centre. Also accessible from the B6315 (leave at High Speen).

The Black Horse is a sturdy stone roadside building dating from 1887, with super views over open countryside from the back rooms. The interior is delightfully traditional, with lots of beams, plaster or bare stone walls and plenty of comfortable leather sofas or upholstered chairs set at polished darkwood tables. A log fire burns in a hearth set in a massive stone surround adorned with brass warming pans and a stag's head. Enthusiastic owner Steve Lancaster offers a good choice of ales and wines, and in the restaurant home-cooked pub classics (steaks a speciality) are served from 6 o'clock in the week and from 12 to 4 on Sunday.

Steve is very interested in local history, and the area around Barlow is rich in reminders of the Northern industrial and social heritage. The North of England Open Air Museum at Beamish illustrates life in the late 19th and early 20th centuries with shops and offices, a chapel, trams and steam trains, farms and gardens. Close by is the famous Causey Arch, claimed to be the world's first single-arch railway bridge, which carried the preserved Tanfield Railway. Derwent Walk is the trackbed of the old Derwent Valley railway and Derwent Walk Country Park covers 425 acres of woodland and riverside meadow. Gibside, also close to the Black Horse, is a National Trust estate with superb gardens.

Opening Hours: 3-11 (Sat 11-11, Sun 12-10.30).

Food: Bar meals.

Credit Cards: None.

Accommodation: None.

Facilities: Car park, outside seating.

Entertainment: Occasional live music.

Local Places of Interest/Activities: Derwent Walk 1 mile, Gibside 2 miles, Beamish 5 miles.

The Bridge 119

Annitsford,
Cramlington,
North Tyneside
NE23 6QH
Tel: 0191 250 0288

Directions:
Annitsford is located 4 miles north of Newcastle on the A189

The mother-and-daughter team of Jennifer and Nicola have worked tirelessly in their short time at the **Bridge**, providing good hospitality for a mainly local and business clientele. A Grade III listed building dating from the late-19th century, the Bridge has a huge frontage on the road and an interior that is laid out for comfort and space. A warm welcome is guaranteed in the carpeted, oak furnished bar, and the 36-cover restaurant owes its style and taste to Jennifer's keen eye for design. The cooking is wholesome and unpretentious, with generous portions at kind prices; pasta dishes, fresh fish and beef are always popular, and the Bridge's rack of lamb is a surefire favourite with many of the regulars.

The Bridge has a car park and a beer garden with a play area for children. Newcastle, a short drive south of Annitsford, is one of Britain's most exciting and vibrant cities, with endless things to see and do, while to the east is the coast. Blyth's heritage is mainly industrial, but it also has some lovely sandy beaches, one of which extends down to Seaton Sluice, the nearest point on the coast to Annitsford. Further south, towards the mouth of the Tyne, are Whitley Bay and St Mary's Lighthouse on a bird sanctuary island that is accessible at low tide.

Opening Hours: 12-11 (Mon-Sat), 12-10.30 (Sun)

Food: Bar meals.

Credit Cards: None.

Accommodation: None.

Facilities: Car park, garden, children's play area.

Entertainment: None

Local Places of Interest/Activities: Seaton Delaval Hall (superb Vanbrugh mansion) 2 miles, Blyth 4 miles, Newcastle 4 miles.

120 The Masons Arms

Front Street,
Dinnington,
Tyne & Wear
NE13 7LG
Tel: 01661 872618

Directions:

Dinnington is
located 3 miles east
of Ponteland on a
minor road
between the A696
and the A1.

By a sweeping bend on the main road through the village of Dinnington, the **Masons Arms** is a substantial cream-painted inn which boasts a lovely colourful show of flowers in the spring and summer. It started life in 1823 as a coaching inn, and the owner since the autumn of 2001 is Terry Bosley, a businessman whose fresh ideas are already beginning to transform the look of the place. He has engaged the services of an interior designer to put the ideas into practice, and the bar and separate non-smoking lounge are very pleasant spots to enjoy a glass of real ale in the company of the locals and the staff, who all come from the village. Dave also has the services of a talented chef who produces a fine variety of dishes highlighted by fish specials, super steaks and puddings for which space should definitely be left. Food is served at lunchtime, and also in the evenings in the summer season.

There are real ales and good wines, and in summer it's nice to enjoy a drink in the garden. The setting, by the village green, is agreeably rural, nut the pub is conveniently close to Newcastle Airport, with the city itself an easy drive away. Four miles to the west is the small town of Ponteland, with its 12th century Church of St Mary. Nearby are Kirkley Hall Gardens, where visitors can see the National Collections of beech, dwarf willow and ivy and 35,000 different species of labelled plants.

Opening Hours: 11.30-11.

Food: Bar meals.

Credit Cards: None.

Accommodation: None.

Facilities: Car park, garden.

Entertainment: None

Local Places of Interest/Activities:
Ponteland 4 miles, Kirkley Hall Gardens 6 miles, Newcastle 8 miles.

The Queens Head 121

Birtley Road,
Birtley,
Co Durham
DH3 2PH
Tel: 0191 410 4706

Directions:

Birtley lies just off
J65 of the A1(M)
south of Gateshead
on the A167. The
inn is in the centre
of Birtley.

Early in 2002 the **Queens Head** welcomed a young and enthusiastic new landlord in Matthew Arthurs, who has every intention of realising the considerable potential of the inn. Dating from the last decade of the Victorian era, the inn is a handsome redbrick building on a prominent elevated site. Inside, it's bright, spacious and totally unpretentious, with an open fire, pine floors and staff who really know their jobs. John Smith's Special is one of a good range of draught beers on sale to quench a thirst or to accompany one of the simple, tasty bar dishes, which could be a toastie, a savoury pie or a plate of chicken and chips.

The Queens Head has car parking space and a beer garden, and the regulars make good use of the pool table. A clear mind is an advantage on Monday, which is quiz night, and there's live music on Saturday. Birtley, on the A617, is close to Chester-le-Street, Washington and Gateshead, and the North of England Open Air Museum at Beamish is just a few minutes down the road. There are several other reminders of the area's industrial past, including the Bowes Railway at Springwell. Next to the A1 on the southern approach to Gateshead is one of England's most important and best known modern icons, the Angel of the North, made from 200 tons of steel, 65 feet high and with a wingspan of 175 feet. To the west of Birtley there is pleasant walking in open countryside, while in the other direction is the Washington Wildfowl and Wetlands Centre, home to over 100 different species of birds.

Opening Hours: 11-11 (Sun 12-10.30).

Food: Bar meals.

Credit Cards: None.

Accommodation: None.

Facilities: Car park, beer garden.

Entertainment: None

Local Places of Interest/Activities:
Gateshead 1 mile, Washington 2 miles,
Beamish 3 miles.

122 Run of the Mill & Chaplins Restaurant

Winlaton Mill,
Blaydon-on-Tyne,
Tyne & Wear
NE21 6RT
Tel: 0191 414 2731
Restaurant/Fax:
 0191 499 0404

Directions:

5 miles from
Newcastle city
centre. A1 then
A694.

Ian, Ian and Trevor have invested a great deal of time, money and expertise in totally refurbishing the **Run of the Mill**, which looks set to become one of the major social venues around the metropolis of Newcastle. Thick pile carpets and solid oak furnishings typify the high standards evident throughout, and in the new restaurant locally sourced produce features prominently on the à la carte menus. Lighter eating is available on the well-balanced bar menu, and to accompany the food are four cask ales and a comprehensive choice of wines. Regular entertainment is provided by live music and discos, and the recent work is enhancing the inn's popularity as a venue for wedding receptions, parties and functions of all kinds.

Blaydon, on the south bank of the Tyne, was once famous for its races ("ganning along the Scotland road to see the Blaydon races") but racing ceased here in 1916; Newcastle's racecourse is now at Gosforth Park to the north of the city. A visitor attraction close to the inn is the 18th century Park Head Water Mill.

The city of Newcastle, more or less on the doorstep, has a host of things to see, including magnificent public buildings, the revitalised quayside, the ancient city walls, museums and galleries galore and shops to rival the best in the land. Opposite Run of the Mill is Derwent Country Park - a former coke works reclaimed with EEC grants. It has a river, lake, fishing, walks, tennis courts and cycle route.

Opening Hours: 12-11 (Sun to 10.30).

Food: Bar and restaurant menus.

Credit Cards: Amex, Mastercard, Visa.

Accommodation: None.

Facilities: Car park, garden.

Entertainment: Regular live music and discos.

Local Places of Interest/Activities: Newcastle 5 miles. Beamish Open Air Museum 6 miles, Metrocente 2 miles.

The Stackyard 123

St Cuthbert's Road,
West Herrington,
Houghton-le-Spring,
Co Durham
DH4 4NB
Tel: 0191 512 4901

Directions:

From the A1(M) or Durham. J62 then A690 to Houghton-le-Spring and fork left on to the A182. Newbottle is half a mile on.

Whitewashed and smartly painted, the **Stackyard** is located in the small community of Newbottle, on the A182 by Houghton-le-Spring. Landlord Pat Glendinning welcomes locals and visitors throughout the day into very civilised surroundings with gentle background music playing in the inviting, spotlessly kept bar and lounge. A full selection of draught beers is available, and in the conservatory-style restaurant a splendid variety of dishes guaranteed to please all tastes and appetites is served in an ambience that takes diners far away from the hustle and bustle of the daily routine.

The lunchtime menu offers starters, quick snacks (sandwiches, burgers, jacket potatoes) and main courses, all priced at a kind £4.50, that run from broccoli and potato bake to lasagne, scampi, chicken tikka masala and rump steak. In the evening (not Sunday) the full scope of the kitchen comes into play on a long and tempting menu that takes its inspiration from around the world: gingered duck and noodle broth, game terrine with home-made chutney, seared loin of swordfish with a sun-dried tomato and butter sauce, pork escalope with wholegrain mustard. Pasta dishes can be ordered as starter or main course, and there's always a good choice for vegetarians and some hard-to-resist desserts. The Stackyard is located in St Cuthbert's Road: the local church and many others around here are dedicated to St Cuthbert, the shepherd saint of Northumbria, whose tomb is in Durham Cathedral.

Opening Hours: 11-11 (Sun 12-10.30).

Food: Bar lunches, evening à la carte.

Credit Cards: All major cards except Amex

Accommodation: None.

Facilities: Car park, beer garden.

Entertainment: Live music Thursday.

Local Places of Interest/Activities: Durham 5 miles, Seaham (on the coast) 5 miles.

124 The Wheatsheaf

St Nicholas Road,
West Boldon,
Tyne & Wear
NE36 0QR
Tel: 0191 536 5107

Directions:

West Boldon is located on the A184 between Gateshead and South Shields.

The Wheatsheaf, a cream-painted building adorned with attractive greenery, is a 100-year-old pub on a corner site near the A184 between the built-up areas of Gateshead, Sunderland and South Shields. Inside, there's plenty of well-carpeted floor space and cosy seating, with some handsome panelling contributing to a good traditional feel. Tenant Debbie Brown cooks tasty no-frills food for her many local customers; dishes are served from 12 to 7 in the week and from 12 to 4 on Sunday. The pub has a pool table, and every Friday and Sunday karaoke sessions take centre stage.

Though West Boldon is almost surrounded by built-up areas there is a surprising amount of open space around, and there are several varied attractions within an easy drive. At Washington, the Wildfowl and Wetlands Centre and the Glaxo Wellcome Wetland Discovery Centre are both very popular with visitors, and Washington Old Hall is a 17th century manor house with memorabilia celebrating George Washington, and a re-created Jacobean garden. On the A183 at Whitburn is the National Trust's Souter Lighthouse, one of the first to be equipped with electric light. To its north is The Leas, a 2½-mile stretch of beach, cliff and grassland; the cliffs are a gathering place for thousands of sea birds.

Opening Hours: 11-11 (Sun 12-10.30).

Food: Bar meals.

Credit Cards: None.

Accommodation: None.

Facilities: Car park, outside seating.

Entertainment: Karaoke Friday and Sunday, occasional disco.

Local Places of Interest/Activities: Whitburn 4 miles, Washington 4 miles, Newcastle 4 miles.

5 Northumberland

PLACES OF INTEREST:

PUBS AND INNS:

The Hidden Inns of The North of England

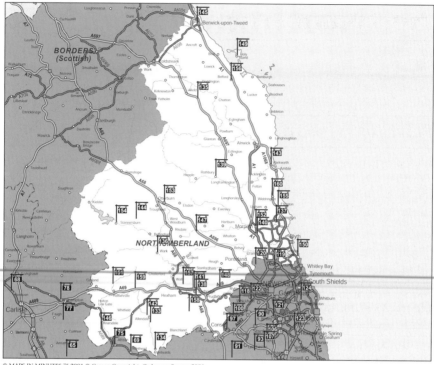

© MAPS IN MINUTES ™ 2001 © Crown Copyright, Ordnance Survey 2001

Please note all references refer to page numbers

Northumberland

The area from the edge of the Cheviots to the coast, and from Berwick-upon-Tweed in the north to the River Blyth in the south, is predominantly rural, though there is some bleak moorland as well as some industry around the south east. Here you'll find what most people consider to be the finest coastline in England - that stretch that goes from the Scottish border above Berwick down to Cresswell, a distance of 40 miles. It's been designated as the North Northumberland Heritage Coast, and takes in such historical places as Bamburgh Castle, Lindisfarne, the Farne Islands and Dunstanburgh Castle.

For all its beauty, it's a quiet coastline, and you can walk for miles along the dunes and beaches without meeting another soul. No deck chairs or chiming ice cream vans here - just a quietness broken occasionally by the screeching of gulls. At Cocklawburn, just south of Berwick, you'll find fossil beds, and Coquet Island is a renowned bird sanctuary where the visitor can see puffins, roseate terns, razorbills, cormorants and eiders.

The most evocative place of all on the coast is Lindisfarne, a small island lying between Bamburgh and Berwick. It was to here that St Aidan and a small community of Irish monks came from Iona in AD635 to found a monastery from which missionaries set out to convert northern England to Christianity. And it was on Inner Farne that St Cuthbert, Bishop of Lindisfarne, lived an austere and simple life. Inland from the coast the land is heavily farmed, and there is a pleasant landscape of fields, woodland, country lanes and farms. The villages are especially fine, most with their ancient parish churches and village greens. The green was essential in olden times, as the Scots constantly harried this area, and the villagers needed somewhere to guard their cattle after bringing them in from the surrounding land.

West Northumberland, where the North Pennines blend into the Cheviots, is an exhilarating mixture of bleak grandeur, beauty and history. Stretching to the north, towards the Scottish border, are the 398 square miles of the Northumbrian National Park and the Kielder Forest Park, which crosses into Cumbria on the west and into Scotland on the north. To the south is Hadrian's Wall, that monumental feat of Roman civil engineering built on the orders of Emperor Hadrian in AD122.

PLACES OF INTEREST

ALNWICK

The town is dominated by the massive bulk of **Alnwick Castle**, which began, like most of the Northumberland castles, as a Norman motte and bailey. In the 12th century this was replaced by a stone castle, which was much added to over the centuries. In 1309 it came into the possession of Henry de Percy, who strengthened the fortifications. Henry's great grandson was made an earl, and eleven earls later, the male Percy line died out. It then passed through the female line to Sir Hugh Smithson, who took the Percy name and was created Duke of Northumberland.

In the 18th century, the castle was falling into disrepair, and Robert Adam was commissioned to make improvements. However, these were largely swept away in the 1850s and 1860s when the 4th Duke commissioned the Victorian

Alnwick Castle

128

architect Anthony Salvin to transform the castle into a great country house with all modern comforts while recapturing its former medieval glory. The castle is still the home of the Percys to this day, and is a favourite location for making films, including the Harry Potter film, where it doubles as Hogwart's School.

A number of rooms are open to the public, and among its treasures are paintings by Titian, Tintoretto, Canaletto and Van Dyck, collections of Meissen china and superb furniture. There is also an extremely important archaeological museum and extensive archive collections, as well as the **Royal Northumberland Fusiliers Museum** in The Abbot's Tower.

Hulne Park, landscaped by the great (and Northumbrian-born) **Capability Brown**, encompasses the ruins of **Hulne Priory**, the earliest Carmelite foundation in England, dating from 1242.

Alnwick town itself is worthy of an afternoon's exploration with its ancient narrow streets retaining such evocative names as Fenkle Street, Pottergate, Green Batt, Bondgate Without and Bondgate Within. One road leads through the narrow arch of **Hotspur Tower**, the one surviving part of the town's fortifications, built by the second Duke of Northumberland in the 15th century. And all that's left of the once mighty **Alnwick Abbey** is its 15th century gatehouse, situated just beyond Canongate Bridge.

St Michael's Church overlooks the River Aln, and dates from the 15th century. It was unusual in a place as lawless as Northumberland at that time to build a church as large and as splendid as St Michael's.

The popular and colourful **Alnwick Fair**, dating from the 13th century, takes place each June.

BAMBURGH

Bamburgh Castle is epic in scale, even by the standards of this coastline of spectacular castles, and dominates the village of the same name. Situated on a dramatic outcrop of the Whin Sill rock overlooking the sea, it was almost certainly the royal seat of the first kings of Bernicia from the 6th century onwards. The dynasty was founded by the Saxon King Ida in AD547 and mentioned in the "Anglo-Saxon Chronicle". Ida's grandson Ethelfrid united the kingdoms

Bamburgh Castle

of Bernicia and Deira, and thus created Northumbria, a kingdom that stretched from the Humber to the Forth, and which in turn was ruled from Bamburgh.

In those days, the castle would have been of wood - a mighty stockade surrounding a great royal hall, sleeping quarters, stables, workshops and a garrison for troops. Later on, when Northumbria embraced Christianity, chapels would have been added, and the whole palace would have been an ostentatious declaration of the Northumbrian kings' power and wealth.

The present stone castle covers eight acres, and has a massive 12th century keep around which three baileys were constructed. The castle was extensively rebuilt and restored in the 18th and 19th centuries, latterly by the first Lord Armstrong.

Bamburgh is open to the public, and rooms on display include the Armoury, King's Hall, Court Room, Cross Hall, Bakehouse and Victorian Scullery, with collections of tapestries, ceramics, furniture and paintings. In the Laundry Room is an exhibition about the first Lord Armstrong and his many remarkable engineering inventions.

The village was the birthplace of Grace Darling, the celebrated Victorian heroine, who, in 1838, rowed out with her father from the **Longstone Lighthouse** in a ferocious storm to rescue the survivors of the steam ship *Forfarshire* which had foundered on the Farne Islands rocks. She died of tuberculosis only four years later, still only in her twenties, and is buried in the churchyard of St Aidan's. The **Grace Darling Museum**, in Radcliffe Road, also contains memorabilia of the famous rescue.

Just offshore are the **Farne Islands**. This small group of 28 uninhabited islands of volcanic Whin Sill rock, just off the coast, provides a sanctuary for many species of sea birds, including kittiwake, fulmar, eider-duck, puffin, guillemot and tern. It is also home for a large colony of grey seal which can often be seen from the beach of the mainland.

The islands have important Christian links, as it was on **Inner Farne** that St Cuthbert died in AD687. A little chapel was built here to his memory and restored in Victorian times. The nearby **Tower House** was built in medieval times by Prior Castell, according to legend, on the site of Cuthbert's cell. Landings are permitted on **Inner Farne** and **Staple Island**, though times are restricted for conservation reasons and advance booking is urged in the busy times of year.

BARDON MILL

Bardon Mill, a former mining village, stands on the north bank of the South Tyne. An important drovers' road crossed the river here and cattle were fitted with iron shoes at Bardon Mill to help them on their way to southern markets. The village is a convenient starting point for walks along **Hadrian's Wall**. The Roman forts of **Vindolanda** and **Housesteads** are nearby, and both are popular with visitors, having plenty of Roman remains and accompanying exhibitions.

Between Bardon Mill and Haydon Bridge lies the confluence of the South Tyne and the River Allen, which, like the Tyne, comes from two main tributaries - the East Allen and West Allen.

The valleys of the East and West Allen really are hidden jewels. The 22,667 acres of Allen Banks, as the lower part of the valley near the Tyne is known, is a deep, wooded, limestone valley, rich in natural beauty, now owned by the National Trust.

BERWICK-UPON-TWEED

Along part of its length, the River Tweed serves as the border between Scotland and Northumberland. But a few miles to the west of Berwick, the border takes a curious lurch north, and curls up and over the town to the east before reaching the coast. So, while Berwick is on the north bank of the Tweed, it's well and truly within Northumberland.

For centuries, the town was fought over by the Scots and the English, and changed hands no less than 14 times until it finally became part of England in 1482. But even now, Scotland exerts a great influence. The local football team, Berwick Rangers, plays in the Scottish League,

and in 1958 the Lord Lyon, who decides on all matters armorial in Scotland, granted the town a coat-of-arms - the only instance of armorial bearings being granted in Scotland for use in England.

But for many years after becoming English, the town was a curious anomaly. It was declared a 'free burgh', a situation that lasted in one form or another right up until 1885. When war was declared on Russia in 1853, it was done in the name of "Victoria, Queen of Great Britain, Ireland, Berwick-upon-Tweed and all the British Dominions". When peace was announced in 1856, no mention was made of Berwick. So technically, the town remained at war with Russia.

The situation was rectified in 1966, when a Soviet official made a goodwill visit to the town, and a peace treaty was signed. During the ceremony, the Berwick mayor told the Soviet official that the people of Russia could at last sleep easy in their beds.

Berwick's original medieval walls were built in the 13th century by Edward I. They were subsequently strengthened by Robert the Bruce when he recaptured the town in 1318, and finally rebuilt by Italian engineers at the behest of Elizabeth I between 1558 and 1569, though the work was never completed. They are regarded as being the finest preserved fortifications of their time in Europe. These

Berwick Ramparts

130

walls can still be walked, their length being about one and a half miles.

The many fine buildings include the **Berwick Barracks**, designed by Nicholas Hawksmoor and built between 1717 and 1721. They were the first purpose-built barracks in Britain, and within them you'll find the **King's Own Scottish Borderers Museum**. This is another anomaly, as the KOSB, as the name suggests, is a Scottish regiment. Here visitors will learn about a regiment that was raised in 1689 by the Earl of Leven, and which is still in existence today.

In the clock tower of the barracks is the **Berwick-upon-Tweed Borough Museum and Art Gallery**, which explores the history of the town. At nearby **Hutton Castle** lived Sir William Burrell, famous for collecting the works of art that can now be seen in the Burrell Art Gallery in Glasgow. But what is less well known is that he donated 300 works of art, sculpture and pottery to Berwick as well. This wonderful collection can be seen in the Borough Museum. Within the barracks is also the **Gymnasium Gallery**, opened in 1993 and housing changing exhibitions of contemporary art.

The Tweed estuary is spanned by three distinctive bridges linking the town centre with the communities of Tweedmouth and Spittal. The oldest of these is the 17th-century **Berwick Bridge**, a handsome stone bridge with 15 arches completed in 1626. **The Royal Tweed Bridge** is the most modern, having been completed in 1928 with a concrete structure built to an iron bridge design. The enormous 126 feet high, 28-arch **Royal Border Bridge**, carrying the East Coast main-line railway, was built between 1847 and 1850 by Robert Stephenson.

The Berwick skyline is dominated by the imposing **Town Hall** with its clock tower and steeple, which rise to 150 feet, and which is often mistaken for a church. Built between 1754 and 1761, this fine building has a façade as elaborate as its well-documented history. On the ground floor, markets were held in the Exchange and shops and cells existed where now a gift shop and coffee house stand. Guided tours in the summer enable visitors to explore the upper storeys, where there are civic rooms and the former town gaol. A small **Cell Block Museum** is located there.

Facing Berwick Barracks is the church - one of the most interesting in the county. **Holy**

Trinity Church was built between 1650 and 1652, during the Commonwealth of Oliver Cromwell, to replace a dilapidated medieval church which stood on the same site. It was built to one overall plan, and is one of the few Commonwealth churches in England.

On the north west side of the town are the remains of **Berwick Castle**. Built in the 13th century, it was demolished in 1850 to make way for the railway station, and the platform now occupies the site of the former Great Hall. The ruins are in the care of English Heritage.

CRASTER

Craster is a small, unpretentious fishing village which is nationally known for its oak-smoked kippers. At one time herring were caught around this coast in vast quantities, but a possible combination of over-fishing and pollution resulted in a decline in numbers, so the fish now have to be imported. During the kipper curing season visitors can peer into the smoking sheds where the herring are hung over smouldering piles of oak chips.

South of Craster is **Howick Hall**, built in 1782, and having long associations with the Grey family who have produced many famous public figures - most notably the 2nd Earl Grey, the great social reformer and tea enthusiast. The gardens are open to the public in spring and summer and are noted for their beauty.

Craster Quarry closed in 1939, and is now a small nature reserve called the **Arnold Memorial Site**, managed by the Northumberland Wildlife Trust. It was this quarry that supplied London and other large cities with its kerbstones.

KIELDER

Kielder village was built in the 1950s to house workers in the man-made **Kielder Forest**, which covers 200 square miles to west of the Northumberland National Park. Initially the planting of the trees brought employment to this area, and families came here from Tyneside and beyond for work and a home. Technology has since taken over and very few workers are now employed.

Here at Kielder Forest you'll find one of the few areas in Britain that contains more red squirrels than grey ones, and an area that abounds with deer and rare birds. Rare plants also grow here, and there's some excellent walking to be had. There are routes to suit all abilities, from a leisurely stroll to an energetic climb, with maps and leaflets to guide you round. There are also cycle routes, including the 17 mile Kielder Water Cycle Route, and bicycles can be hired from the local visitors centre.

Within the forest is **Kielder Water**, opened by the Queen in 1982, and the largest man-made lake in Northern Europe. It has 27 miles of shoreline, and there's an art and sculpture trail laid out in the forest round its shores. The visitor can even take a pleasure cruise aboard the Osprey, an 80 seat passenger cruiser.

To the north west is **Kielder Castle**, at one time a hunting lodge for the Duke of Northumberland, and later offices for the Forestry Commission. It is now a fascinating visitor centre with exhibits describing the development of the forest, and an exhibition on the birds of Kielder.

LINDISFARNE, OR HOLY ISLAND

Visitors can get across to this magical place only at low tide along the three-mile long causeway from Beal. Tide tables are published locally and are displayed at each end of the road and there are refuges part way along for those who fail to time it correctly. Alternatively there are bus services from Berwick, which run according to tides. As you cross, note the 11th-century **Pilgrims' Way**, marked by stakes, still visible about 200 metres south of the modern causeway. This route was in use until comparatively recent times.

This, most evocative of English islands, was known as Lindisfarne until the 11th century when a group of Benedictine monks settled here

Holy Island

giving it the name Holy Island, although both names are now used. The ruins of their great sandstone **Lindisfarne Priory**, in massive Romanesque style with great pillars, can still be explored. They are now looked after by English Heritage

The links with early Christianity go further back than the Benedictines. It was here, in AD635, that St Aidan and his small community of Irish monks came from Iona to found a base from which to convert northern England to Christianity. This led to the island being called one of the cradles of English Christianity.

These early monks are also remembered for producing some of the finest surviving examples of Celtic art - the richly decorated **Lindisfarne Gospels**, dating from the 7th century. When the island was invaded by Vikings in the 9th century the monks fled taking their precious gospels with them. These have, miraculously, survived and are now in the safety of the British Museum. Facsimiles are kept on Lindisfarne and can be seen in the 12th-century parish church on the island.

St Cuthbert also came here, living on a tiny islet as a hermit before seeking even further seclusion on the Farne Islands. A cross marks the site of his tiny chapel.

Lindisfarne is the finishing point for the 62-mile long **St. Cuthbert's Way**, a long distance footpath which opened in 1996. It finishes at Melrose, across the Scottish border, and along the way passes through the Northumberland National Park and the Cheviot Hills. On the English side, it is managed by both Northumberland County Council and the Northumberland National Park. It's clearly marked along its whole length, and trail guides and leaflets are available.

Lindisfarne Castle was established in Tudor times as yet another fortification to protect the exposed flank of Northumbria from invasion by the Scots. In 1902 it was bought by Edward Hudson, the owner of Country Life magazine, and he employed the great Edwardian architect Sir Edward Lutyens to rebuild and restore it as a private house. It is now in the care of the National Trust, and the house and its small walled garden are open to the public during the summer months.

Holy Island village is a community of around 170 people who work in farming, in the island's

132

distillery (noted for excellent traditional mead) and in the tourist trade. Much of the island is also a nature reserve, with wildflowers and a wide variety of seabirds. **St Mary's Church** in the village has some fine Saxon stonework above the chancel arch.

MORPETH

Morpeth, Northumberland's county town, seems a long way from the mining areas further down the Wansbeck, both in spirit and appearance. It was a stopping point on the A1 from Newcastle and Edinburgh, and some fine inns were established.

The first of Morpeth's castles was Norman, and stood in what is now Carlisle Park. It was destroyed by William Rufus in 1095. The second was built close by, but was destroyed by King John in 1215. It was subsequently rebuilt, but was destroyed yet again by Montrose in 1644, though substantial ruins remain. The third - which isn't really a castle but has all the appearance of one - was built by John Dobson in 1828 as the county gaol and courthouse. It still stands.

The **Town Hall** was built to designs by Vanbrugh, and a handsome bridge over the Wansbeck was designed by Telford. The **Clock Tower** in the middle of Oldgate has been heightened several times. It probably dates from the early 17th century, though medieval stone was used in its construction. In its time it has served as a gaol and a place from where the nightly curfew was sounded. Its bells were a gift from a Major Main, who was elected MP for the town in 1707. He had intended them for Berwick, but they didn't elect him, so, as a local saying goes, "the bells of Berwick still ring at Morpeth". The Clock Tower is one of only a handful of such buildings in England.

Somewhere not to be missed is the 13th century **Morpeth Chantry** on Bridge Street, close to the bridges over the Wansbeck. Originally the Chapel of All Saints, it has been in its time a cholera hospital, a mineral water factory and a school where the famous Tudor botanist William Turner was educated. Nowadays it houses a museum of the Northumbrian bagpipe, a musical instrument that is unique to the county, There is also a tourist information centre, a silversmiths and a mountain sports shop.

St Mary's Church, lying to the south of the river, dates from the 14th century. In the churchyard is the grave of **Emily Davison**, the suffragette who was killed under the hooves of Anmer, the king's horse, during the Derby of 1913. He funeral attracted thousands of people to Morpeth. About a mile west of the town are the scant remains of **Newminster Abbey**, a Cistercian foundation dating from the 12th century. It was founded by monks from Fountains Abbey in Yorkshire.

OTTERBURN

The village of Otterburn stands almost in the centre of the National Park, in the broad valley of the River Rede. It makes an ideal base for exploring the surrounding countryside, an exhilarating area of open moorland and rounded hills. It was close to here, on a site marked by the 18th century **Percy Cross**, that the **Battle of Otterburn** took place in 1388 between the English and the Scots. The battle continued for many hours, gradually descending into a series of hand to hand fights between individual soldiers. Gradually the Scots got the upper hand, and captured both Percys. But it was a hollow victory, as the Earl of Douglas was killed. A second force under the Bishop of Durham hurried north when it heard the news, but it wisely decided not to engage in battle. A series of markers known as 'Golden Pots' are said to mark the journey of Douglas's body when it was taken back to Melrose.

Otterburn Mill dates from the 18th century, though a mill is thought to have stood on the site from at least the 15th century. Although production of woollens ceased in 1976, the mill is still open, and on display are Europe's only original working tenterhooks (hence the expression, 'being on tenterhooks'), where newly woven cloth was stretched and dried.

North of the village are the remains of **Brementium** Roman fort. It was first built by Julius Agricola in the 1st century, though what the visitor sees now is mainly 3rd century. It could hold up to 1000 men, and was one of the defences along the Roman road now known as Dere Street. And close by is the **Brigantium Archaeological Reconstruction Centre**, where you can see a stone circle of 4000BC, Iron Age defences, cup and ring carvings and a section of Roman road.

The Allendale Inn 133

The Square, Allendale,
Nr Hexham,
Northumberland NE47 9BJ
Tel: 01434 683246

Directions:

Allendale is about 10 miles from Hexham; take the B6305 out of Hexham, left on to the B6304, left on to the B6295.

Local man Henry Stoelk was fulfilling a long-cherished ambition when he took over the **Allendale Inn** towards the end of 2001. On the main road through the town, the inn is a favourite place of refreshment for the local community, for sportsmen, for walkers and for cyclists, as well as tourists in this peaceful and picturesque part of the world. An open log fire assists the warm, easygoing atmosphere in the spacious bar, where a large selection of sandwiches, light snacks, tea and coffee are available in addition to the usual liquid offerings. Happy hour on beers, lagers and selected spirits operates every day between 4 and 7. In the recently refurbished restaurant, which can seat 50 in comfort, an extensive menu of traditional dishes makes excellent use of local produce. Lunch is served from 12 to 2 (till 3 on Sunday) and the evening meal from 6 to 9.

Private parties can be catered for, children are welcome, and the inn has ample parking space. Allendale lies on the River East Allen, with a backdrop of heather-clad moorland. It grew prosperous as a centre of the lead-mining industry and has many grand and attractive houses. It also has the distinction of being the midway point between Beachy Head in Sussex and Cape Wrath in Scotland. The mining heritage of the area is remembered in two museums within an easy drive of the inn. The Weardale Museum at Ireshopeburn includes a re-creation of a typical lead-miner's cottage kitchen, while Killhope Mine, in a hollow between Cowshill and Nenthead, is the focal point of the superb North of England Lead Mining Museum.

Opening Hours: 11-11 (Sun 12-10.30).

Food: Bar and restaurant menus..

Credit Cards: All the major cards.

Accommodation: None.

Facilities: Car park, outside seating.

Entertainment: None

Local Places of Interest/Activities: Hexham 10 miles, Weardale Museum 12 miles, Killhope Mine 12 miles.

134   The Allenheads Inn

Allenheads,
Northumberland
NE47 9HJ
Tel: 01434 685200

Directions:

From Hexham take
the B6305, then
the B6295 to
Allenheads.

Visitors come from all over the North to enjoy the lively, friendly ambience, the fine ales, the excellent food and the first-class accommodation provided at the **Allenheads Inn**. Set in the heart of a pretty village high in the Northumberland Pennines, the inn, run in fine style by the affable Steve and Sue Wardle, was built as the family home of Sir Thomas Wentworth and retains all the character and charm of a bygone age. Its imposing frontage is virtually unchanged down the years, and inside, where the sturdy walls, the low ceilings and the original walls and doors continue the old-world feel, the pub is festooned with antiques and memorabilia.

    This free house serves a wide range of real ales, wines and spirits, and a varied menu of bar snacks and evening meals including splendid home-made pies and a big Sunday lunch. The inn has eight letting bedrooms with shower/bath, tv and tea/coffee facilities providing comfortable double, twin and family accommodation. There is also a sitting room with tv, and a non-smoking lounge. An alternative to the in-house bedrooms is a self-contained cottage which can sleep up to 6 guests, with a choice of B&B or self-catering. The village of Allenheads is a convenient stopping-off point on the coast-to-coast cycle route and is also an excellent base fro walkers and hikers. The nearby town of Hexham provides good shopping facilities and among its other attractions are 9- and 18-hole golf courses and a racecourse offering excellent racing under National Hunt rules.

Opening Hours: 12-4 & 7-11 (Mon to Thurs); All day Fri, Sat, Sun

Food: Bar snacks, evening meals, Sunday lunches

Credit Cards: All the major cards

Accommodation: 8 en suite rooms and self-catering/B&B cottage.

Facilities: Car park, garden.

Entertainment: None

Local Places of Interest/Activities: Golf and horseracing at Hexham 10 miles, Derwent Reservoir 8 miles, Killhope Lead Mining Centre 5 miles.

Internet/website:

e-mail: theallenheadsinn@yahoo.co.uk
website: theallenheadsinn.co.uk

The Black Bull   135

High Street, Wooler,
Northumberland
NE71 6BY
Tel: 01668 281309

Directions:

Wooler is located on the
A697 20 miles north of
Morpeth.

The Black Bull is a sturdy,
traditional pub-hotel on the
main street of a small town on
the northern edge of the Cheviot
Hills. Partners Stephen Duke and
John McGleeve, ably assisted by
pub manager Christine Clow,
offer a smiling welcome and
genuine hospitality at their late-
Victorian hostelry, with is at once
spacious and cosy behind its solid
stone frontage. Wooler is a rural,
mainly agricultural community,
and the Black Bull is in the forefront of restoring morale after the town suffered greatly
during the foot 7 mouth crisis. No visitor goes hungry here, as the food - sourced locally as
much as possible - is served freshly cooked in generous portions and at extremely reasonable
prices. Food is served every session (Sunday night for residents only).

This is a great part of the world for keen walkers, who can head for Wooler Common,
climb Humbledon Hill just outside town or head off into the Cheviots or the glorious hills
and valleys of Northumberland National Park. A lane runs along the valley of the little
River Harthope to a footpath that leads up to the top of The Cheviot, which stands 2,800
feet above sea level. The Black Bull is a splendid base for a walking or touring holiday and its
11 en suite letting bedrooms offer ample space and comfort, three of the rooms are in an
adjoining cottage. A large car park and the town's Tourist Information Centre are also situated
next to the Black Bull.

Opening Hours: 11-11 (Sun 12-11).

Food: Bar meals.

Credit Cards: Mastercard, Visa.

Accommodation: 11 en suite rooms.

Facilities: Car park.

Entertainment: None

Local Places of Interest/Activities:
Bamburgh Castle 12 miles, Flodden Field 7
miles, The Cheviot 2 miles.

136   The Black Bull Hotel

Wark,
Nr Hexham,
Northumberland
NE48 3LG
Tel: 01434 230239
Fax: 01434 230514

Directions:
From Hexham,
take the A6079,
then the B6320 to
Wark. Approx 8
miles in all.

The attractive village of Wark is situated on the edge of Northumberland National Park, between Hexham and Otterburn and close to Kielder Water and Hadrian's Wall. Scottish kings are said to have held court here in the 12th century, and centuries later the **Black Bull** was used as a trading point for local farmers. A fine greystone building with a huge hotel sign on its slate-tiled roof, the Black Bull has a compact, well-stocked bar and a lovely bright, inviting lounge with a separate restaurant area. Farmers still use the hotel as an unofficial local headquarters and they, together with other locals and the more-than-occasional tourist, make for an excellent, cheerful atmosphere.

    Hearty country appetites are satisfied by a good, well-balanced menu of straightforward dishes prepared and presented with care. Food is available lunchtime and evening seven days a week, cooked by Angie Cowen, who runs the inn with her husband. The Black Bull also offers comfortable overnight accommodation in six en suite guest bedrooms with tv and tea/coffee tray, making it a very pleasant and convenient base from which to explore the scenic glory and historic sites that are all around. The Northumberland National Park, with forests, fells and the huge man-made Kielder Water. Hadrian's Wall is a short drive south, and on the slopes overlooking the North Tyne, on which Wark stands, are the remains of several prehistoric settlements.

Opening Hours: 11-11 every day

Food: Bar meals.

Credit Cards: All the major cards.

Accommodation: 6 en suite rooms.

Facilities: Car park, garden.

Entertainment: None

Local Places of Interest/Activities: Walking, cycling, fishing; sailing and water-skiing on Kielder Water 10 miles, Hadrian's Wall 4 miles, Hexham 8 miles.

The Black Diamond Inn | 137

*29 South View,
Ashington,
Northumberland
NE63 0SF
Tel: 01670 851511*

Directions:

Ashington is
located 5 miles
northeast of
Morpeth on the
A197.

On a main street of the town where the footballing Charlton brothers were born, the **Black Diamond** is a smart modern redbrick building with a contemporary open-plan design masterminded by the go-ahead owner Dave Langdown. A wide range of beers, lagers and spirits is served in the bar, and a three-page list of wines offers an amazing choice to accompany the simple, satisfying bar food that is served in man-size portions from 11.30 to 9.30 seven days a week. Dave's plans include the development and extension of the restaurant and also adding to the overnight accommodation - there are currently four guest bedrooms, all with en suite facilities.

Ashington grew up around the River Wansbeck, and the 2-mile-long Wansbeck Riverside Park, which has been developed along the embankment, offers lovely walks, sailing and fishing. Other attractions in the locality are the Woodhorn Colliery Museum in the QEII Country Park and Woodhorn's St Mary's Church, said to be the oldest church building in the county. The enterprising owner has another string to his bow in the adjacent Bubbles, a free house serving hot and cold snacks and bar meals, cask ales and cocktails. Bubbles holds regular quiz nights and live music evenings aimed at the younger set; on music nights it is open until 2am.

Opening Hours: Black Diamond 11-11 (Sun 12-3 & 6-10.30).

Food: Bar meals and snacks.

Credit Cards: Mastercard, Visa.

Accommodation: 4 en suite rooms.

Facilities: Car park.

Entertainment: Quiz and live music nights in Bubbles.

Local Places of Interest/Activities: Morpeth 5 miles, Woodhorn 2 miles, Newbiggin-by-the-Sea 3 miles.

Internet/website:

e-mail: info@blackdiamond.co.uk
website: www.blackdiamond.co.uk

138

The Blue Bell

Hill Street,
Corbridge,
Northumberland
NE45 5AA
Tel: 01434 632789

Directions:

Corbridge is on the A69 six miles east of Hexham.

One of the oldest public houses in the resort town of Corbridge on the River Tyne, the **Blue Bell** stands in a broad, fashionable street of shops, restaurants, pubs and houses. Inside, all is simple and cosily old-fashioned, with thick stone walls and original wooden floors, and mine host Ian Young has a warm welcome for a broad cross-section of locals, and also for the large numbers of visitors to a part of the world that is particularly rich in historic and scenic attractions. Food is served from 11 to 3 Monday to Saturday and from 12 to 3 on Sunday. Plain and wholesome, with everything prepared on the premises, the choice includes lasagne, Cumberland sausage, steak pies and the great favourite, liver and onions. Pool and darts are played in the bar, and Sunday brings regular entertainment by a singer or a duo. There's a garden at the back of the pub. One of the most interesting buildings in Corbridge is the Peel Tower, built in the 14th century to protect the vicar of St Andrews from marauding Scots. But the history of the place goes back much further, to the Roman fort - Corstopitum - built to guard the bridge over the River Tyne. Visitors can explore the extensive site, which includes the remains of a storehouse that was possibly the largest Roman building in Britain. Hadrian's Wall is also very close, and there's plenty more history to discover in nearby Hexham.

Opening Hours: 11-11.
Food: Bar lunches.
Credit Cards: None.
Accommodation: None.

Facilities: Garden.
Entertainment: Singer or duo on Sunday.
Local Places of Interest/Activities: Roman Corbridge 1 mile, Hadrian's Wall 1 mile, Hexham 6 miles.

Coquet Vale Hotel 139

*Station Road,
Rothbury,
Northumberland
NE65 7QJ
Tel: 01669 620305
Fax: 01669 621500*

Directions:

From the south: A1 then A697 to junction with B6344; take this road to Rothbury. From Otterburn: A696 for half a mile then B6341 to Rothbury.

In the historic village of Rothbury in the heart of the lovely Coquet Valley, the **Coquet Vale Hotel** is an imposing stone-built Victorian mansion with a fine, well-earned reputation for quality, service and friendly informality. That reputation is currently being maintained and enhanced by Greek owner Socrates Giazitzoglu, a skilled and experienced chef who is putting increasing emphasis on the food side of the operation. On the ground floor is a pizza and pasta outlet, while above it are the bar and the hotel's main restaurant, where the food is exciting, inventive and full of variety. Greek dishes are naturally included on the menu, which also includes a number of fish and seafood specialities such as fresh crab, red snapper and salmon. This excellent food, served every day from noon onwards, is complemented by an equally varied and interesting wine list.

The hotel has an elegant lounge, a spacious conference/function room and, for guests staying overnight, ten attractively furnished, well-appointed bedrooms, eight of them en suite, with tv, telephone and tea/coffee making facilities. Rothbury is a natural focal point for touring the Coquet Valley, which offers delightful scenery and pleasant walks along the valley or through nearby woodland. Fishing can be arranged by the hotel on the Coquet, a salmon river, or on several trout lakes within easy reach. Just outside Rothbury is the National Trust's Cragside, a Victorian estate and mansion with rock gardens and a remarkable orchard house.

Opening Hours:

Food: Pizza, pasta and à la carte menus.

Credit Cards: All the major cards.

Accommodation: 10 rooms, 8 en suite.

Facilities: Car park, garden.

Entertainment: None

Local Places of Interest/Activities: Salmon and trout fishing nearby; Cragside 1 mile, Otterburn 12 miles.

Internet/website:

e-mail: vale@rothbury.com
website: www.rothbury.com/vale

140 The Cornerstone Inn

Bridge Street,
Morpeth,
Northumberland
NE61 1PQ
Tel: 01670 510434

Directions:

Morpeth is 10 miles
north of Newcastle
on the A197 (off
the A1).

Long experience with the Courage Brewery gave Cyril Turnbull an excellent background to running a pub, and since arriving as the new tenant in the autumn of 2001 he has made great strides towards his goal of making the **Cornerstone Inn** the best bar in Morpeth. Occupying a prestigious corner site, the pub is looking very smart after a repaint, and from spring through to autumn hanging baskets and window boxes add an extra splash of colour to the street. Inside, all is neat and bright, and a mixed clientele of local residents, business people and tourists enjoy a drink and perhaps a simple bar snack.

The Cornerstone has a pool table, and weekly entertainment includes a quiz on Thursdays and a disco Friday and Sunday. It's especially handy for visitors to this historic town, as a large car park and the Tourist Information Centre are just across the road. Morpeth, now the county town of Northumberland, was a stopping point on the A1 Newcastle-Edinburgh coaching run, and today's motorists will find it well worth while breaking their journey to see what the town has to offer. Among the places of interest are the Vanbrugh-designed Town Hall, the castle ruins, St Mary's Church (the suffragette Emily Davison is buried in the churchyard) and, in the same street as the Cornerstone, the Chantry, which houses a museum of the Northumbrian bagpipes.

Opening Hours: Winter: Mon, Tue & Thu 6-11.30, Wed 12-3 and 6-11.30,Fri-Sat 12-12.30,Sun 12-10.30. Summer: Mon-Thu 12-11.30, Fri-Sat 12-12.30, Sun 12-10.30

Food: Bar snacks.

Credit Cards: None.

Accommodation: None

Facilities: Car park opposite.

Entertainment: Quiz Thursday, disco Friday and Saturday.

Local Places of Interest/Activities: Wansbeck Riverside Park 5 miles, Woodhorn Colliery Museum & QEII Country Park 6 miles.

The Golden Lion

Hill Street,
Corbridge,
Northumberland
NE45 5AP
Tel: 01434 632216

Directions:

Corbridge lies just off the A68/A69 8 miles west of Newcastle.

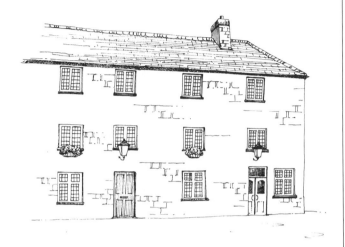

On a prominent corner site in what was once the capital of the ancient Kingdom of Northumbria, the **Golden Lion** has recently been given a major facelift by owner Linda Peel and her family. Dating from the late-19th century, the pub has an open-plan interior with masses of space, well furnished and carpeted throughout and a comfortable for relaxing over a glass or two of real ale. The Golden Lion is also a very good place to take an appetite, as everything on the menu is fresh, wholesome and home-made; food is served from 11 to 3 and 5 to 8.30 Monday to Friday, 11.30 to 9.30 on Saturday and from 12 to 5 on Sunday.

Pool and darts are the favourite pub games, and there's karaoke every Friday and occasional live music nights. Corbridge lies in the Tyne Valley, and evidence of its long history can be seen at the site of the original Roman settlement of Corstopitum, once the nerve centre for the Roman legions' campaigns in Scotland. In the town are two fortified medieval towers (one housing the Tourist Information Office) and a splendid parish church with many Saxon features. Hadrian's Wall is close by, and Newcastle is easily reached along the A69 eastwards; in the other direction the wide-open spaces of Northumberland National Park beckon. Corbridge is also the site of the annual Northumberland County Show.

Opening Hours: 11-11 (Sun 12-10.30).

Food: Bar meals.

Credit Cards: Mastercard, Visa.

Accommodation: Planned.

Facilities: None

Entertainment: Karaoke Friday.

Local Places of Interest/Activities: exham 3 miles, Hadrian's Wall 3 miles, Wylam (George Stephenson Birthplace) 6 miles, Newcastle 8 miles.

142

The Hare & Hounds

Allendale,
Nr Hexham,
Northumberland
NE47 9ND
Tel: 01434 683325
Fax: 01434 618086

Directions:
Allendale Town is situated on the B6295 8 miles southeast of Hexham.

Denise Smith moved to the **Hare & Hounds** at the end of 2001 having previously run a night club in Wales. The new realm of Denise and her husband is a 300-year-old coaching inn of high renown - small, inviting and little changed in appearance down the years. Sturdy stone walls, slate floors and low ceilings present a traditional picture, assisted by a fine selection of old prints and two open fires always blazing. Denise intends to keep all the period character intact while brightening up the interior, and a new upstairs restaurant is just one of many improvement plans.

Fresh, home-cooked food is served lunchtime and evening Monday to Saturday and lunchtime on Sunday to an appreciative clientele that includes local residents, farmers and visitors to the region. For the last group the Hare & Hounds has three letting bedrooms - a double, a twin and a family room, all with en suite facilities, tv and tea/coffee makers. Allendale Town lies on the River East Allen, with a backdrop of heather-clad moorland. A sundial in the churchyard records that the village is exactly halfway between Beachy Head and Cape Wrath, making it the very centre of Britain. Walking is a popular activity hereabouts, along with many other outdoor pursuits including fishing and golf.

Opening Hours: 11-11 (Sun 12-10.30).

Food: Bar meals.

Credit Cards: Planned..

Accommodation: 3 en suite rooms.

Facilities: Beer garden.

Entertainment: Occasional live music nights.

Local Places of Interest/Activities: Hexham 8 miles, Allenheads 5 miles, Cowshill (lead mining museum) 7 miles, Stanhope Castle 15 miles.

The Hermitage 143

23 Castle Street,
Warkworth,
Northumberland
NE65 0UL
Tel: 01665 711258

Directions:

Warkworth is 6
miles south of
Alnwick on the
A1068 Ashington
road.

The Hermitage is a grand old coaching in classic style standing on a curve in the main street of Warkworth. From spring onwards, hanging baskets and window boxes make a colourful sight on the whitewashed frontage, behind which the well-lit, smartly decorated public rooms are hung with a profusion of paintings and prints. In the restaurant the emphasis is on local produce, handled with care to produce tasty, satisfying dishes including excellent home-made pies. The main menu is available every session, and a popular carvery comes into operation at the weekend; the Hermitage also has a function room that is a perfect venue for private parties and special occasions. The food is prepared by Maurice Abbott, who runs this delightful place with his wife Lorna.

With history all around and the coast a short drive away, Warkworth is much visited by with tourists, and the Hermitage provides an excellent base with five letting bedrooms, three of them en suite, all with tv and tea-coffee making facilities. At the southern end of Alnmouth Bay, on the River Coquet, Warkworth is looked over from the head of the steep main street by the impressive ruins of its castle, where Henry Percy (Harry Hotspur) was born in 1364. At the opposite end of the main street is the Church of St Lawrence with a late-Norman chancel and Perpendicular aisle. Opposite it is the other Hermitage, a tiny chapel hewn out of solid rock. The town's stone bridge has an imposing gatehouse that was fortified by the Percys.

Opening Hours: Winter: Mon-Thu 11.30-3 & 6-11, Fri-Sun all day. Summer, all day every day

Food: A la carte menu, weekend carvery

Credit Cards: All the major cards.

Accommodation: 5 rooms, 3 en suite.

Facilities: Car park.

Entertainment: None

Local Places of Interest/Activities: Warkworth Castle, Alnwick 6 miles, Amble 2 miles.

144 The Hollybush Inn

Greenhaugh, Tarset,
Nr Hexham,
Northumberland
NE48 1PW
Tel: 01434 240391

Directions:

From Hexham take the A6079 to the junction with the B6320. Turn left and follow the B6320 to Bellingham and turn left towards Kielder. At Lanehead, turn right to Greenhaugh.

Built over 200 years ago on an old drovers' road, the **Hollybush Inn** is set in the heart of the North Tyne Valley in countryside of breathtaking beauty. The inn, which is owned and managed by Ian and Gloria Armstrong, retains much of its original rustic character, with low doors leading from the main street into the bar with its beamed and planked ceiling and welcoming open fire. Bed & Breakfast accommodation comprises three attractively furnished bedrooms with bathroom or shower room en suite, radio alarm clocks, tea/coffee making facilities and hairdryers. A full English Breakfast is served in the dining room, and bar meals are served daily, with packed lunches by arrangement. The inn has a pleasant garden with a heated patio, where guests can take in the glorious view of the beautiful Tarset Valley. Next door to Hollybush Inn is Blacksmith's Cottage, which is available for self-catering accommodation. It has three bedrooms, a bathroom, fully equipped kitchen and cosy living room with a wood-burning stove, three-piece suite, dining table and chairs and tv.

The area is ideal for peace and relaxation, for admiring the views or for walking or fishing. For the more adventurous there's sailing, water-skiing on Kielder Water or mountain biking on the many forest trails in the locality. Kielder Water, opened by the Queen in 1982, is the largest man-made lake in Northern Europe, with 27 miles of shoreline. A road leads northwest from Greenhaugh to the village of Otterburn, almost in the middle of the Northumberland National Park. Around the village are the remains of Iron Age and Roman forts, and it was close to here that the ferocious Battle of Otterburn was fought in 1388 between the English and the Scots; the site is marked by the 18th century Percy Cross.

Opening Hours: 1-11 every day

Food: Bar meals (also packed lunches).

Credit Cards: Mastercard, Visa.

Accommodation: 3 en suite rooms and self-catering cottage.

Facilities: Car park, garden.

Entertainment: None

Local Places of Interest/Activities: Walking, bird-watching, fishing; sailing and water-skiing on Kielder Water 4 miles, Bellingham 3 miles, Otterburn 7 miles, Hexham 15 miles.

Internet/website:

website: www.hollybushinn.net

The Kings Head 145

50-56 Church Street,
Berwick-upon-Tweed,
Northumberland
TD15 1DX
Tel: 01289 331491

Directions:

The inn has a central location in town.

The Kings Head is a splendid old coaching inn which has retained many period features from its 300 years of existence. The roomy public area comprises a comfortable bar, a games room with pool and darts, a lounge and restaurant, all recently refurbished and recarpeted by owner Ian Stewart. Here since the early 1990s, Ian attracts a wide cross-section of customers, including local shop and office workers at lunchtime, when the central location is a great advantage. The bar menu and daily specials always provide plenty of choice, with curries and giant cod among the favourites.

Food is served every lunchtime and all day in the summer, when the beer garden comes into its own. Berwick-upon-Tweed is a town of unique historical interest, fought over incessantly between England and Scotland before finally becoming part of England in 1482. The town has many attractions for the visitor, including museums, art galleries and some very splendid bridges, and the Kings Head is an excellent base from which to explore the sites and the surrounding area. The eight bedrooms are neat, bright and comfortable, and six of them have bathrooms en suite. The inn is a very friendly, sociable place, with darts and pool played in the games room and karaoke every Saturday night.

Opening Hours: 11-11 (Sun 12-10.30).

Food: Bar meals.

Credit Cards: Amex, Mastercard, Visa.

Accommodation: 8 bedrooms (6 en suite).

Facilities: Beer garden.

Entertainment: Karaoke every Saturday.

Local Places of Interest/Activities:
Museums and art galleries in Berwick, Norham Castle 6 miles, Holy Island (Lindisfarne) 10 miles.

146 Kirkstyle Inn

Slaggyford,
Nr Brampton,
Northumberland
CA8 7PB
Tel: 01434 381559

Directions:
Slaggyford is situated on the A689 4 miles north of Alston.

Samantha and David Basset gave up lives and careers in London when they took over the **Kirkstyle Inn** in the summer of 2001. The contrast in the pace of life and the ambience is great indeed, and their ancient stone inn is set in scenery of breathtaking beauty. A wood burning stove warms the unfussy interior, where farmers and other local residents are joined by tourists and walkers on the Pennine Way. Hearty home-cooked dishes satisfy fresh-air appetites; steak and mushroom pie, served in big portions with plenty of fresh vegetables, is among the favourites, washed down perhaps with a glass or two of Yates or Boddingtons. Opposite the inn is Church Cottage, a sturdy stone building where the Bassets offer self-catering accommodation for up to 4 guests.

The owners are still making plans for their new venture, including the creation of a beer garden. The nearest community of any size is Alston, 1,000 feet up in the Pennines, which was transformed into Bruntmarsh for the filming of Alan Bleasdale's reworking of Oliver Twist. The town council has devised an Oliver Twist Trail, and another attraction here is the narrow gauge South Tynedale Railway. Beyond Alston, at Little Salkeld, is one of the most impressive prehistoric sites in the country; this is Long Meg and her Daughters, a stone circle second only in size to Stonehenge. There are other villages and other places of interest in the vicinity, but first and foremost the Kirkstyle Inn is a place for relaxing, walking at whatever pace suits, eating and drinking well and revelling in the stupendous scenery.

Opening Hours: 12-3 & 6-11; closed Tuesday lunchtime

Food: Bar meals.

Credit Cards: Mastercard, Visa, Switch

Accommodation: Self-catering cottage for 2/3. Continental breakfast

Facilities: Car park.

Local Places of Interest/Activities: Pennine Way, Alston 4 miles, Haltwhistle 8 miles, Long Meg 10 miles. Hadrians Wall

Internet/website:

e-mail: sam@kirkstyle.demon.co.uk

Knowesgate Inn 147

Knowesgate,
Kirkwhelpington,
Nr Newcastle-upon-Tyne,
Northumberland
NE19 2SH
Tel: 01830 540336
Fax: 01830 540449

Directions:

From the south, follow
the A1 to Newcastle
Airport and Ponteland,
then A696 through Belsay
and 10 miles on. From
the north, follow the
A696 through Jedburgh
and Otterburn and 8
miles on.

Easy to find on the A696 between Belsay and Otterburn, the **Knowesgate Inn** offers quick and easy access to both town and countryside. Run in fine style by Robbie Jackson, Ann Dalton and their caring, attentive staff, the inn is a sturdy stone building on the fringe of the Northumberland National Park. Comfortable, practical overnight accommodation is provided in 16 en suite guest rooms with telephone, teletext tv, radio-alarm and hospitality tray. Top of the range is a suite with a four-poster bed and whirlpool bath. There's a hunting theme in the day rooms.

A full menu, with fresh local produce used wherever possible, is served lunchtime and evening in the 80-cover restaurant, and the inn is also open for morning coffee and bar meals. It's also a popular venue for functions and conferences, with seats for up to 120 in the banqueting suite. The Knowesgate provides a convenient stopover on the journey to or from Scotland and is also a convivial base well placed for exploring the spectacular countryside and the many places of historic interest in the vicinity. Wallington Hall, lying deep in the heart of the countryside, is one of the most elegant houses in the county and stands in really delightful grounds. Nearby Cambo was the birthplace of Capability Brown and at Belsay, along the A696 towards Newcastle, is one of the best English Heritage properties in the area, Belsay Hall with its magnificent gardens.

Opening Hours: 8am-12pm every day

Food: Bar and restaurant meals.

Credit Cards: All the major cards

Accommodation: 16 en suite rooms.

Facilities: Car park, beer garden.

Entertainment: Occasional live music.

Local Places of Interest/Activities: Cambo 2 miles, Wallington Hall 3 miles, Harwood Forest 5 miles, Otterburn 8 miles, Belsay 10 miles, Newcastle 19 miles.

Internet/website:

e-mail: knowesgate@btconnect.com

148   The Lion & Lamb

Horsley,
Newcastle-upon-Tyne,
Northumberland
NE15 0NS
Tel/Fax:
  01661 852952

Directions:
Horsley lies on the
A69 about 10 miles
west of Newcastle.

Owner Tony Milne has carefully moulded the **Lion & Lamb** into a little gem of an inn that caters for today's clientele while retaining all the best features of its past. AD 1718 is carved into the whitewashed wall above the entrance, and the promise conveyed by that date is fulfilled within, where the look and feel are delightfully old-world. This is an excellent spot for anyone with a serious thirst or appetite: four real ales are always on tap, and a fine wine list complements the wide range of food that is served every session except Sunday evening. The choice runs from light snacks to hearty pub classics, an evening à la carte and a traditional Sunday lunch.

The Lion & Lamb, which is open all day, every day, has a games room with multi-channel tv, a beer garden with a children's play area, and outside seating on patios that overlook the pleasant rural scenery. The inn is located just off the A69, exactly halfway between Newcastle and Hexham, in a part of the world that is rich in history, particularly of Roman Britain. Hadrian's Wall is close by, and at Corbridge is the site of the mighty Roman fort of Corstopitum. History moves on a short drive south of Horsley at Prudhoe Castle, completed in the 12th century and still impressive in its ruined state, and the National Trust's Cherryburn, the home of the illustrator and engraver Thomas Bewicke. At Wylam, another National Trust property is the modest stone house where George Stephenson was born.

Opening Hours: 12-11.

Food: Bar meals and evening à la carte.

Credit Cards: Mastercard, Visa.

Accommodation: None.

Facilities: Car park, garden, patio, children's play area

Entertainment: None

Local Places of Interest/Activities: Hadrian's Wall 1 mile, Hexham 10 miles, Newcastle 10 miles, Prudhoe Castle 3 miles.

The Manor House Hotel | 149

Holy Island,
Berwick-upon-Tweed
TD15 2RX
Tel: 01289 389207
Fax: 01289 389310

Directions:
Holy Island, 10 miles
south of Berwick-
upon-Tweed, can be
reached by car from
Beal, or there is a bus
service from Berwick.

The 1,000-acre Holy Island, or Lidisfarne, offers a variety of scenic and historic attractions, and the Manor House Hotel is the ideal base for a holiday on this most evocative of islands. Owned and run by George and Jennifer Ward and located in the market square, the early-19th century hotel has nine letting bedrooms, two with four-poster beds, all en suite with bath or shower; rooms are equipped with tv, hairdryer and tea/coffee-making facilities. Rooms are let on a dinner, bed and breakfast basis, and the hotel is also open for morning coffee, snacks, lunch, afternoon tea and dinner for non-residents.

The lunch and dinner menus feature a wide range of dishes, including game, vegetarian meals and locally caught crab, lobster and salmon, as well as much-loved classics such as haddock and chips or steak & kidney pie. The bar and dining room overlook the atmospheric ruins of Lindisfarne Priory, and the hotel has a private garden and ample residents' parking. Holy Island's many attractions include the Priory, the Castle (a Tudor fort rebuilt by Lutyens with a walled garden planned by Gertrude Jekyll), a heritage centre, a winery famous for its mead and a shoreline rich in flora and fauna. The island is linked to the mainland by a causeway that is covered by the sea twice a day for about five hours, so a little planning ahead is needed and safe crossing times can be obtained from the Hotel.

The hotel is open from mid February to the end of December.

Opening Hours: 12-3 & 7-11.

Food: Table d'hote, à la carte and snack menus.

Credit Cards: All the major cards.

Accommodation: 9 en suite rooms.

Facilities: Car Park, Garden

Entertainment: None

Local Places of Interest/Activities: Lindisfarne Castle and Priory; Belford 10 miles, Bamburgh Castle 15 miles, Berwick-upon-Tweed 13 miles.

Internet/website:
e-mail: jan@lindisfarne97.fsnet.co.uk

150 The Melton Constable Hotel

Seaton Sluice,
Northumberland
NE26 4DP
Tel: 0191 237 7741

Directions:
Seaton Sluice is on
the A193 north of
Tynemouth and
Whitley Bay.

A warm welcome and friendly atmosphere are complemented by real ales and excellent home cooking at the **Melton Constable**, which stands near the sea on the A193 north of Whitley Bay. Run by the husband-and-wife team of Karen and Paul Tait, the pub is a substantial late-Victorian redbrick building overlooking Holywell Dene from the conservatory and the Northumbria coast from the front. Inside, the Melton Constable is roomy and comfortable, and there's a good local following of local residents and business people who come to enjoy a drink, a chat and something from the varied menu.

The Melton Club double-decker Toastie, with cheese, ham, tomato and onion, served with chips and salad, is a meal in itself, and other favourites run from poached salmon to spicy chicken dippers and the super Directors Pie, a home-made traditional steak & kidney pie cooked in Directors Bitter gravy and topped with a puff pastry lid. Steaks are a Thursday special, brunch is served on Saturday, and traditional roasts on Sunday, and a selection of wines is available by bottle or glass. Entertainment at this convivial pub, which takes its name from the Hastings family seat in Norfolk, includes folk music on the last Sunday of the month and a quiz every Wednesday. The coastal resorts of Blyth and Whitley Bay are close by, and inland from Seaton Sluice is Seaton Delaval Hall, one of the finest houses in the North of England, built by Vanbrugh in the Palladian style for Admiral George Delaval.

Opening Hours: 12-11 (Sun till 10.30).

Food: Bar meals.

Credit Cards: Visa.

Accommodation: None.

Facilities: Car park.

Entertainment: Quiz Wednesday, folk music

last Sunday of the month, occasional other live music.

Local Places of Interest/Activities: Seaton Delaval Hall 2 miles, Blyth 4 miles, Whitley Bay 4 miles, Newcastle 8 miles.

Internet/website:
e-mail: paultaity@hotmail.com

Milecastle Inn

Cawfields,
Nr Haltwhistle,
Northumberland
NE49 9NN
Tel: 01434 320682
Fax: 01434 321671

Directions:

Cawfields lies on
the B6318 just
north of
Haltwhistle.

A gem of a pub, with good ale, good food and super staff. **The Milecastle Inn** dates from the 17th century and stands on a corner site in a country setting very close to Hadrian's Wall. Often used as a location site for films and advertisements, the inn's sturdy stone exterior is more than matched inside, where the tiny bar and adjoining snug are exactly in keeping with the age of the place.

Attached to the snug is a restaurant where regulars come from near and far to enjoy Margaret Payne's outstanding cooking. Assisted by husband Ralph and daughter Sarah, she produces meals to remember on a menu that always offers quality, variety and interest, with daily specials adding to the already excellent choice. Beef comes from a local farm, and other splendid dishes include wild boar, duck with dumplings and a truly magnificent smoked fish pie. This fine food is served from 12 to 2 and from 6.30 to 9 every day of the week, and many of the Milecastle's devotees pay several visits during the week, such is the variety and appeal of the food. The beer is excellent, too, with Northumberland Castle and guest ales on tap. The inn has a beer garden and off-road parking.

Hadrian's Wall, built when the Roman Empire was at its height, is naturally a major attraction, and a particularly impressive two-mile stretch runs along Great Whin Sill crest. At Cawfield Crags is the site of a Roman mile castle, and the Roman Army Museum is also nearby. Beyond the Wall, the scenic delights of Northumberland National Park and Kielder Forest await ramblers and lovers of the great outdoors.

Opening Hours: 11-11.

Food: A la carte menu.

Credit Cards: Amex, Mastercard, Visa.

Accommodation: None.

Facilities: Car park, garden.

Entertainment: None

Local Places of Interest/Activities:
Haltwhistle 1 mile, Hadrian's Wall 1 mile,
Northumberland National Park 2 miles.

152 The Oak Inn

Causey Park Bridge,
Morpeth,
Northumberland
NE61 3EL
Tel: 01670 787388

Directions:

The inn is situated
very close to the A1
about 4 miles north
of Morpeth,
signposted at the
southern end of the
village .

Just yards from the
busy A1 a few miles
north of Morpeth, the
Oak Inn is a very
pleasant, unpreten-
tious place to take a pause for refreshment. Motorists who follow the signs from the main
road will find the warmest of welcomes from Mr and Mrs Atkinson in a late-19th century
hostelry with an attractive conservatory restaurant extension. Oak beams and oak furniture
feature in the bar, which is designed for space and comfort, with plenty of seats and some
intimate little corners. In the 40-cover restaurant the emphasis is on freshness, quality and
value for money; portions are generous, and the food is served lunchtime and evening
seven days a week.

The Oak has a good-sized car park and a beer garden; visitors arriving on the last Tuesday
should have their brains in good working order, as that is quiz night. A road off to the right
at the top of the village leads eastwards across the A1068 to the Northumberland Heritage
Coast at beautiful Druridge Bay, which sweeps all the way from Cresswell up to Amble.
Morpeth is a quick drive to the south, while the next important place up the A1 in a northerly
direction is the historic market town of Alnwick.

Opening Hours: Mon-Sat 12-3 and 6-11; Sun
12-4 and 6-10.30

Food: Bar meals.

Credit Cards: All the major cards

Accommodation: None.

Facilities: Car park, garden.

Entertainment: Quiz last Tuesday every
month.

Local Places of Interest/Activities:
Morpeth 4 miles, Druridge Bay 6 miles.

The Otterburn Tower Hotel | 153

Otterburn,
Northumberland
NE19 1NS
Tel: 01830 520620
Fax: 01830 521504

Directions:

Otterburn stands in
the Northumberland
National Park on the
A696, 25 miles
northwest of
Newcastle. From
Corbridge, A68 then
B6320.

The Otterburn Tower is a truly distinctive and imposing fortified Northumbrian country house founded by a cousin of William the Conqueror in 1076. Touched by history at key moments down the centuries, it became a hotel after the Second World War, and the present owner, John Goodfellow, has renovated and refurbished the property in a way that is sympathetic to the history while providing the best of modern amenities. The hotel is a perfect base for a getaway break, and the 17 bedrooms, each with its own individual style and character, have en suite facilities and everything needed for a comfortable stay; top of the range is the bridal suite with four-poster bed and original fireplace. The day rooms are dignified, civilised and superbly relaxing, with log fires and inviting sofas, and in the attractive restaurant guests and non-residents can enjoy the best of local produce prepared with skill and flair and accompanied by an extensive choice of wines.

Friendly staff are on hand to look after guests' daily needs, and the hotel has long experience in organising meetings, conferences, weddings and other special occasions. It's also an ideal base for guests with sporting interests, including fishing for salmon and trout (the hotel has extensive rights on the River Rede), rough shooting and clay pigeon shooting. And to make sure that guests are ready for a day of healthy outdoor exercise the hotel has recently added gym facilities to its amenities. The village of Otterburn is well worth taking time to explore, and within an easy drive are the scenic delights of Kielder Forest, the Northumberland National Park and the Cheviots, and a number of historic sights, including Hadrian's Wall, other Roman monuments and an amazing number of castles.

Opening Hours: Open 24 hrs to residents.

Food: A la carte and fixed-price menus.

Credit Cards: All the major cards.

Accommodation: 17 en suite rooms.

Facilities: Car park, garden, keep-fit equipment.

Entertainment: Special events with local entertainers

Local Places of Interest/Activities: wide range of sporting activities arranged by the hotel; Otterburn Mill, Kielder Forest and Kielder Water 15 miles.

Internet/website:

e-mail: reservations@otterburntower.co.uk
website: www.otterburntower.co.uk

154 The Pheasant Inn

Stannersburn,
Falstone,
Kielder Water,
Northumberland
NE48 1DD
Tel: 01434 240382

Directions:

From the A69, exit
near Hexham turning
on to the A6079, then
the B6320 towards
Bellingham, then the
C200 towards Kielder.
Stannersburn is about
8 miles down this
road. From the A68,
take the B6320 then as
before.

Entering the **Pheasant Inn**, visitors are immediately aware of the warm, welcoming atmosphere of this old one-time farmhouse, which has been owned and run by the Kershaw family since 1985. Original beams, open fires and old farm implements paint a traditional scene in the bar, whose bare stone walls are covered with prints and pictures of the surrounding area. The dining room, furnished in mellow pine, is the place to enjoy some of the finest traditional home-cooked food in the area; everything on the extensive menu is individually prepared using fresh local produce whenever possible.

Round a courtyard next to the inn are eight en suite bedrooms, each with tv and tea/coffee making facilities and all enjoying beautiful views over the glorious local countryside. The Kershaw family also offer a selection of luxurious self-catering accommodation, from a one-bed studio to a three-bedroomed cottage. The Pheasant is the ideal spot for a break, be it a weekend pick-me-up or a full touring holiday, and the hosts and their friendly staff will ensure that every stay is a memorable one. The Pheasant Inn is situated by Kielder Water in an area that can cater for a tremendous range of recreational interests, from walking, mountain biking, sailing and fishing to exploring Roman remains and ancient castles and shopping and sightseeing in Hexham ....or simply relaxing and revelling in the unforgettable scenery.

Opening Hours: 12-3 and 6.30-11 every day

Food: Extensive à la carte menu

Credit Cards: All the major cards except Amex

Accommodation: 8 en suite rooms and self-catering.

Facilities: Car park, garden.

Entertainment: None

Local Places of Interest/Activities: Diverse recreational activities on the doorstep, Kielder Water, Kielder Forest.

Internet/website:

e-mail:
thepheasantinn@kielderwater.demon.co.uk

The Plough
155

***Front Street,
Ellington,
Northumberland
NE61 5SJ
Tel: 01670 860340
Fax: 01670 861380***

Directions:

Ellington is located by the A1068 Ashington-Alnwick road, about 3 miles north of Ashington.

The delights of both coast and countryside are more or less on the doorstep at **The Plough**, a large and handsome stone pub built in the early 1800s. From the outside it has something of the look of a grand manor house, and the interior does not disappoint, with sturdy stone walls, low ceilings, good-quality carpeting and splendid oak tables and chairs. The owner since the summer of 2001 is Dawn Barrett, a young and very enthusiastic lady with the determination to succeed at this, her first venture into the business. Her clientele is broad-based, from the young to the retired, and The Plough's varied attractions cater for all, with pool, darts, live music, karaoke and a weekly quiz.

Well-kept ales and lagers are on tap in the bar, and in the adjoining restaurant traditional home-cooked dishes provide satisfaction and excellent value for money. Lunch (with roasts on Sunday) is served from 12 to 3, dinner from 6 to 9, and a new kitchen has been fitted to cope with this growing aspects of the inn's trade. The Plough has a beer garden and plenty of parking space.

Nearby Cresswell has a beach sheltered by a reef from the North Sea, while stretching beyond it up to Amble and the seabird sanctuary of Coquet Island is the broad sandy sweep of Druridge Bay backed by golden sand dunes and grassland. Among other local attractions are the Colliery Museum and Queen Elizabeth Country Park at Woodhorn, and Wansbeck Riverside Park at Ashington.

Opening Hours: 12-3 & 6-11 (Sat & Sun 12-11); closed Wednesday in winter.

Food: Bar meals.

Credit Cards: None.

Accommodation: None.

Facilities: Car park, beer garden.

Entertainment: Quiz Sunday, singer or karaoke once a fortnight.

Local Places of Interest/Activities: Cresswell 1 mile, Coquet Island (from Amble) 8 miles, Newbiggin 3 miles.

156

The Salmon

*High Street,
Belford,
Northumberland
NE70 7NG
Tel: 01668 213245*

Directions:

Belford is located 14 miles south of Berwick-upon-Tweed just off the A1.

The husband-and-wife team of Robert and Ann Sim arrived at **The Salmon** in the summer of 2001 with ambitious plans to extend its scope and improve its facilities. It's a delightful little country pub built in 1837, the year Queen Victoria came to the throne, and the bar and lounge are cosy spots for settling down with a glass of one of the good selection of ales always on tap. Robert is in charge of the bar, while Ann does sterling work in the kitchen, producing wholesome, good-value dishes such as lasagne or shepherd's pie every lunchtime and every evening.

The food is an important side of the business and the Sims have recently completed an extension to house a restaurant. They have also created a beer garden and are livening up the social side with karaoke, live bands and discos planned for the weekends. The Salmon has ample car parking space. An important stop on the Great North Road in coaching days, Belford is now an ideal holiday base, with many attractions both inland and on the coast - and indeed off the coast, as the Farne Islands can be visited at certain times of the year and Holy Island is a short drive north. Many outdoor pursuits, including fishing, riding and golf, are available in the vicinity.

Opening Hours: 11-11 (Sun 12-10.30).

Food: Bar meals and restaurant menu.

Credit Cards: None.

Accommodation: None.

Facilities: Car park, beer garden.

Entertainment: Music at the weekend.

Local Places of Interest/Activities: St Cuthbert's Cave 2 miles, Kyloe Hills 4 miles, Bamburgh Castle 4 miles.

The Sun Inn

Main Street,
Acomb,
Nr Hexham,
Northumberland
NE46 4PW
Tel: 01434 602934

Directions:

Acomb is situated just above Hexham, on the A69 between Haydon Bridge and Corbridge.

Alan and Elaine Burrows, both from Scotland, crossed over the border and took over the reins at the **Sun Inn**. Dating from the mid-19th century, the inn is a fine stone building in a long row of neat houses in the main street of Acomb. Inside, the Sun is comfortable, well appointed and spotlessly kept, with open fires - maintaining some of the old-world appeal.

Alan does the cooking, offering restaurant-quality food at pub prices, with great care taken in both preparation and presentation. There are always two or three guest ales on tap to quench thirsts or accompany a meal. This is a place of wide appeal, attracting a mixed, well-balanced clientele, and it's also a very sociable spot, with pool and darts, occasional live music, a family room and a beer garden.

The Sun is also a good base for visiting the many places of historic in the area, and there are four bedrooms for Bed & Breakfast guests, two of them with en suite facilities. In neighbouring Hexham there's plenty to interest the visitor, including the famous abbey and an old jail that is now a museum and Tourist Information Centre. The site of the Roman camp at Corstopitum is also nearby, along with Aydon Castle, one of the country's finest fortified manor houses.

Opening Hours: Mon-Fri 12-2 & 5-11; Sat 11-11; Sun 12-10.30.

Food: Bar meals.

Credit Cards: All the major cards.

Accommodation: 4 rooms (2 en suite).

Facilities: Garden.

Entertainment: Pool, darts, occasional live music.

Local Places of Interest/Activities: Golf Course 1 mile, Hexham 1 mile, Aydon Castle 4 miles, Corbridge & Roman site 6 miles.

Internet/website:
e-mail: alanmcjannet@aol.com

158 The Travellers Rest

Slaley, Nr Hexham,
Northumberland
NE46 1TT
Tel: 01434 673231
Fax: 01434 673906

Directions:

The inn is situated on
the B6306 between
Slaley village and
Hexham.

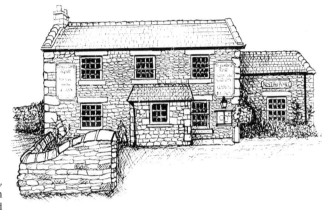

The Travellers Rest,
built in the mid-19th
century as a grand
farmhouse, has long
been a popular place of refreshment for travellers from near and far. In the four years since
the arrival of Jed and Lucy Irving its popularity has increased still further, and it has become
one of the places for a meal in rural Northumberland. Jed is in charge of the bar, which
features pine and slate floors, an open log fire and wooden church-style pews.

Here he dispenses a good variety of liquid refreshment, including four real ales, while in
the kitchen Lucy prepares a wide selection of splendid dishes to be enjoyed at the bar or in
the 40-cover pine-furnished restaurant. The lunchtime menu runs from sandwiches, warm
baguettes and savoury pancakes to goujons of sole, omelettes and the day's roast, with lots
of scrumptious puddings and a special menu for children. In the evening (not Sunday) Lucy
gives full rein to her considerable talents with such super dishes as duck breast marinated in
honey and ginger, roasted and toped with crispy leeks, or a mighty mixed grill with steak,
pork chop, lamb cutlet, liver, sausage, black pudding, tomato, mushrooms, egg and chips.
Fresh fish specials are always something to seek out, and this terrific food is complemented
by an extensive wine list. After dining regally, travellers can look forward to a restful night
in the two well-appointed bedrooms, a double and a twin, both with en suite facilities. The
inn has a huge beer garden and plenty of parking space.

The Travellers Rest is the ideal base for combining the enjoyment of the great outdoors
with the exploration of historic sites and churches. Slaley Hall is one of many local places of
interest, and Hexham has a famous abbey, a 14th century moot hall and a Museum of
Border History. To the south lie Slaley Forest, the peaks of the northern Pennines and Derwent
Reservoir, a 3-mile stretch of water set in heathery moorland.

Opening Hours: 12-11.

Food: Lunch and dinner à la carte menus.

Credit Cards: Mastercard, Visa, Switch

Accommodation: 2 en suite rooms.

Facilities: Car park, garden, adventure
playground

Entertainment: None

Local Places of Interest/Activities: Hexham
4 miles, Derwent Reservoir 3 miles.

Internet/website:

e-mail: enq@travellersrest.sagehost.co.uk
website: www.travellersrest.sagesite.co.uk

The Twice Brewed Inn | 159

Bardon Mill,
Northumberland
NE47 7AN
Tel: 01434 344534

Directions:

Bardon Mill is located 10 miles west of Hexham on the A69.

Situated at the heart of Hadrian's Wall country and next to the Northumberland National Park Information Centre, the **Twice Brewed Inn** has recently acquired new owners in Brian and Pauline Keen. They ran another establishment in the locality for many years, and familiar faces and first-timers can expect an equally warm welcome at their family run pub. Real ales, including the local Twice Brewed ale, are served in the spacious lounge bar, which is warmed in cooler months by a log-burning stove. Local produce is used for a menu of no-frills traditional pub dishes cooked by Pauline and served in generous portions.

Meals can be taken either in the bar or in the cosy little restaurant behind it; food is served throughout opening hours. Guests can stay overnight at the Twice Brewed Inn, which has 12 very reasonably priced letting bedrooms. In addition the inn is also available all year round for breakfasts - both residents and non-residents are welcome - a useful prelude to a day's walking or touring.

With Hadrian's Wall more or less on the doorstep, this is a popular spot with walkers, and other nearby attractions for visitors include the Roman forts of Vindolanda and Housesteads.

Opening Hours: 11-11 (Sun 12-10.30).

Food: Breakfasts, bar meals served til 6.00 pm, evening menu from 6.00pm onwards

Credit Cards: Mastercard, Visa.

Accommodation: 12 budget rooms.

Facilities: Car park.

Entertainment: Quiz night every Tuesday and frequent live music nights in either bar or function room.

Local Places of Interest/Activities:
Hadrian's Wall ½ mile, Haltwhistle 5 miles, Hexham 10 miles.

Internet/website:
e-mail: twicebrewed@hotmail.com
website: www.twicebrewedinn.co.uk

160

Widdrington Inn

Widdrington Village,
Nr Morpeth,
Northumberland
Tel: 01670 760260

Directions:

From Morpeth, take
the A197 to
Ashington, then the
A1068.

North of Morpeth on the road that leads up to Amble and beyond (A1068), the **Widdrington Inn** stands on its own just off the village green. Built in 1906, it has a private garden, a good-sized car park and picnic benches at the front and on the green. Inside, oak is a major feature, for the floor, the bar and the tables and chairs, and the whole place is kept in excellent order. The tenants are Scotsman Billy and Julia, and while Julia takes care of the bar Billy takes care of the cooking. Food is becoming an increasingly important part of the business, and the accomplished home cooking can be enjoyed from 11.30 to 3 and from 5 to 9 every day except Sunday evening.

The Shaws and their staff create a delightfully relaxed, convivial atmosphere that attracts a good cross-section of the local community to enjoy a drink and a snack and perhaps a game of pool or darts. Widdrington Village is a very short distance inland from the coast at Druridge Bay, which stretches all the way from Cresswell up to Amble. The National Trust owns a mile of this beautiful coast backed by golden sand dunes and grassland. Druridge Bay Country Park offers sailing and windsurfing, activities guaranteed to generate a thirst which the Widdrington Inn is perfectly placed to satisfy.

Opening Hours: 11-11 Mon-Sat, 12-10.30 Sunday

Food: Bar meals.

Credit Cards: None

Accommodation: None.

Facilities: Car park, garden.

Entertainment: Pool, darts.

Local Places of Interest/Activities: Druridge Bay 2 miles, Cresswell 3 miles,

ALPHABETIC LIST OF INNS

ALPHABETIC LIST OF INNS | 163

164   *Alphabetic List of Inns*

ACCOMMODATION

ALL DAY OPENING

CHILDRENS FACILITIES

170 | CREDIT CARDS ACCEPTED

CREDIT CARDS ACCEPTED

172 CREDIT CARDS ACCEPTED

GARDEN, PATIO OR TERRACE | 173

174 GARDEN, PATIO OR TERRACE

GARDEN, PATIO OR TERRACE | 175

LIVE ENTERTAINMENT

178 RESTAURANT/DINING AREA

RESTAURANT/DINING AREA   179

180 INDEX OF PLACES OF INTEREST

Hidden Inns Order Form

To order any of our publications just fill in the payment details below and complete the order form *overleaf*. For orders of less than 4 copies please add £1 per book for postage and packing. Orders over 4 copies are P & P free.

Please Complete Either:

I enclose a cheque for £ [   ]   made payable to Travel Publishing Ltd

Or:

Card No: [   ]

Expiry Date: [   ]

Signature: [   ]

NAME: [   ]

ADDRESS: [   ]

POSTCODE: [   ]

TEL NO: [   ]

Please either send or telephone your order to:

Travel Publishing Ltd   Tel : 0118 981 7777
7a Apollo House   Fax: 0118 982 0077
Calleva Park
Aldermaston
Berks, RG7 8TN

The Hidden Inns of The North of England

	PRICE	QUANTITY	VALUE
Hidden Places Regional Titles			
Cambs & Lincolnshire	£7.99	....	....
Chilterns	£8.99	....	....
Cornwall	£8.99	....	....
Derbyshire	£7.99	....	....
Devon	£8.99	....	....
Dorset, Hants & Isle of Wight	£8.99	....	....
East Anglia	£8.99	....	....
Gloucestershire & Wiltshire	£7.99	....	....
Heart of England	£7.99	....	....
Hereford, Worcs & Shropshire	£7.99	....	....
Highlands & Islands	£7.99	....	....
Kent	£8.99	....	....
Lake District & Cumbria	£8.99	....	....
Lancashire & Cheshire	£8.99	....	....
Lincolnshire and Nottinghamshire	£8.99	....	....
Northumberland & Durham	£8.99	....	....
Somerset	£7.99	....	....
Sussex	£8.99	....	....
Thames Valley	£7.99	....	....
Yorkshire	£8.99	....	....
Hidden Places National Titles			
England	£10.99	....	....
Ireland	£10.99	....	....
Scotland	£10.99	....	....
Wales	£10.99	....	....
Hidden Inns Titles			
Central and Southern Scotland	£5.99	....	....
Heart of England	£5.99	....	....
Lancashire and Cheshire	£5.99	....	....
North of England	£5.99	....	....
South East England	£5.99	....	....
South of England	£5.99	....	....
Wales	£5.99	....	....
West Country	£5.99	....	....
WelshBorders	£5.99	....	....
Yorkshire	£5.99	....	....
TOTAL			

For orders of less than 4 copies please add £1 per book for postage & packing. Orders over 4 copies P & P free.

Hidden Inns Reader Reaction

The *Hidden Inns* research team would like to receive reader's comments on any visitor attractions or places reviewed in the book and also recommendations for suitable entries to be included in the next edition. This will help ensure that the *Hidden Inns* series continues to provide its readers with useful information on the more interesting, unusual or unique features of each attraction or place ensuring that their stay in the local area is an enjoyable and stimulating experience.

To provide your comments or recommendations would you please complete the forms below and overleaf as indicated and send to:

The Research Department, Travel Publishing Ltd,
7a Apollo House, Calleva Park, Aldermaston, Reading, RG7 8TN.

Your Name:

Your Address:

Your Telephone Number:

Please tick as appropriate: Comments ☐   Recommendation ☐

Name of *"Hidden Place"*:

Address:

Telephone Number:

Name of Contact:

Hidden Inns Reader Reaction

Comment or Reason for Recommendation:

....

....

....

....

....

....

....

....

....

....

Hidden Inns Reader Reaction

The *Hidden Inns* research team would like to receive reader's comments on any visitor attractions or places reviewed in the book and also recommendations for suitable entries to be included in the next edition. This will help ensure that the *Hidden Inns* series continues to provide its readers with useful information on the more interesting, unusual or unique features of each attraction or place ensuring that their stay in the local area is an enjoyable and stimulating experience.

To provide your comments or recommendations would you please complete the forms below and overleaf as indicated and send to:

The Research Department, Travel Publishing Ltd,

7a Apollo House, Calleva Park, Aldermaston, Reading, RG7 8TN.

Your Name:

Your Address:

Your Telephone Number:

Please tick as appropriate: Comments ☐   Recommendation ☐

Name of *"Hidden Place"*:

Address:

Telephone Number:

Name of Contact:

Hidden Inns Reader Reaction

Comment or Reason for Recommendation:

....

....

....

....

....

....

....

....

....

....